Michele MacDonald

Sam MacDonald lives with his wife and four children in rural Ridgway, Pennsylvania, where he was born and raised. He currently writes, teaches, and travels across the state's northern tier doing community outreach and economic development work.

Also by Sam MacDonald

•

The Agony of an American Wilderness

Sam MacDonald

THE
URBAN HERMIT

A MEMOIR

PICADOR
ST. MARTIN'S PRESS
NEW YORK

www.picadorusa.com

Picador® is a U.S. registered trademark and is used by St. Martin's Press under
license from Pan Books Limited.

For information on Picador Reading Group Guides, please contact Picador.
E-mail: readinggroupguides@picadorusa.com

Design by Kathryn Parise

LIBRARY OF CONGRESS CATALOGING-IN-PUBLICATION DATA

MacDonald, Samuel A., 1972–
    The urban hermit : a memoir / Sam MacDonald. — 1st Picador ed.
        p. cm.
    ISBN 978-0-312-42915-7
    1. MacDonald, Samuel A., 1972– —Anecdotes. 2. Maryland—Biography—
Anecdotes. 3. Pittsburgh (Pa.)—Biography—Anecdotes. I. Title.
    CT275.M4324A3 2009
    975.2'043092—dc22
    [B]

                                                          2009032108

First published in the United States by St. Martin's Press

First Picador Edition: December 2009

10 9 8 7 6 5 4 3 2 1

A woman may live a whole life of sacrifice and at her death meekly says, "I die a woman." But a man passes a few years in experiments of self-denial and simple life, and he says, "Behold a God."
—Miss Anna Page,
as quoted by Abigail Alcott,
wife of Transcendentalist Bronson Alcott, 1843

To my wife, Michele,
for making the sacrifices this book entailed

Acknowledgments

The Urban Hermit is a work of nonfiction. I did not compose characters or alter the sequence of events. I ran the manuscript past many of the people involved. Their recollections occasionally differed from mine. When they turned out to be right, I rewrote the offending passages. When they were wrong, I didn't. When we couldn't figure it out, I tried to flag my uncertainty in the text. The Urban Hermit plan was not a literary gimmick. This is the way I lived my life, for better or worse. It never dawned on me to record conversations or keep a diary. The dialogue is as accurate as I could make it. Any deficiencies are, of course, my own.

Beyond that, countless people worked extremely hard to make this book possible. My wife deserves extra thanks because she met me halfway through the Urban Hermit plan and for some reason stuck around. My mother and father, my sisters, Molly, Lucy, and Gracie, my brothers-in-law, John, Dave, and Andy, and all my nieces and nephews all made immense contributions. Bonnie and Kenny Ramsburg and Doug and Allison Duck were constant sources of support. My cousin Rena served as a sounding board for my ridiculous dietary ideas.

Then there is Skippy, my faithful companion and partner in

absurdity, who lived this with me. Master Bernard Lytton and Dean Mark Ryan gave me a chance, and all my friends in New Haven helped me survive. Jason Finestone and Richie Bugden offered generous feedback on the manuscript. At the *Laurel Leader,* Joe Murchison was a great newspaperman and a wonderful mentor. Melanie, Harold, Stephanie, and David were great friends and colleagues. John Stafford provided an impossible service. In Baltimore, JJ kept me in good spirits and pocket change. Troy, Shane McShane, the Chance brothers, Patrick, and a host of others were pals of the highest order. Justin, Heavy, Bobby, Greg, Michelle, and everybody else at Kisling's deserve credit for running such a bizarre, fantastic place. Thanks also to Jesse Walker and Nick Gillespie for giving me a shot. Dr. David Shi helped me track down some important materials.

Meg Guroff at Johns Hopkins University was one of the first people to support this as a book. At the University of Pittsburgh, professors Lee Gutkind, Bruce Dobler, and Faith Adiele let me run with this project, offered crucial feedback, and gave me the space I needed to figure it out. Professor Jeanne Marie Laskas was particularly generous with her time, expertise, and support. Drs. Troy Boone, David Bartholomae, and Jim Seitz were fantastic. Dr. Dennis Looney and Dr. William Fusfield re-introduced me to Aristotle and Thoreau. The young men and women I taught and those with whom I learned offered constant inspiration, as did the late, great Hunter S. Thompson. My apologies, sir.

Byrd Leavell and Michael Homler had faith in this project and allowed it to be what it needed to be. Thanks. Meg Drislane and David Rotstein at St. Martin's also made crucial contributions.

I also would like to thank my children for being patient while I finished this book. And for waiting until they are mature enough to read it. When that time comes, I pray that they will do me the honor of trying to understand what this is really about, and exactly what it is that I am celebrating here.

Finally, my cousin and friend Aaron Ross, who played such a central role in this story, died of a rare medical condition in 2003. He was a good man and a hard worker, and nobody can ask for more than that. He taught me many things. We miss him dearly.

Introduction: Flee!

The Terrible Flight of a Broken Fat Man

> *It would be some advantage to live a primitive and frontier life,*
> *though in the midst of an outward civilization, if only to learn*
> *what are the gross necessaries of life and what methods have been*
> *made to obtain them.*
>
> —Henry David Thoreau, *Walden*, 1854

I was somewhere around Thurmont on the edge of the forest when the hunger began to take hold. I remember feeling light-headed and wondering about the tiny Tupperware container inside my enormous backpack and thinking something like, "I could eat the lentils; but then there's nothing for tomorrow except the tuna . . ." And suddenly there was a terrible roar all around me as my innards unleashed another round of churning and screeching that devoured all the other sounds in the car, which was struggling to maintain fifty miles per hour as I pushed higher into the mountains. And a voice weak with famine ignored the monstrous noise, whispering: "My God. Is there any place in this fucking wilderness to get something to eat?"

Then the screeching stopped. I shifted to catch a breath and felt my belly ooze over the seat belt, come to rest on my thighs, and jiggle as the car bounced in and out of a pothole. "Fuck it," I thought. "You're too broke to do anything about it now."

I stomped on the accelerator and felt the transmission slip—that goddamn, soul-crushing transmission—until the fading red Taurus, built the year I graduated from high school, finally responded with a surge. No point thinking about the pain. Or the car. I would deal with both of them soon enough. But first I had some bills to pay.

And some time to kill. God, the time was getting to me. The boredom. I wondered what was happening in Baltimore. The guys at the bar hadn't seen me in a week. They were probably calling the house. "Hey, asshole! Where are you? What do you think you're doing?" I had heard it before. And it could be persuasive stuff. I mean, really: Where *was* I? And what *was* I doing?

Escaping, that's what. Escaping the dollar drafts that morphed into three-dollar shots that somehow became a twenty-five-dollar hit of Ecstasy, then a bit of ratty marijuana and some meat loaf on the side. None of that going on in Thurmont. The mountains were home to Camp David, the presidential retreat, but not much else. This is where I would kill the time. Until it was dead. Or at least until the morning and the drive back to the city.

It was only a temporary escape, but a crucial one. It was late April, the year 2000—the first weekend of this ridiculous plan. Starving myself out of financial insolvency was one thing on a Monday and Tuesday, or on a Wednesday and Thursday, even. But I almost buckled on Friday night. There was no way I could make it through Saturday. I had to get out of town.

It was getting hard, so much harder than I thought it would be. And I was only five days into it. Spending the gas money was a breach of the code, the first stain on the purity, but it had to be done. And so what? Even Thoreau cheated. He borrowed an ax to cut down the logs for his precious cabin on Walden Pond. And he paid cash for an old shack that he tore down to salvage the boards for his walls.

So much for living lightly. A real prick, that guy. I could relate.

The year 2000 was an age of excess. NASDAQ. Enron. Reality TV. People were fat and happy. But things were about to change. That's why I was in my car, hurtling through the mountains of western Maryland, away from the excess and the excitement and the fun. Hurtling into boredom and starvation.

Into reality.

I was a big, fat bastard. No excuses. No complaints. That's just the way it was.

I didn't have an eating disorder or a glandular problem. I was not from a broken home. I was not so stupid as to be duped by crafty advertisers into eating too many McRib sandwiches. The problem, if you call it that, was me.

I was in good shape when I graduated from high school in 1991. I had a thirty-two-inch waist. Then I grew up and started making my own decisions. An Ivy Leaguer, don't you know. But that's when I got fat. By 1999 my waist had ballooned to something like forty-four inches. I never bought a pair of 44s, but the 42s I had were getting tight. Then that summer I was the best man in a friend's wedding. I had to call in the measurements. Yep. Forty-four. What that translated to in terms of weight I'll never know, because I never stepped on a scale. It's not like I didn't know I was fat. I just didn't care.

Sure, I probably would have taken a pill that made it all melt away, but that pill didn't exist. Losing the weight would have required cutting out the fun. And that was a trade-off I wasn't willing to make. The fat rolls never had that kind of power over me.

Hell, no. It was the creditors who finally did me in.

It was already midafternoon when the Taurus rattled into the empty dirt parking lot in the woods outside of Thurmont. I had never been to Catoctin Mountain Park. I had never even heard of it until I did a bit of emergency research earlier that day. I had no idea where I was going next.

I saw the outline of a rocky, lonely path winding its way up a steep embankment into the trees. I planned to follow it. But then what? Backwoods camping was forbidden, so I would have to find one of the designated areas for overnighting. There was one a few miles down the path, according to the map. It would have to do.

It was springtime in the mountains—far too chilly for the shorts and T-shirt I was wearing. I opened the front passenger door and grabbed a pair of jeans off the seat. I had seen people change their drawers standing up—take off one boot, change that leg, then put the boot back on and move to the other leg—but I didn't even try. I knew I'd end up face-first in a puddle. Instead, I squeezed myself into the front of the Taurus, pushed the seat all the way back to make some legroom, and got to work.

Finally finished after a few minutes of graceless squirming and grunting (it's not so easy for a fat man to change pants in the confines of a midsized American sedan), I threw on a sweatshirt and a fleece jacket, congratulated myself for thinking to bring them, and headed for the trunk. I popped the lock, grabbed the top of the backpack, and heaved.

"Oof!" It was heavy, at least seventy pounds of tent, tarp, sleeping bag, rainwear, pots, pans, lanterns, shovel, hatchet, flashlight, batteries, propane stove, propane canister, a few books, and Lord knows what else. Other than food, I had enough supplies for an extended trek in the wilderness. The real wilderness. Fresh water? I had a hand-pumped purifying system that had cost me eighty dollars the previous summer. It would transform my own piss into potable water in a pinch. I didn't know how to use it, but the instructions were still in the box. I was beginning to question my packing strategy, though. All this crap for an overnight stroll in the woods? It didn't seem that heavy when I'd carried it to the car that morning, but it felt like a real load in the shadow of that embankment.

Oh, well. No time to unpack now. Big boy like me ought to be able to haul it anyway. So I slammed the trunk shut, hoisted the pack onto the rear of the car, backed myself up to the burden, and lifted. It was heavy, but it was a good pack, designed for the job. I braced myself, stepped away from the car, and started walking up the path.

It was tough going, but it felt good to do something. The terrain was steep and damp, but the footing was solid. The air was brisk. I was alone. Back to my roots.

Sure.

The straps started cutting into my shoulders before long. Then my legs started to quiver. My lungs began to strain. I was losing my balance. Is this pack adjusted right? Maybe the weight is supposed to be higher. Or maybe lower. What are all these straps supposed to do? And—*clang, clang, smash*—what's that noise? Is that the pans banging around inside the pack? Am I going to have to listen to that godawful racket all fucking day? And when is this mother god bitch of a hill going to end, dammit!

Out of breath, I stopped and let the backpack drop. It hit the wet leaves with a thud, a final clang of the pans, then tipped over onto its side. A rush of cold mountain air slid inside the fleece jacket and up my sweaty back. Frustrated and confused, I turned back to contemplate my progress. I could still see the Taurus through a quarter-mile of branches.

Something was wrong. Sure, I was out of shape. Really out of shape. But I was twenty-seven years old. If called upon, I easily could lift a man off his feet with one hand on his throat, the other on a frosty mug of beer. Slow to anger. Good-natured. Jolly, even. But strong. I ought to be able to walk for more than ten minutes.

Right on cue, my stomach chimed in with an explanation. It was empty. Angry. And growling.

In the five previous days I had consumed fewer calories than I normally would have during a decent night at the bar. Twenty Rolling Rocks add up to more than twenty-six hundred calories. And I could drink twenty. Easy. Plus shots.

Damn. I would have lived that way forever if I could have. I just couldn't. It cost too much. Ten years of eating and drinking and spending had finally come crashing down that April. I needed a new angle, and fast. Something to get those vicious creditors off my back. Some resources. But where to find them? There are only so many corners to cut. And living costs what it costs.

Or does it? That's what I wanted to find out. That's why I was climbing that hill. How much does it cost to *make it?* In basic animal terms, what does it take for a human being to survive? Maybe I didn't really need to swallow half of the Rolling Rock and Ecstasy for sale in central Maryland. Maybe I didn't need a lot of the things I consumed.

What if I just stopped consuming them? What if, like a bear in winter, I viewed past excesses not as an obstacle, but as an opportunity? What if I could find a way to turn the terrible, seductive beast of indulgence against itself? I certainly had stored up enough reserves. My fingers were fat. My neck. My thighs and calves. Hell, my body was bursting with opportunities. Literally.

The plan I devised called for eight hundred calories a day, about half of it in the form of lentils. And that was hard enough, to tell the whole truth. But the weakness was only beginning to settle in as I climbed that path into the woods. I still had a whole year of pain and poverty and boredom to endure. And I didn't even know it.

At the time, all I could feel was the hunger. I thought about the lentils in the backpack again, then remembered that they were at the bottom of all that gear. This, I thought, was a very good time to be in the woods. Had I been within reach of a telephone, I would have called for a pizza. One I couldn't really afford.

No sense complaining. You had it coming and you know it. Suck it up. Grab the backpack. Keep walking.

I never did make it to the camping spot on foot. After walking for an hour or two, I started to worry about setting up camp in the middle of the woods in the dark. So I turned back and made it to the car at dusk.

I was dead tired, but it was barely six P.M. I didn't have a lot of options. Heading to Baltimore was out of the question. That would put me right back in the teeth of things. So I tossed the pack into the trunk and started driving nowhere in particular. Ten minutes later I blazed right past the designated camping area.

I did a quick three-pointer and—what a place! The campground had a series of well-manicured pull-offs. A few of them were occupied with pop-up campers, pickup trucks, and minivans, peopled with shadowy figures wandering in and out of extravagant tent-mansions as they tended to their hibachis and beer coolers and fire pits. I noticed a squat concrete structure near the center of the action. It was a bathroom, men's and women's, with flush toilets and showers. It was pretty much the Ritz-Carlton of camping.

The road made a large, lazy loop into the woods. I pointed the Taurus toward an open spot. The setup seemed ideal until I turned off the ignition and wobbled into the cool evening air. That's when I saw the official notice strung on a wire between two trees in my woodsy little cul-de-sac. It informed me that I needed to report to the "host," the guy in charge of collecting twelve dollars from everyone utilizing the campground.

Twelve dollars! What kind of half-ass Gestapo-tactic wilderness experience is this? They won't let you pitch a tent in the woods, and they force you to pony up cash? Yeah, the shitters are a nice touch, but this sure as hell doesn't seem like camping.

I considered driving away in protest, but the backseat of the Taurus was packed with empty Marlboro boxes, fast-food wrappers, and other symbols of the good times. Changing pants in the front of the car had been difficult, but sleeping in the back would have been far worse.

I walked about a hundred yards down the dry, paved road to the host's camper—a little motor home complete with an awning that covered two plastic chairs and a cooler. I knocked on the hollow plastic door, heard the hum of a generator in response. Maybe they were out.

But they were efficient hosts. They had set up a secure box so people could deposit the fee through a slot. They even provided little envelopes to hold the money. Each one had lines on it so campers could write down their license plate number and the number of the site they had occupied.

I didn't know either, of course, so I trudged back to my car, scribbled down the information, stuffed twelve wilted dollar bills into the envelope, then headed back and shoved it through the slot. Then I returned to the campsite. Finally.

It took me about an hour to set up my gear. It was dark, but I had a picnic table to use as a staging area and the car's headlights to illuminate the scene. Still, I wondered how my stupid little trip had devolved into such an embarrassing failure. I was supposed to be saving money, but somehow I had managed to burn twenty dollars on gas and twelve dollars on a campground. Thirty-two dollars. Enough for thirty-two pints of Rolling Rock at the bar.

Worse, the campground was getting rowdy. The hibachis were under wraps, but the beer coolers were still open for business. Every campsite had an enormous dog, a blaring stereo or an arsenal of illegal fireworks. The group closest to me had all three, not to mention a litter of anxious children who had free run of the place. These fuckers are lucky, I thought. One week earlier and I would have shown them a thing or two about rambunctious camping.

But not tonight.

Cold, lonely, beerless, drugless, and thirty-two dollars closer to penniless than I had been that morning, I crawled into the tent and located the ninety-five-dollar sleeping bag I had bought the previous summer. It was a "mummy" bag, designed to wrap a body tightly, exposing only the nose and mouth to the elements. I had never used it. I couldn't zip it up past my belly. I was too fat.

Lucky for me it was spring rather than winter, brisk rather than freezing. I didn't bother undressing. I draped the unzipped bag over my aching corpse and used a cheap foam-rubber camping pad for insulation against the cold, hard ground.

It was only nine P.M. When was the last time I had been in bed at nine on a Saturday? Seventh grade? It smelled like mildew in the tent. I must not have dried it off the last time I used it. How long had it been? Two years? I tried reading by flashlight but quickly abandoned that in favor of sleep. Oh, well. At least I wasn't buying shots at the bar and negotiating for a better price on illegal pills. Thirty-two dollars down the drain instead of two hundred. That was a minor victory, I guess.

But then, as I was drifting off, crushed under the weight of the poverty and the boredom and the dogs and the drunken campers . . . something strange.

My pants. They were loose.

Had I been walking around with them undone all day? No. Had I forgotten to button up? To cinch my belt? No. It was cinched where it was always cinched. And it was loose. By an entire notch.

I squeezed my hand between the hard leather and the soft, sickly heat of my belly fat, then immediately withdrew the hand. Lying on my back, I pulled the belt tight.

Five days. One inch. Gone.

Holy shit.

Eight hundred calories a day. They said it couldn't be done. Not for long. But I figured I had amassed enough soft tissue to make it work. It was a strange calculation, and by all accounts a dangerous one. But there was no turning back—at least no turning back worth considering. I just never figured it would cost me 160 pounds of real human flesh, swallow the better part of a year, serve as a passport to war-torn Eastern Europe, land me across a campfire from a vicious biker in the midst of thirty thousand hippies, score me a job, land me a wife, and otherwise make things extremely weird.

Could I do it again? I don't know. Would I? I'm even less sure. But I do know this: Hunger is power. And everything else is bullshit.

PART I

Most illustrious Drinkers and you, most precious Syphilitics, for it is to you, not to others, that my writings are dedicated . . .

However, you are to interpret all that I do and say in the very best part, holding in reverence the cheese-shaped brain that feeds you these fine puff-balls; and to the best of your ability, always keep me good company.

And now, my dears, hop to it, and gaily read the rest, wholly at your bodies' ease and to the profit of your loins. But listen, asswallopers—may a chancre lame you!—remember to drink a like health to me, and I will pledge you on the spot.

—François Rabelais, author's prologue to *Gargantua*, 1532, translated by Samuel Putnam.

Getting Fat and Going Broke
From Ivy League to Big and Tall

Some men spend their whole lives, from their infancy to their dying day, in going down the broad way to destruction. . . . The way to Heaven is ascending; we must be content to travel up hill, though it be hard and tiresome, and contrary to the natural bias of our flesh.
—Great Awakening preacher Jonathan Edwards,
"The Christian Pilgrim," c. 1745

MacDonald, perhaps you could trade this in for a six-pack.
—Dr. Bernard Lytton, Master of Jonathan Edwards College,
Yale University, upon handing me my diploma, 1995

I was a football player in high school. Never a great football player. Probably not even a good one. But I loved it.

Even in ninth grade, when I didn't get to play a single down. Even sophomore year, when I had to give my cleats up in the Coudersport game because our star fullback forgot his and everyone knew I wouldn't need mine. I had to warm up in regular sneakers. It was raining. I fell on my face. Repeatedly.

But it was a small town, so I got to play eventually. Especially senior year. There were only twenty-three guys on the team. At five feet eleven inches and a solid two hundred and fifteen pounds—a thirty-two-inch waist and a forty-four-inch chest—I never came off the field.

We finished the season with one win, seven losses, and a tie. But I didn't care. I loved it. Hitting people. Talking shit. Joking around with the guys. Wearing my jersey to school on game day. I was a starter, man. A starter on the worst team in town history, but that didn't matter. It was 1990. I was eighteen years old. A bit bookish, perhaps, but strapping in my own fashion. And I didn't have to give up my fucking cleats to anybody.

Sports gave way to booze when the season ended, though, and that's when I discovered that I had real talent. I'm not saying that my tolerance was world-class: I understand that Andre the Giant could suck down more than a hundred beers in one sitting. I couldn't touch that, but I could kill an entire Stroh's thirty-pack over the course of an evening, with a bit of Southern Comfort thrown in for effect.

So I drank a lot. And I had fun. Loads of it. And not the kind of fun people look back on ten years later and regret. I didn't hurt anybody. I didn't steal anything. I didn't wreck any cars. It was a good time, plain and simple.

Besides, it's not like I was a complete degenerate. My parents rode me pretty hard. I delivered home-cooked meals to dying widows. I got good grades. I got accepted to a fancy college. I was a decent kid, for the most part. One who liked to drink beer.

That carried over into college. I shot on the trap and skeet team. I completed a community service fellowship at a home for wayward children. One summer I worked my ass off in a brake factory. I washed dishes in the dining hall. I completed a double major in four years and maintained a respectable GPA.

And I drank.

By sophomore year the renowned British urologist Bernard Lytton, who served as master of my residential college, began checking into my antics. One morning he strolled into our suite unannounced. The stereo was playing GWAR at top volume; a smashed wheelchair was smoldering on the floor. I was sitting on a dirty love seat contemplating a Barbie doll. I had given her a Mohawk haircut to match my own the night before. I had not been to bed yet, and looked it.

Aghast at the scene, Master Lytton asked where the smoldering wheelchair had come from. I said I didn't know. Which was true. He muttered something about turning down the music and bolted.

A few months later I sold some books and bought a very expensive bottle of scotch with the proceeds. That night the master barged in on a small party I was attending. He complained that the noise we were making was ruining a symphony in the dining hall. Or maybe it was an opera. Either way, I tried to smooth things over by offering him a pull on the bottle, which I was holding in my right hand. "It's really good scotch," I said.

He seemed to mellow a bit. Really he did. And he seemed to be considering the offer until his glance shifted to the red plastic cup I was holding in my left hand. "What are you mixing it with?" he asked.

"Gin and tonic," I said.

He looked at me, perplexed.

"Well . . . gin, really," I said.

He did an about-face and bolted once again.

We had a series of similar run-ins throughout my time in New Haven. Once, he called me on the phone at six o'clock Sunday morning: "MacDonald," he said in his grim, groggy English accent, "it appears that you had a party last night."

"Yes, Master Lytton. Didn't see you there. Too bad, we—"

"MacDonald."

"Yes, Master Lytton?"

"It appears that one of your guests attacked my *buuuuhhhd-baaaahhhth*."

"Your birdbath, Master Lytton?"

"Yes, MacDonald. My birdbath is on its side. You will kindly come and right it."

"Yes, Master Lytton. Sorry about—"

Click.

And what a birdbath. It was concrete or marble or something equally heavy. And it was huge, apparently built for a condor or a family of ostriches. The bowl alone must have been three feet across. Or . . . Actually, maybe it was a sundial. Either way, I bet it weighed three hundred pounds. It had come detached from the base (which probably weighed another three hundred pounds) and was embedded eight inches deep in the master's lawn. It took me and two roommates thirty minutes to fix the cursed thing.

Senior year I personally purchased more than fifty kegs for parties in a suite known as the JE Sextet. I was a better customer than all the jocks at the SAE house combined, according to the woman who owned the liquor store.

My once-solid frame was showing signs of that excess, of course. My waist had expanded to thirty-eight inches. Or maybe it was forty. I should remember getting to forty inches. It seems like a landmark moment. Like turning sixteen or twenty-one. Or your first kiss. But I don't remember it.

I vaguely remember forty-two, though. Forty-two inches is closer to fifty than thirty. That's what struck me about it at the time. That, and the fact that most stores didn't stock anything bigger. Even Wal-

Mart. Forty-two was the end of the rack. It was the big-and-tall store after that. Where fat people shop.

I didn't hit forty-two until some time after graduation. When I moved to Baltimore. That's where everything hit the shits.

It was spectacular.

I moved to Maryland with my cousin. John Paul MacDonald. We called him Skippy.

Skippy had been my steady drinking partner for years. Then in 1996—the year I walked away from a half-assed career in computers and the year he graduated from college—we headed to Baltimore together. My sister taught middle school there. We crashed on her floor for a few months while we looked for real jobs. Then a few months more while we lowered our expectations and looked for jobs waiting tables.

We were bouncers at a Fell's Point bar called the Horse You Came In On Saloon. We also tended bar at the Waterfront Hotel, where they filmed scenes for the television show *Homicide*. Every afternoon it filled up with starstruck old ladies who asked if we knew any of the actors. The old ladies never tipped, so Skippy always told them they had the wrong place and sent them to a dirty dive bar about five blocks away. We thought that was pretty funny, but the comedy act didn't last long. I refused to work Labor Day because the owner didn't tell me I was scheduled until the night before. He fired me. Skippy went to work the next morning and called him an asshole. Skippy got fired, too.

So we moved from job to job, apartment to apartment. Two good-natured, booze-soaked idiots who loved drinking and spending money and letting the dealer come over with the Ecstasy and cat tranquilizer when things got strange. We spent most of our nights in a bar called Kisling's. It was a fantastic place. Just a few blocks from the gentrified nicety of Fell's Point, Kisling's was more of an every-man's joint. There were yuppies, sure, but the place was lousy with motorheads, skinheads, bikers, young couples, and just about every other kind of degenerate. We were especially fond of an ancient lady named Miss Jenny, a tough old bird who usually started drinking early in the afternoon. By early evening she would tell us all about her parents, her children, and how someone tried to slit her throat in a robbery. She had the scars to prove it.

Kisling's was especially popular with a peculiar breed of young tradesmen who had grown up thereabouts. Electricians, plumbers, carpenters. A few of them had started their own businesses, buying houses and refurbishing them. It was the nineties, dammit, and they were getting rich. Just like everybody else. A few of them became hard-charging real-estate tycoons, flipping house after house, work-ing like hell and drinking whenever they got the chance. Those guys could put away the booze. It was a privilege to waste my time with them. Really it was.

A pint of Rolling Rock at Kisling's was a dollar. Shots were free if you knew the right people. I always knew the right people. So I was always there. Tuesday became known as "boys' night," when a few hard-core regulars bellied up and enjoyed the midweek quiet. Wednesday was five-dollar all-you-can-drink night. (Those of us who were not real-estate gurus—mostly the college graduates— threw a handful of nickels and dimes at the bartender when we were low on cash. He never counted it.) Fridays and Saturdays were a given. Somebody called to demand my presence if I failed to show, which wasn't often.

When Kisling's commissioned a commercial and began searching for someone to play the lead—a big fat guy who sat around and drank a lot—I was the natural choice. A production crew transformed half the bar into a living room. I put on a Ravens jersey, drank a bunch, and danced around. The camera focused on me, then slowly pulled back to a wider shot revealing that the living room was actually part of the bar, which was full of other patrons. They did it over and over, trying to get the drinking and the dancing just right. I am not sure what the message was. Something about mixing your living space and the ambience at the bar. Like it was a second home. Which to me it was. All the commercial did was make it official. For a whole year, every place I went in Baltimore, I'd hear people say, "Hey, is that the Kisling's guy?"

Kisling's. Man, I loved that place.

I quit one job after another during those four years in Baltimore, moving from bouncing and bartending to investment banking and financial publishing. It's not that I couldn't do the work. Even with all the drinking, the late nights, the ever-expanding waistline, I was a good employee. In fact, I hardly ever quit until I got a promotion. The last thing I wanted was a job that called for nice clothes, a respectable car, and a decent apartment.

Journalism, I figured, was my last resort. Hemingway made it sound easy enough. Boozing it up in Paris. Bullfighting in Spain. *The Sun Also Rises* even revealed what I consider the first and only rule in journalism. According to Hemingway, for journalists, "it is such an important part of the ethics that you should never seem to be working."

Never seem to be working? Hell. I'd been a journalist for years and I didn't even know it. So in 1999 I signed on as a reporter at a small weekly newspaper twenty miles south of Baltimore. It was a good paper with a real newspaper guy in charge, but the pay was not what I might have hoped for four years gone from the Ivy League. One of my college friends was already a day-trading millionaire in Manhattan. He owned three apartments in the Village. He even rented a beach house in Montauk for a whole summer and purchased a new Audi to get himself there.

Rumor had it that another classmate was making inroads as a head-office guy in professional baseball. He had lived on my floor junior year. (His name was Theo Epstein. He eventually became the youngest general manager in the history of baseball and led the Boston Red Sox to the World Series in 2004.)

Another friend from college was selling paintings on a city street until a rich guy bought one for something like fifteen thousand dollars. So the painter took the money and hopped a flight to Morocco. Someone told me he was paying less than fifty dollars a week for his apartment, which came complete with a girl who provided cooking, cleaning, hashish, and blowjobs. I never bothered to confirm any of it. All I could do was imagine. What would that kind of life cost in New York? Baltimore, even? The blowjobs alone would have been astronomically expensive.

My monthly encounter with the Yale alumni magazine was becoming a tense affair. *So-and-so has recently finished her third year at Harvard Law. . . . Such-and-such has been named a partner at Goldman Sachs . . . tenure track position . . . travels through Europe and Africa . . .* It was the late 1990s and everyone was loaded. Even the heavy drinkers. Sure, a few of my classmates were living on credit, but most of those were the long-view types who decided to forgo in-

stant riches for med school or academia, or artsy types who laughed at
the blind ambition corrupting everybody else.

I tried to join the second crowd and blame my relative poverty
on my profession—journalism just doesn't pay. Which is true, in a
sense, but my classmate who was working as an editorial page editor for *The Wall Street Journal* was doing all right. One guy who
graduated a year behind me already had a piece published in *Playboy*. In fact, they published it while he was still in college. That's
the Big Time. The major freaking league. I consoled myself by re-
calling his last name—a name hinting that his grandfather might
have invented the atomic bomb. Tough to compete with that kind of
pedigree, that driven Ivy League type. I was just a hillbilly.

Still. I bet he got invited to the Playboy Mansion. Imagine. An
uptight Yale guy wallowing around in the Grotto, trying to get a
handful of sopping-wet Girl Next Door in all her coked-up, silicon-
stiff absurdity.

Or maybe that's just projection. Come to think of it, if he ever
did make it to the mansion he probably selected a manly-looking
cocktail and nursed it just long enough to chat up a features editor,
or line up an interview with someone who mattered. Yeah. It's only
important to never *seem* like you're working. Had he figured that
out? Who knows? I never knew him all that well. I don't even know
if he's related to the atomic-bomb guy. That's just the kind of thing
you tell yourself when someone makes it to the Big Time and you
don't.

In the meantime, I could barely pay my living expenses as I
scrambled to account for a decade of drinking on credit and borrowed time. These pipers, they were vicious, and they demanded to
be paid. And not in an angry bookie sort of way. Flight from an angry bookie allows for radical action. Friends converge. Siblings

rally. Parents hawk heirlooms: Silver, china, everything goes except the rosaries. Anything to protect the prodigal prodigy from shattered teeth and broken thumbs.

Or so I imagine. My financial crisis was doubly cruel in its dullness and the damnable respectability of my pursuers.

Despair finally descended on me in April 2000, almost a full decade after I had embarked on my long, raucous march into irresponsible living.

The first disaster played out on a visit home when my father took my aging Ford Taurus for a spin. He meant to fill it with gas, a generous paternal gesture that morphed into a nine-hundred-dollar calamity by the time I stumbled out of bed later that afternoon.

He immediately recognized the awful metallic rumble—the strange symphony I had been ignoring for months—as the last gasps of a shattered machine. "Even the tires are shot," he explained in the driveway as I tried to shake off a hangover. "The belts are exposed. They're rubbing on the road. Can't you hear it on the highway?"

"Well, yeah. I thought I heard something, but . . ."

"And the CV boots are gone," he said. "Can't you hear it when you turn?"

"Yeah, I guess so," I said. "Yeah. I was going to get it fixed, but the money . . . you know. I'm waiting until I get my tax return."

"You can't drive this car back to Baltimore like this," he said.

So I didn't drive it back to Baltimore like that. Because he got the car fixed. Four retread tires. CV boots. Thermostat. Battery. Headlights. Wipers. Oil change. A few bits and pieces I had never heard of.

It was another in a long line of bailouts. My parents bought me the car after college to help me get on my feet. I still wasn't on my feet when the transmission crapped out six months after that, so they paid for a rebuild. And another rebuild when the damn transmission died again a year later.

But this time was going to be different. The tax return. I was going to use it to pay my parents back for the repairs. That glorious, ass-saving tax return. It meant responsibility. Self-sufficiency. Independence. Potential fulfilled. So I limped back to Baltimore, chastened yet again, but convinced that salvation was just a 1040EZ away.

So Sunday night, after arriving at the crusty townhouse Skippy and I shared on South Chapel Street, I sat down to fill out the forms. No going out tonight. It was mid-April. The filing deadline was upon me. Ignoring the fragile state of the secondhand recliner (the footrest had collapsed in tatters months earlier), I leaned my hefty frame forward and balanced a burning cigarette on top of an empty beer can amid the paperwork on the floor. I snatched up an official-looking envelope, slipped my pudgy pinky finger under the wilted flap, ripped it open, and yanked out the form.

"Ten-ninety-nine?" I wondered as I retrieved the cigarette. "What the hell is a 1099?"

Uh-oh.

Turns out freelance work is taxable. Worse, the bastards who hired me as a freelancer told the IRS how much they paid me. Where's the decency? Isn't there some kind of unwritten code? Great Christ. Had I really made that much? I had quit a job as managing editor of a financial newsletter in early 1999. They had offered a promotion, but made some ominous squawkings about a lucrative future in the world of direct-mail copywriting. Oof! That smacked of responsibility and measurable success. No thanks. Still, I left on good terms and they sent some editing work my way. A hell of a lot more work than I remembered. About ten thousand dollars' worth. Taxable. Every cent of it. Shit.

I leaned forward again and slipped the burning cigarette into the mouth of the beer can. It hit the bottom with a hollow clink. I picked up the can by its beveled top and gave it a shake, heard the quick reassuring sizzle within. I retrieved another cigarette from my chest pocket. I grabbed the Zippo.

Click. Clink. Puff.

My fat tax return had suddenly become a thirteen-hundred-dollar federal tax liability. And a few hundred more in state taxes. All of it due immediately.

The boys at the bar are going to love this one, I thought.

I was slumped in that same wrecked recliner a few days—and a few hangovers—later when the final blow slipped through the mail slot. Rattled awake by the ominous plunk of correspondence on the living room rug, I did my best version of a sit-up to get out of the recliner, slumping forward to grab the pile of mail that had fallen at my feet.

I was worried. I didn't have a penny to pay for the car repairs and the back taxes, and here was a whole new pile of bills. Credit card. Credit card. Credit card. No surprise there. But then another envelope caught my eye. Student loans. Dammit, dammit, dammit. I forgot the damn student loans. Again.

For a while I didn't have to worry about student loans because another Sam MacDonald, bless his heart, lost everything in a flood in South Carolina. He applied for a deferral that somehow, miraculously, got attached to my account. Those were happy times. Until someone in charge realized the error. Then it all got very messy and I slipped further and further into arrears.

I slid the letter out of the envelope. What did I owe? How far behind? Two months? Three? Three would mean I owed four hundred and fifty dollars, plus late fees. That would be the kind of humiliating blow that leaves a man gasping for breath and defenseless, the financial equivalent of a rabbit punch to the throat.

What I got was far worse. An ice pick to the eyeball. A shotgun blast to the nuts. A somersault-savate kick to the base of the skull followed promptly by a shiv to the small intestine.

Yeah, I was three months behind. But I also owed extra. *One thousand four hundred dollars extra.*

The letter mentioned something about transferring my loan to another bank. There was something about the flood and another coupon book that I should have received. The bottom line: I had been paying the wrong amount for a long time (when I had been paying at all). It was my fault. And they wanted me to make up the difference. Now.

So . . . in a ten-day span, between the car and the taxes and the student loans, I had leapt out of a precarious paycheck-to-paycheck existence and into something far worse. I was suddenly around four thousand dollars in debt—all of it due yesterday. Throw in back rent, utility bills, and a couple thousand dollars on credit cards—all of which I paid sporadically, if ever—and my troubles were into the five-figure range.

I know. That might not seem like a lot. Other people my age owed a lot more, but most of them had something to show for the red ink. A hulking SUV. A hip town house. Fancy clothes. A master's in philosophy. A fucking CD collection. At least the guy in Morocco was getting hashish and blowjobs. All I had was a bloated midriff and a growing catalog of barroom stories.

To be fair, they were good stories. How about that time we blew up the street? The Chinese guy we carried home on New Year's? The time that guy with the harelip attacked me at the convenience store and I knocked him out cold with a stiff right cross? The Hispanic dude with the machete? (Or was it a piece of broken glass? It's so hard to remember details like that.) The run-in with state troopers at the wine festival? Such memories are priceless, to be sure, but sorely lacking in terms of liquidity.

I knew people who had run up a load of debt by living irresponsibly, but most of them were positioning themselves to pay the money back. My fellow Yalies on Wall Street and in Silicon Valley were finally coming into their own. And not just the high achievers. We're talking the B-plus masses. They would soon rule the free world, or so we were told, and the holdover cost of a few indiscriminate nights on the town, even with compound interest, would be nothing more than fodder for self-deprecating memoirs fifty years hence.

So it was time. Time for action. But what kind of action? The beast of indulgence is not so easily tamed. Besides, even if I did clean up my act, I still couldn't cover my monthly bills *and* the debt.

Bankruptcy seemed appealing. At least on the surface. Seven years and in the clear. But then what? What would the alumni magazine say in 2007? *Perfect Perfectson recently received tenure at Stanford and finalized plans to kick off his congressional campaign next fall. In the meantime, Sam MacDonald reports that he is still living in a decrepit Baltimore town house but has recently emerged from bankruptcy with his fat ass intact. He writes for a weekly news-*

paper and has a lot of good stories, although none of them involves the Playboy mansion.

I knew there had to be another way. So I made a plan. It was a strange and dangerous plan. A shitty plan, actually. But it was something.

I took a deep breath and issued a warning to myself: "Get ready. This is going to hurt."

2

This Grocery Store Is Decadent and Depraved

The outside relaxes the belly; the inside constricts. It is digested with difficulty, generates black bile and creates scaly skin disease, causes flatulence and a stuffed feeling, harms brain and chest, dulls the eyes, and represses passion.

—Bartolomeo Platina, discussing lentils,

in *De Honesta Voluptate et Valetudine*, c. 1470 A.D.

Lentils are known throughout the world, particularly in India and the Middle East, as "the poor man's meat."

That is because lentils suck.

I know. I'm going to catch all sorts of flak: *But lentils form the basis of many traditional world cuisines.* Indeed. *But lentils form the basis of harira, the national soup of Morocco.* Yes. *But lentils form the basis of fakes, the ancient soup of the Greeks.* Quite accurate.

These things are all true. But none of them can overcome the terrible fact that lentils are horrible. Awful. And bad.

Everyone knows it. And they always have. In the play *Plutus*, written by Aristophanes in 380 B.C., a character named Chremylus discusses what happens when a man gets a bit of cash in his pocket: "When poor, he would devour anything; now he is rich, he no longer cares for lentils."

Why would such a man no longer care for lentils? Because he

could afford something else. Anything else. Try them once. You'll see.

And it's not just rich Greeks. In *A History of Food*, Maguelonne Toussaint-Samat reveals the following:

> In the reign of the Emporer Caligula, the obelisk which now stands in St. Peter's Square in the Vatican was brought by ship from the banks of the Nile, nestling among 120,000 measures of lentils. The Athenians made a fortifying lentil broth called a *ptisane*, and the lentil soup provided for the Roman legions by the consuls sustained their iron morale. . . . Later, in the seventeenth century, people came to despise them, and declared them fit only for horse fodder.

Here's my take: To say that lentils taste like dirt would be to state the case exactly backward. Dirt, it turns out, tastes like lentils. I am confident that, had the lowly lentil plant never evolved, the world's soil might today deliver a palate-pleasing sensation akin to ripe cantaloupe, fresh honey, or perhaps a Twix bar.

But it was not to be. The aggressive chalkiness of the lentil—the dry, pasty, unstoppable blandness—eventually pervades all it touches. And thousands of years of cultivation have poisoned the earth with the vast vacuum of lentil-taste.

Okay. Sure. Give me a nice hot bowl of Moroccan harira any day. The lusty tomato and curry can overpower the intruding lentil for a while. But given enough time—maybe an hour, maybe a day—all taste would disappear into the abyss.

How do I know? I happen to be an expert on lentils. I matched Caligula in the several months that marked the opening stage of the Urban Hermit plan. Bested him, actually. One hundred and twenty thousand measures of lentils to support an obelisk? Please. I must have eaten twice that to support my own bloated carcass.

And I am not talking *ptisane* or harira or some kind of special Greek soup. That would have been cheating. I am talking about lentils. Boiled. With salt.

Horse fodder. If you hate your horse.

Perhaps I seem bitter. And perhaps that's true. But allow me to explain how lentils—those despicable lentils—came to play such a critical role in my experiment. How they saved me from myself. Maybe then you'll understand.

I came up with the basic plan on my own: Spend as little money as possible for a month. And no messing around. Rip life down to the basics. No more Kisling's. Eat the bare minimum required to stay alive. Send the savings to the creditors. Simple.

But I had to come up with something more. I needed specifics. Immediately. The weekend coming up was Easter. I was heading home. I still had to explain to my parents why they weren't going to get that tax return check. Worse, if I wasn't careful I would end up taking another check from Mom and Dad to cover the back taxes and the student loans. All to be paid at some future date. Just like all the other times.

I had to find another way.

I had the phone to my ear and I could hear what she was saying. "You can't do that," she said. "Your kidneys will fail. You'll die eventually."

But I wasn't listening.

I acted like I was mulling it over. I owed her that much. Rena was more than my cousin. She grew up two houses down the street from us. In Aunt Inez and Uncle Paul's house. The house my mom grew up in. Rena was more like a sister. And she was a registered dietician. That's why I called her.

"Come on, Rena," I said. "It's just for a month. How many calories do I need to keep me alive for a month? People get stuck on life rafts for that long, right? I don't want to get sick. Scurvy or rickets or something. But how many calories do I *need* every day? Six hundred?"

"I'm telling you," she said. "You need at least twelve hundred calories a day. And you need that just sitting around the house. You're a big guy. Your heart beats. You digest food. All that takes energy. Any less than twelve hundred calories and you could get sick."

"Okay," I said. "But could I start out lower and move up if I don't feel good after a few days? I'm fat. Can't I, like, hibernate? Live off reserves? What about six hundred?"

"Twelve hundred," she said.

"Eight hundred?"

"You're not listening," she said. "Twelve hundred."

"A thousand?"

"Twelve hundred."

I decided right then and there that it would be eight hundred calories. Sure, she was a professional nutritionist. But twelve hundred calories? I was tough. Any sane medical professional would have advised me against guzzling a Stroh's thirty-pack and a pint of Southern Comfort in one sitting. Against pounding one Rolling Rock after another for an entire decade. And all that did was make me fat and broke. Twelve hundred calories was for supermodels on crash diets. Soccer moms who needed to lose five pounds fast. Accountants making New Year's resolutions.

Pussies.

I was serious. My mind was made up: eight hundred calories a day.

Reactions to the plan were mixed.

"You're going to do what?"

"How many calories?"

"Yeah, right."

"How much money do you *owe*, dude?"

Which was understandable. I revealed the details over Easter weekend, during which time I consumed approximately five pounds of candy, at least a dozen hard-boiled eggs carefully colored by my nieces and nephews, and an enormous holiday feast. I also got rip-roaring drunk three times. So yeah, the Urban Hermit story seemed pretty far-fetched. Even to me. I'll admit it.

I don't know what made the idea stick. Maybe the mixed reaction. The notion that maybe I *couldn't* do it. The idea that maybe I *was* out of control. Perhaps it was mom's frustrated but kindhearted offer: "We can help you," she said. "Really, we can." Maybe so. But how many thousands of dollars would it take? For how long?

No.

Skippy was the last one to see me before it got started. When I still had a chance to change my mind. Fucking Skippy. It seems right and good that he was there to see the old me waddle off into oblivion.

He wasn't nearly as fat as I was. His chemistry was different. It was the Crohn's disease that nailed him. All that pain and the cramps and the surgical bowel resections. He could drink whiskey like a son of a bitch—which was quite courageous, given his condition—but he wouldn't have lasted a week on eight hundred calories a day. Not because he wasn't tough-minded or disciplined. He couldn't have handled it physically.

We met at the door of our crappy rowhouse. It was Easter Sunday. Late afternoon. I had just dropped off my stuff from the weekend and was headed back out the door. He was just getting in.

"Where you going?" he asked.

"Grocery store," I said.

"Hold up," he said as he dropped his bag on the seat of my recliner, the one with the broken footrest. "I'll go."

It was an awkward moment.

"Well," I said, "I'm just getting all that junk I was talking about. The lentils and stuff."

"Holy shit," he said. "You're really doing that?"

"I know," I said. "I'm just going to try it. Maybe a few weeks. A month or something."

Silence.

"I'm really in trouble with the fucking bills," I said.

"Yeah," he said.

And then I died.

The grocery store used to be a place of wonder. Happiness. Plenty. Especially this grocery store. It was on Boston Street. When we moved to Baltimore the street was basically impassable. Broken concrete. Potholes. A real dump. There was a gay bar called the Unicorn. A ratty dance club called the Spot. The Captain James, a diner designed to look like the bow of a ship, complete with porthole windows. And another diner called the Sip 'n Bite. Skippy and I loved the Sip 'n Bite.

But the neighborhood was changing, and it started with the

grocery store. It was brand-new, built to serve the influx of yuppies paying top dollar for the townhouses that the drunks at Kisling's had been so busy converting. These new city dwellers demanded a salad bar, a hot bar, green tomatoes, Black Angus beef, fresh white asparagus, yellowfin tuna, bluefin tuna, white albacore tuna, seventy-eight varieties of orange juice, and service with a smile. A Starbucks in the store, right next to the checkout lanes.

The old American Can Company next door to the grocery store was next. Developers converted it into a Borders bookstore. A tuxedo shop. A barbershop staffed with young, large-breasted Australian chicks who charged thirty-five dollars for a high-and-tight. Why not? It was the year 2000 and all was well. Only it wasn't anymore. At least not for me as the electronic doors parted and I entered the Boston Street Safeway.

It's a good thing Skippy didn't come. There was always some kind of fancy stuff on sale, and Easter Sunday was even worse. The aisles were packed with loads of high-end groceries that the store overstocked for the holidays. Shrimp—fresh, frozen, and steamed. Enormous hams. Tiny hams. Pre-sliced. Spiral-sliced. Free-range honey-baked hams, corn fed, coddled, and slaughtered in the most humanitarian Midwestern American fashion. So many marshmallow Peeps that it made my nuts ache just looking at the gargantuan piles. The place was hell on earth for an Urban Hermit. But I was determined.

I had originally planned to snap up a few cases of ramen soup. That would have been some cheap living. But it also could have been a death wish. Too much salt. Too many carbs. Not enough *protein*, Rena said.

Protein is easy if you're just dieting, of course. Just swing by the meat counter and get yourself some of that Black Angus. Or try the yellowfin. Yeah, that's good shit. But at $16.99 a pound, it didn't fit into my scheme.

No. I needed a different kind of tuna fish. So I made my way to the canned meats aisle. And there it was. The cheap stuff. I'm talking shredded tuna. Store brand. Packed in water. A six-ounce can. One hundred and fifty calories. Fifty cents each. *Clink, clatter, clang*, into the cart.

And then the rest of it: Store-brand cheese. Pre-sliced. Fifty calories per slice. *Sold.* Eggs. Grade "A" large. Seventy calories each plus the protein. *Delicious.* White bread. The cheapest. Fifty calories a slice. *That'll do.* Green cabbage. One head. Calories negligible. But you have to have greens, Rena said, and broccoli is expensive. *To hell with broccoli.*

And finally . . . the lentils. Rena told me that lentils were a "wonder food." What people ate to stay alive. A plant with protein. And dirt cheap. The poor man's meat. But even she blanched at my proposal. "I think you have to cook them with something," she said. "A ham hock, you know. Lentil soup."

No. No ham hock. A ham hock will cost. Even on Easter Sunday in the world's most dangerous grocery store.

So I made my way down the dry-foods aisle and found my salvation: a gray, dusty bag of lentils, one pound for fifty-nine cents. I picked it up and inspected the dull little lenses, felt them fold over my hand. Ooze. Rattle. Like they were alive.

The nutrition label told an impressive tale. One serving packed 160 calories. I would have two servings per day. A bag would last me four days and then some. Half my calories for the week for $1.18. Fantastic.

I tossed that bag into the cart, grabbed another and did the same. You are what you eat, they say. So I started getting used to the idea of being a poor man's meat and headed for the counter.

That food—enough for an entire week—cost me a grand total of eight dollars. Not even, actually, because there was enough bread and cheese to last two weeks. And the bread and cheese was high-dollar stuff compared to the lentils.

Eight dollars. A lunch at Applebee's for everyone else in the world. But not for me. The Urban Hermit.

My daily menu on the Urban Hermit Financial Emergency Rotgut Poverty Plan:

BREAKFAST
Two eggs, hard-boiled (140 calories)

LUNCH
One serving lentils (160 calories)

DINNER
One serving lentils (160 calories)
One tuna fish sandwich—consisting of two slices bread, one can tuna, one slice cheese (300 calories)
Boiled cabbage if you can stomach it, up to 40 calories' worth

TOTAL: 800 CALORIES

Or 760 if you forget the cabbage. And I recommend that you do.

Eight hundred calories a day. Desperate? Sure. But the only other option was . . . well, I don't know that there was another option. Especially after I made a point of explaining the plan to everyone. Once I did that I was finished.

Being a screw-up is a personal failing. But making a plan and not sticking to it? That's a *failure*. And those are completely different things.

I had never actually *failed*. As fat as I was, I had never gone on a diet. So I had never failed to stick to one. As far as finances go, yeah, I was broke. But that was also by choice, in a way. I never applied for a job and failed to get it, as far as I could recall. And other than that job at the bar, I had never been fired. So as screwed up as my life was, I could always fall back on the notion that I could straighten it out if I *wanted* to. Or if I *had to*.

Well, now it seemed like I had to. The old way was getting old. Even for my parents. Even for my dad, who knows a thing or two about self-induced financial distress. As a young drinking man in the early 1950s, one of his favorite stunts was to stand on the margins of a crowded dance floor, rip open a roll of quarters, and toss them at everyone's flailing feet. Ten dollars was a lot of money at the time, but he thought it was funny to watch people scramble for change.

He took this passion to extremes as an Army engineer during the Korean War. On leave, he had his pay exchanged into the nearly worthless local currency. Impressed by the enormous bulk of all those foreign bills, he filled a bushel basket and dumped it out of his hotel window. Just to watch people scramble for it. Besides, he says, they needed it more than he did.

My dad never scrambled for money. He worked for it. And he worked hard. He just never let it master him.

He was an automotive machinist. Not a body man or transmission guy. That's a mechanic. My dad did the serious stuff. Boring-out blocks, turning cranks. He was good at it, too. He worked sixty hours a week well into his sixties. How the hell else is a machinist supposed to pay what Yale costs?

He had to give up his wild ways when he started a family, but he still managed to control things in his own peculiar way. When I was in college, I came home for the summer and discovered that someone had painted the eaves on our house. I mentioned it to my dad, who gave a chuckle and led me into the backyard. "See that?" he said, pointing to a dingy spot way up high on the house.

"Yeah," I said. "Missed a spot."

"I didn't miss it," he said. "I just didn't finish it."

"Why?" I asked.

"I hate painting houses," he said. "This way, I can still say I never really painted one."

After that I noticed that the freshly mowed lawn occasionally had patches of long grass scattered here and there. The freshly shoveled sidewalk a patch of ice in the corner. Were these oversights? Maybe. But I don't think so. My dad did what he needed to do. Always. But he found a way to do things on his own terms. Strange as they might have been.

Most of the people I grew up around were like that. It was a hardworking bunch, but not serious or grim. People loved their families. They went to church, volunteered as scout leaders and coaches. They punched the clock and lived their lives as best they could.

And they drank. Some of them better than others, but everyone drank. To celebrate. To mourn. To think. To share their lives. Drinking was an important thread in the social fabric, one that was neither dysfunctional nor destructive for people who knew how to handle their moderation in moderation.

My family was full of masters. The men specialized in beer. Whatever was cheapest. Genesee, usually, but Hamm's or anything else when it was on sale. The women drank Manhattans that were dry enough to qualify as a glass full of whiskey. That would not have been very ladylike, though, so they always kept a dusty bottle of vermouth on hand and stuck to the Manhattan story. And there wasn't a single drunk in the bunch.

But something had gone wrong. I got the gene that told me to dump a bushelful of foreign cash out the window. And I sure as hell understood about Manhattans. But that moderation-in-moderation gene? I don't know what happened to that.

So I was a hundred and twenty pounds overweight and dead-ass broke on Easter Sunday in the year 2000 as I walked through the front door of my crappy Baltimore row house, began reading the preparation instructions on a bag of lentils, and started counting the days.

· 3 ·

Preparation

The Color of (No) Money

Of all the deadly sins currently tempting us, envy is topping the charts. Who wants to get rich? Everyone! Who wants to work for it? No one!

—*The New York Times Book Review*, April 23, 2000

April 23, 2000. The kitchen was clean for once.

I spent about forty-five minutes scrubbing the filthy dishes. The ones in the sink had been soaking all weekend in water that had gone from orange greasy suds to a sad sort of gray. But at least they had been soaking. The ones on the counter had developed an angry crust reminiscent of concrete. But I cleaned them. One at a time.

Then I chiseled the burnt cheese and petrified elbow noodles off the stovetop. Then I emptied the half-empty beer bottles that we used as ashtrays. Then I swept all the cat litter off the floor. Then it was time to cook.

So there I was, boiling a dozen eggs. Boiling lentils. And boiling half a head of cabbage. I was cooking enough for a few days. Might as well make things easy. Only I never counted on the smell. Good God. It didn't waft off the stove like smoke. It was an aggressively earthy stench, blasting my nostrils, burning them. No sweetness. No humor. It made me feel even poorer. And fatter.

Skippy looked in and gave me a grave, skeptical look. "Dude," he said.

"Dude, seriously," I replied.

Skippy went to bed, but I had work to do. After the eggs were cooked I cooled them in ice water. I had seen Martha Stewart cook her eggs this way on the Food Network. (We watched it incessantly.) It was supposed to keep the yolks from turning green.

Then the lentils. I had never cooked them before. They had been boiling for about twenty minutes. I dipped the spoon into the water and snagged a few of the little bastards. They had plumped up substantially, bursting out of their skins. I took a bite. Bad stuff. They were mushy on the outside, but somehow underdone. Crunchy in the center. I added more salt.

After a few more minutes I tossed a strainer into the sink and, *plop*, dropped the whole mess of them in there to drain. Wow. It was a lot of lentils, a sloppy mound of them about as big as a softball. Or maybe a brain. Enough for four days. So I grabbed eight plastic containers—two servings per day—and parceled them out.

By the time I was done I could smell the smoke coming out of the cabbage pan, which had boiled dry. I lifted the lid, looked in, and saw a pile of putrid green leaves perched on a thin layer of charred black leaves. Shit. I tossed it in the sink and ran it under water. *Tssssss!* Green leaves. Black leaves. Brown water. And still the smell. But there was no looking back. I grabbed the other half of the cabbage, cut it up, and started boiling it in the lentil pan.

While that was cooking I walked into the living room and got on my knees directly between the two recliners and the television. I fell forward a bit and put my hands on the floor. Then I walked my feet back until I was positioned to do a push-up. My arms quivered, sending a little wave through my soft flesh. It became a bigger wave as I bent my elbows and felt the full weight of my history pulling me into the center of the earth.

I dipped down, closer and closer to the floor. My belly, swinging loosely below me, hit bottom before anything else. I tried to control the descent as best I could until my nose was an inch from the dirty carpet. I let out a little grunt and paused before trying to reverse the motion. I unclenched my eyes for a split second and contemplated the floor. It was brown. Our entire house was brown, to be honest. Browner than any of the other places Skippy and I had occupied. Which was saying something.

The first place we considered renting, way back in late 1996 or early 1997, was next to a used-appliance store on Eastern Avenue. The apartment was dark and crooked. All the floors seemed off by a few degrees—just enough to make us nauseous. But it was cheap, and two blocks from Kisling's. The guy showing the place was old, round, and bald. He wore a tight white T-shirt that revealed lumps, nipples, and skin tone. He kept asking where our furniture was.

"We're just looking," I said, a little confused by the question. Why would we bring our furniture to look at the place? "We're living with my sister. Once we get settled we'll—"

"You don't want this fucking place," he whined. "You don't got no fucking furniture."

No fucking furniture, indeed. The accusation was irrefutable. So we spent a few more weeks looking. Responding to ads. But mostly we went to Kisling's. Which is where we met Eric.

We had been drinking—a lot—and complaining about the house hunt when he overheard our chatter and swooped in. He was extremely tall. Extremely thin. Leather jacket. Slicked-back hair.

Pencil-thin mustache. Eric was so singular in his tallness and his thinness and his mustache-ness, in fact, that I sometimes wonder if he really ever existed. But I know he did. Because the next day he walked us through a row house he owned. It was right up the street.

The living room had brown carpet and wood paneling on one wall. The other had an enormous mirror that reflected the brown into infinity. Rounding out the décor was a faux fireplace, an old gas log, and a four-foot palm tree in a green plastic pot. "That's Robert," Eric said, pointing to the palm. "He stays."

"Robert?" I replied.

"Yeah, Robert," he said with a huge grin, waiting. Waiting. Waiting for what seemed like hours. *Robert Plant.*

And that was only the beginning. The living room gave way to an outdated kitchen, which gave way to a mudroom, which gave way to a large fenced-in concrete yard. It had a huge deck—in dire need of weather treatment—and a "hot tub." It was just a black plastic tub sunk into the deck. No drain. No jets. No way to heat the water. It was full of dead leaves.

Back inside, we went up the tight spiral staircase. The railing was an extremely thick rope, heavily shellacked for stiffness. The second floor had one bedroom, a laundry, and a tiny spare room overlooking the backyard. The third floor had a bedroom, a bathroom with a red shag carpet, plus a utility room occupied by a rusty weight bench.

We signed a lease on the spot. Because it was cheap and close to Kisling's. And there were only two rules: No more than two tenants, and no pets.

Within three months we had another tenant. Richie, our good friend from back home. Eric, who had a troubling habit of stopping by, noticed the sleeping bag and started asking questions. Which we never answered. So he stopped asking.

A few months later we got a dog. A ridiculous black-and-white mutt with a pointy nose, puffy fur, and a curly tail. Maybe part Pomeranian. Definitely part idiot. It was the kind of dog that loved to drink whiskey, but only if someone put it in a bowl with mustard. I'm not sure how we discovered that. But we did. We named the dog Bootjack.

Eric dropped by a week or so later and discovered about seven hundred dog turds on the back deck. Probably enough to fill the hot tub. He warned us about the rules. Then he built us a doghouse.

And the row house kept getting browner. We were all heavy smokers. There was no air-conditioning. We were terribly inept at house-training Bootjack. Which was becoming a real problem. Until one Sunday morning when Richie woke me up to go drinking at Double Dans, a dive bar down the street. I stuck with beer, but he started in with the cheap tequila. He was in trouble by noon, when he decided to drive somewhere. I hopped in the car to talk him out of it. And we were off.

We rear-ended a convertible by Camden Yards. The guy we hit took pity on us. "You guys need to get the fuck out of here," he said. We didn't ask questions. We bolted.

I went upstairs to take a shower when we got home. Richie only made it halfway through the door. His head and chest were on the living room floor. His legs were on the stoop in front of the house. He was propping the door open, giving Bootjack access to the great outdoors. We never saw the dog again.

After a year of that we decided it was time to clean up our act. We started looking at apartments in better neighborhoods, but we could never agree on a place. Pretty soon we had a week left on our lease and nowhere to go. Then Richie noticed that the three hot girls living next door to us were moving out. (We had never spoken

to them. Maybe all the stumbling and dog shit had turned them off.)
Richie talked to their landlord. The house seemed a bit bigger. And
a bit nicer. So we moved our crap one house over.

It was blue inside. Ostensibly. But we quickly realized that it was
even browner than Eric's place. The kitchen was in the basement,
the refrigerator directly under the first-floor shower, which leaked
like a sieve. And there's nothing quite as brown as water damage.

Except maybe the smell. The place had a horrible stench that
quickly overpowered the lingering scent of powder and bath prod-
ucts that the girls had left behind. We chalked it up to man-smell
and tobacco, or something equally wet and gross, until Super Bowl
Sunday rolled around. We were watching the game at home when we
noticed flashing lights outside. We peeked out the door and saw
about a hundred cops swarming the street. They were hustling in and
out of the row house next door (not Eric's, the one on the other side)
carrying hundreds of huge marijuana plants. One of the cops came to
our door and asked if he could borrow some garbage bags. We said
yes. And scrambled to hide our bong, which was sitting on the coffee
table.

The young couple who lived in the marijuana house seemed normal enough. They even had a little girl. A toddler. But they had a serious system going. Grow lights. Foil on the wall. Special soil. That
was the smell. All that pot and agricultural stuff. We had no idea. Neither did anyone else. Until the guy went to work one day, the woman
sampled some of the merchandise and, allegedly, fell asleep long
enough for the toddler to get loose. Kind of like Bootjack. Only the
neighbors spotted her wandering around on the street and called the
police.

The cops who stormed the place arrested the woman, began
searching for her husband, and seized all the plants as evidence.

When they were done they shoveled all the dirt that was left behind—there must have been a couple tons of it—into the basement. Then they locked the house and left.

About a month later we noticed muddy water seeping through the wall into our basement. We called the fire department. A guy showed up and determined that the pipes in the marijuana house had frozen and burst, turning it into an enormous, icy mud pit. Now it was thawing and oozing into our place.

The fireman promised to turn off the water to the marijuana house. On the way out, he pointed to our coffee table, smiled, and said, "Next time you call the fire department, you might want to hide that."

It was the bong.

Richie eventually left Baltimore when he accepted a job in State College, Pennsylvania. Skippy and I knew we had to move, but where? Mike, one of the owners at Kisling's, mentioned that he had just purchased a row house around the corner from where we were living. "It's a good house," he said, "but eventually I'm going to gut it. I'm not starting work for a few months. You can crash there."

The house was at 315 South Chapel Street. The setting for the Urban Hermit saga.

You want to talk about brown? This place was brown. South Chapel Street was more like an alley. The house was brick, two stories. The front door opened to the living room, with its brown carpet and cheap wood paneling from the seventies. Next came a small kitchen and a utility closet that housed the water heater and a toilet. At the top of the stairs, turning left, we encountered a tiny room, which led into a much larger bedroom overlooking the street. Going straight at the top of the stairs led to the bathroom and a strange room set off by a green shower curtain. Mike called it a walk-in closet.

We took it. Skippy took the big bedroom because he had a big bed. I decided to turn the "walk-in" into my bedroom. We could barely squeeze my mattress into it, but it seemed better than the little room Skippy would have to walk through to get to his bedroom. So I slept three feet from the toilet and had a green shower curtain for a door.

Even more sinister was the closet underneath the stairs. A few days after moving in we worked up the courage to explore it and found an artificial leg—from the knee down—that must have been seventy-five years old. It was heavy. Wood and metal. We joked around with it for a while, but eventually got tired of it and put it back.

We kept to ourselves, mostly. An abandoned row house about four doors up burned a few months after we moved in. Ten or twelve immigrants from El Salvador lived right next to us. They drank a lot and made a whole bunch of noise at odd hours, but so did we. We never complained. Neither did they. They broke the big picture window in their living room about every other week. But they always replaced it the next day.

Then there was the old man who lived across the alley, a frail-looking guy who sat on his stoop at all hours. He never said hello. One day we saw an ambulance there. He was dead. He had been in there for days before anyone noticed. Authorities entered the place and found dogs, cats, and other animals that had been living in filth for years. At least that's what some old lady sitting on her stoop told Skippy.

This went on for months. Mike kept putting off the renovations, and we kept putting off moving. It was a pretty tight deal. When we were late on rent, Mike added it to our tab and we paid it with a credit card.

Like I said, it was brown. Browner than you will ever know. And not just the color. The *feel* of the place. The essence. It was brown like bong water. Brown like artificial limbs. Brown like a fistful of pennies. Brown like a barroom in the morning. Brown like stomach surgery. Brown like 1972. Brown like traffic jams. Brown like your own body odor.

Brown like fender benders and lost dogs and wandering toddlers and water damage. Brown like sweating yourself to sleep three feet from the toilet. Brown like cellulite. Brown like stretch marks. Brown like emphysema.

Brown like you feel right now. Only browner.

That's the brown I saw in that carpet when I did that first push-up. The brown I smelled. The brown I struggled to push myself away from until my arms locked.

Then I paused, took a breath, and did it again. And again. Each time my arms shook a bit more and my grunts got louder, until I had done twenty push-ups. I was out of breath. Exhausted. I told myself I could have done more. But I doubt that. I wondered if the last one even counted. I was strong. But I was heavy.

Besides, twenty was enough. I wasn't trying to get in a good workout. I was playing defense. I ignored everyone who told me that the Urban Hermit plan was dangerous, but some of their warnings seemed pretty gruesome. Like the idea that I might ruin my kidneys, piss out all my muscles, and die. In response, I decided to test my strength through push-ups. I'd do as many as I could once a week to make sure I wasn't getting weaker. And when I started getting weaker I would call it quits. Simple.

So I got up, got the cabbage off the stove just in time, stuck it in the fridge, and went to bed. I was already feeling sore.

· 4 ·

A Day in the Life
"I'll Buy You Lunch," and Other Hateful Things
You'll Hear as an Urban Hermit

[Deepak Jain] started AiNET when he was seventeen, using five computers and his own money. Eight years later, the company is now worth so much that "if somebody offered $50 million to buy this company, we'd laugh at them," said Jain.
— "A Very Exciting Time for Entrepreneurs,"
The Baltimore Sun, April 24, 2000

Given that rising stock portfolios have encouraged high levels of consumer spending, the task for Washington policy-makers is to make sure that the sinking stock market does not take the real economy of jobs and production down with it.
— "Spelling Out Guidelines for Alan Greenspan,"
The Baltimore Sun, April 24, 2000

April 24, 2000. The first full day of the Urban Hermit Financial Emergency Rotgut Poverty Plan. My arms were sore from the push-ups and the house still had a certain stink to it. But I ignored all of that and grabbed two eggs out of the fridge, cracked them on the sink, and peeled them under cold running water. I put them on a saucer. They slid around awkwardly on their own wetness. I sat down in front of the television to eat them and watch the news.

Two days earlier—the Saturday before Easter—federal agents

had invaded a home in Miami to seize a little boy named Elián González so they could return him to his father in Cuba. I was bored with the whole story, which had been dragging on for months. The NASDAQ had stumbled back in March and everyone was still blathering about it. Was it a crash? A correction? I didn't have a single penny invested in the stock market, so I didn't give a shit. Metallica was suing a dot-com millionaire—a teenager who had started a company called Napster. The band was also suing Yale University. I had no idea who was right, although if forced to choose I would probably have sided with Metallica. I was a big fan of their early work, *Ride the Lightning* in particular.

So I just ate my eggs. The yolks weren't green. They were pretty good, actually.

Then I showered, dressed, and grabbed a small container out of the fridge. It contained about a cup of cooked lentils. They looked gray through the cloudy plastic. I shook the container and heard them rattle. I wondered if I'd cooked them enough. But there was nothing I could do about it, so I headed out the door.

Laurel is about twenty-two miles south of Baltimore. The drive can take thirty minutes or two hours, depending on the traffic, so I listened to the radio a lot. Which was weird in April 2000. There was that little Timberlake guy who looked and sounded every bit like Joey McIntyre from New Kids on the Block. Only now the band was called 'N Sync. They had just released an album that had already sold 2.4 million copies. There was a song called "Bye Bye Bye." It was everywhere. The rock stations featured a rising new guitar hero who sounded a lot like Carlos Santana. Mostly because it was Carlos Santana. He had just released an album of collaborations with guys like Rob Thomas, who was the lead singer for the Goo Goo Dolls. Or was it Matchbox 20?

I didn't have to think about it for long. Within a few minutes of leaving home I was speeding past Camden Yards, clenching my teeth, and straining my eyes to catch a glimpse of the traffic on I-95 South. Too many cars, and the commute grinded to a halt. On light days, the cars buzzed by so fast that merging was nearly impossible. I had to get my speed just right. But there was always some asshole in front of me getting it wrong.

Laurel, Maryland, is located in the middle of the highway corridor connecting Baltimore with Washington, D.C. There are loads of federal workers. Others commute for hours on end to the tech companies popping up all over Northern Virginia. There are also a lot of old-time, blue-collar types left over from two or three decades earlier when Laurel was still considered out of the way. Rural, even. Its own place.

Laurel still has an "in between" sort of feel. The city is in Prince George's County, the wealthiest majority-black county in America. Just north is Columbia, a wildly ambitious planned community designed in the late 1960s to be racially harmonious, environmentally friendly, and economically self-sufficient. By the late 1990s it was a lot like Laurel, only newer. With bigger britches and a better mall.

The main difference: Laurel had a Main Street. An old one. With a few bars. A butcher. Some churches. And Main Street was home to the *Laurel Leader*—a scrappy little weekly paper that had been chasing the news in that strange little corner of the universe for more than a hundred years. Weird stuff happened there on occasion. A man named Arthur Bremer gunned down presidential candidate George Wallace in the parking lot of the Laurel Shopping Center in May 1972, about six months before I was born.

Laurel was a good place to be a reporter. It was within a few miles of Fort Meade and the mysterious National Security Agency. It had a horse-racing track. The town was constantly dealing with racial issues. (One of the first stories I covered involved the Ku Klux Klan.) Political issues. (Linda Tripp, who gained notoriety by betraying a young lady named Monica Lewinsky, lived in Columbia.) Sprawl issues. Transportation issues. The kind of issues that spring up when newcomers build $750,000 McMansions next door to trailer parks, and big-box superstores like CarMax set up shop down the road from old standbys like Hubcap City.

April 24, 2000, was a typical day at the *Laurel Leader*. Monday and Tuesday were deadline days. Which was good. It didn't give me much time to think. I was working on a story about a local guy who started a computer company in 1992 and later sold it for $150 million. I was writing another story about the upcoming 2000 census.

All in all, the first day of the Urban Hermit plan wasn't bad in terms of hunger. After all, even a fat bastard like me skipped breakfast from time to time. Lunch, even. So it's not like I was doubled over in pain. But things did get a little strange when I grabbed the lentils out of the fridge and popped them into the microwave.

"What's that?" a coworker asked.

"Lentils."

"Lentils?"

Which, of course, required some explanation. Especially from me. It was a small office. Just a few reporters and our editor. Then there were the art people, the advertising people, and the hot chicks upstairs who sold space in the local phone directory. (A few of them were cheerleaders for the Redskins and the Ravens. I never talked to them.) Still, it was a social office, and I was a go-to guy for lunch. When in doubt, ask the fat guy.

Yes. I was a real lunch-buying, lunch-eating son of a bitch. Or at least I used to be. And opting out required detailing the Urban Hermit plan. But I kept it pretty low-key. Everybody was busy. So I mumbled something about trying to save money, slinked back to my tiny cubicle, and cracked open the lukewarm Tupperware.

I was right. The lentils weren't cooked. Each individual legume gave way with an awkward snap. And they tasted like they smelled. Which was bad. They were dry, pasty, and hard to swallow. I thought about buying a soda from the machine upstairs. Then I remembered I wasn't buying shit. So I choked those bastards down. Spoon after spoon. Until they were gone.

I didn't stop to think about it. I had deadlines. Thank God for deadlines.

I finished my stories, submitted them in the late afternoon, and headed out for the local Quality Inn, where a mob was forming.

At least it was a mob by suburban standards. Commuters were pissed off because the rail line connecting Laurel to Washington was constantly behind schedule, so about sixty of them had crowded into a nondescript conference room to complain.

A state official told the mob that the main culprit was CSX, the huge freight-hauling company that shared the tracks with the commuter trains. He said it was up to CSX to make the trains run on time. Then he introduced the crowd to Rob Gould—a spokesman from CSX.

A thin, dark-haired man in his late thirties, Gould wore a gray suit and clunky black glasses. He tried to explain what was going wrong, but the throng of pasty office workers didn't care. They just wanted to get to work. On time, dammit. Rob Gould told them that probably wasn't going to happen.

So the angry commuters kicked Rob Gould's ass. No, not physically. But they were merciless. People were shouting. Getting red in the face. Swearing. It went on for an hour. There was nothing Rob Gould could do to make things right. Everyone knew that. But they yelled at him anyway.

I talked to him briefly afterward. He looked bewildered. Maybe I would have offered him a bit more of my time if I knew that he would save me from myself in about two months. That he would rescue me completely. But I didn't know that. There was no way I could have.

Besides, the meeting was over and I was done. So I headed for the car. I was hungry, and I had my heart set on a tuna fish sandwich.

The tuna fish sandwich was a calamity. A culinary catastrophe. I was finger-licking fucked and I knew it as soon as I opened the can.

All I saw was gray water with little flecks of pink, and all I smelled was metal. That's what happens when you buy the cheapest tuna fish in the store. It cost half as much as Starkist and the other national brands. I thought I had found a real bargain. I thought wrong.

Things got worse when I tried to drain the tuna. I went to the sink, put my finger on the lid, flipped the can over, and squeezed. And squeezed. I thought the can was empty other than the gray sludge. But no. There was a thin layer of fish product still stuck to the bottom. To call this product "chunk tuna" would be an affront to dead fish everywhere. I mean . . . wow. That was some terrible tuna fish. There were little black specks in it that I can only assume were scales or skin or disease.

But to hell with it. I scraped it out of the can and spread it on a piece of cheap bread. I didn't need to break it up with a fork because it was already sort of a paste. I didn't add any mayo. I couldn't afford any. I just put some salt on it, tossed on a piece of cheese, and put the other piece of bread on top.

I picked up the sandwich. The bottom bread slice had already gone soggy, which in a way was better. I didn't really have to chew it. I just bit pieces off and pressed them against the roof of my mouth with my tongue, like a whale eating plankton. Bad plankton.

Well, at least the cabbage can't be as bad as all that.

Wrong again. Soggy. Stinky. Bad.

All topped off with another spoonful of undercooked lentils. I threw most of that serving away. I was hungry. But not that hungry.

I walked into the living room and leaned back into one of the recliners. I picked up the remote and turned on the television. The news. The NASDAQ had tumbled another 161 points, a full 4.43 percent, making it 14 percent for the year. Rumor had it that Elián González already had a book and movie deal in the works.

Six kids had been shot at the National Zoo.

April 24, 2000.

Things got progressively worse throughout the week. The lentils kept getting drier in the fridge. The cheap tuna stayed cheap.

I was working on a story about plans to build a $3 billion, 300-mile-per-hour magnetic levitation train. Seven states were competing for the project. The Maryland proposal would bring the Maglev barreling right through Laurel. It was Journalism 101, calling transportation officials for comment, knocking on doors for local reaction. But the whole Urban Hermit plan was becoming a distraction.

Tuesday wasn't bad. Deadlines kept me busy. But by Wednesday the hunger had settled in. Not just growls and pangs and cravings. I mean real hunger. Like my stomach was finally putting up a fight. It was a new kind of pain: Self-inflicted pain. Hunger pain.

I could have ended it with a Twinkie. Or a cheeseburger. Or a beer. I thought about it constantly. I saw food on television. On the street. At home. In magazines and newspapers. But I never seriously considered breaking form. The decision was made. The only thing left was the suffering. Buck up, chump. You did it to yourself. You get what you deserve. So try not to think about it.

But the office. It's like I was cursed. Word of my plan had started to spread, and everyone was being so damn *nice*.

"What's this I hear?"

"Lentils? Do you like lentils?"

"Geez. How much money do you owe?"

"What's that smell?"

"I hear you're on a diet."

No. Not a diet. It was a financial issue. I must have explained it a hundred times in three days, and eventually it started to sink in. But then I realized I never should have mentioned that it was about money, because that's when the offers started rolling in.

Melanie was first, I think. She was a part-time editor in charge of the community columnists. She was married. Three kids. The oldest was a junior or senior in high school. She was my colleague, but she was also very protective. Maternal, in a way. She caught me as I was pulling the lentils out of the microwave on Wednesday. "Don't worry," she said when I finished explaining. "I'll bring in some lunch for you tomorrow."

I had to explain why I couldn't accept.

Joe, my boss, also tried to intercede. "Let me buy you lunch," he said. When I refused, he offered to see if he could get me an advance on my paycheck. Or maybe he offered to loan me money out of his own pocket. I can't remember, exactly, except that he tried to help.

This all came to a head late that first week. Thursday, I think. In three days I had consumed 2,400 calories. More like 1,800, actually. (I hardly ever ate any of the cabbage or made a serious dent in the second helping of lentils.) That's less than I would have eaten by noon on a lot of days. And I was feeling it. Oooohhh, I was feeling it. My belly was hungry. My head was hungry. My toenails were hungry. My hunger was hungry. All-encompassing. Stark-raving.

Desire.

Which I tried to ignore as I chatted up structural engineers about the technical specifications of a 300-mile-per-hour magnetically levitated train. How loud is it? How many passengers will it carry? How much will a ticket cost? Will it have a dining car?

That's when I caught wind of it. An office party. A birthday, I think. Or a baby shower. We had them all the time. I saw people milling around. Then someone gave me a card to sign. Then someone came around to collect me. Then I followed some people into the tightly packed meeting room. Then I saw Melanie holding the biggest, best-looking piece of cake in recorded human history. Chocolate. Two layers. White icing, with traces of color that used to be part of a festive, frosted message.

She was looking at me. Smiling. But I was focused on the cake.

"There," she said, holding it out to me.

The room stopped. And I don't mean in the figurative sense, or that it happened in my mind. There were about fifteen people there, and they had all heard about the lentils and why I was eating them. Well . . . How does free cake fit into the scheme? They all wanted to know. So did I. This was a disaster in the making.

Come on, dude. Take the cake. The whole point is to save money, right? Well, it's *free cake*. Take the cake. Eat the cake. Savor a bite of the rich chocolaty goodness of this free-ass cake. Then another. Then another. Delicious cake. It's Melanie, for God's sake. She's a friend. She knows what's best.

Why not? The cake wouldn't cost me a penny. If people are going to offer me things for free, why not take them? Particularly normal everyday things like cake at an office party. The whole point is to see what it really takes to survive, right? Well, free cake is part of the job. Just like deadlines and paychecks. It comes with the territory.

Yes. Take the cake.

Of course, lots of things come with the territory. Pretty soon Skippy is going to get tired of drinking alone. And he's going to offer to pick up the tab at Kisling's. Just one beer. Just one more. Just this once. How about a shot, and another, and a meat loaf platter. And whatever happened to that guy who used to set us up with the Ecstasy? Dammit. I know if I take one bite of that cake I'll be on my second bottle of Wild Turkey by eleven o'clock tonight, swimming in it by morning. Then again, that fucking cake looks pretty good. And I'm starving to death, here, and free cake is free cake and it's just this once and . . .

"No, thanks," I said.

I spent a few minutes trying to explain. It was all or nothing, I said. I appreciated it. Particularly coming from Melanie, who really did have my best interests at heart. But a plan is a plan. And free cake was not part of the plan. Neither was free lunch. Free dinner. Free whiskey. Especially free whiskey. Besides, it's only for a month. I can do anything for a month.

Right?

I went back to the phone to make some more calls. What happens if a Maglev derails?

I faced another hurdle when I got home that night. I had four hard-boiled eggs left, but the first batch of lentils had run out. I pulled the second bag out of the cupboard. Got some water boiling. "Just make sure they're done this time," I told myself.

Then the phone started ringing. Skippy was at work, so I let the machine answer. It was the guys down at the bar. "Haven't seen you all week, asshole. Where you at?"

I didn't return the call.

There was big news in Laurel on Friday. The police found a body in an office along Route 1. It had been there for weeks. Decomposing.

The dead man was a local businessman—a thermal-imaging expert. He was only forty-two. A congressional committee had retained him the year before to study video of the 1993 government assault on the Branch Davidian compound in Waco, Texas. They paid him to analyze footage of the final raid. The FBI still denied that agents had fired their weapons during the showdown, but the guy from Laurel concluded otherwise. Which raised the possibility that maybe some of the seventy-nine people who died in the inferno—including twenty-one children—had tried to escape but were trapped inside by the gunfire.

There was no evidence of foul play in the Laurel man's death, but conspiracy theorists were certain that government goons had him rubbed out. The Laurel Police were getting calls from as far away as New Zealand.

First Elián González, now this guy. It was a bad week for the Clinton Administration.

And for me. I sent Skippy off to the bar by himself that night. I stayed at home and refused to answer the phone, which rang constantly. I guess the guys at Kisling's had finally heard about the Urban Hermit plan, and they didn't like it one bit. I tried to ignore the profanities exploding out of the answering machine as I sat in the recliner and ate my lentils.

This new batch wasn't nearly as bad. I had cooked them longer. But they were still terrible. I forced down the tuna fish sandwich without even thinking about it. Then I thought about going to the bar. Just to say hello. I could manage that. I'd pop in and pop right back out.

Then I laughed and called myself an asshole. A guy who barely survives an office party has no business in a barroom.

What's on TV? I hadn't watched TV on a Friday since *The Dukes of Hazzard* years. Maybe I could read a book? To hell with it. I was hungry and tired. I went to bed early.

I heard Skippy stumble through the door around three in the morning.

I knew I couldn't take another night of this.

5

Porn Shops, Promenades,
and the Sober-Pet People

*One night as I was passing a small pub, I saw through a lighted
window some men having a fight with billiard cues and one of them
being thrown out of the window. At any other time I should have felt
very much disgusted; but at the time I could not help feeling envious
of the fellow who had been thrown out of the window. Indeed, so envious did I feel that I even went into the pub, walked straight into the
billiard room, thinking perhaps that I too could pick a quarrel with
the men there and be thrown out of the window. I was not drunk, but
what was I to do? To such a state of hysteria had my depression
brought me! But nothing happened. It seemed that I was not even
capable of jumping out of the window, and I went away without having a fight.*

Fyodor Dostoevsky, *Notes from Underground*, 1864

I went for a run (With who?) My nuts.
All around the block took no short cuts.
The Fat Boys, "Protect Yourself/My Nuts," 1987

Hunger is horrible. Powerful. Primal. And I was getting hungrier by the hour.

It nearly drove me over the edge that weekend. That's why I es-
caped. That's why I packed up all my shit and headed to the

mountains on Saturday for my half-assed camping trip. Where I cinched my belt that first time. The escape worked, in a way. It kept me away from the refrigerator. And it kept me away from the bar. But when I got back that Sunday I was hungrier than ever.

My night in that wretched tent gave me some time to think, though, and I came to a few conclusions. First, eat the second serving of lentils at night. Eating eight hundred calories a day is stupid enough. Don't make things worse by skipping a hundred and sixty of them. No matter how bad they taste.

And for heaven's sake, go to Sam's Club.

For some reason it hadn't occurred to me. But I was a member. So Monday, on my lunch break, I headed off to the outskirts of Laurel to do a little value shopping.

Sam's Club. What a place. Hot-water heaters. Vibrating chairs. Trampolines. Enough Listerine to fill an Olympic-size swimming pool; enough paper towels to sop it all up. Last year's fashions from designers like Calvin Klein. Batteries. Batteries. Batteries. Cheese puffs. Duct tape. More batteries. Do you have any idea how heavy a ten-pound vat of ranch dressing can be? Sure. Ten pounds. But have you ever *lifted* one? Seen the herbs and spices drifting in that vast sea of white goo? It's thrilling, in a stomach-churning sort of way.

I lingered over these offerings a bit. Touched them. But I passed them, product by product, until I was in the dry-goods aisle. Rice, fifty pounds per bag! Angel-hair pasta in bundles as big as my arm! All at miraculous, unnaturally low prices! And yet . . . not a lentil in sight. The one thing Sam's Club does not sell. You have to be kidding me.

I started making profane oaths about Wal-Mart and America and fairness and all the rest when suddenly, out of the corner of my eye . . . what's that, in the distance? Is it . . . ? Oh, yes. That's exactly what it is. Starkist Tuna. Piled higher than the Eiffel Tower and the Tower of Babel and the Leaning Tower of Pisa combined.

Does it come in an eight-ton can? Can I use that much? Can I make it work?

The packages looked huge from afar, but as I approached I saw that they were ten normal cans shrink-wrapped together. I checked the price, and a little math revealed the full glory of Sam Walton's bulk-buying vision: The Starkist Tuna at Sam's Club was cheaper than the dreadful shit I had been swindled into buying at Safeway.

Real tuna. *Real food*. This was a victory of epic proportions. I grabbed three packages, waited in line, and paid. Then I went back to the office and hurried through the rest of my day.

It was hard to concentrate. My stomach was shrieking like a scalded cat. *Mrrrooowww. Mrrrrooowww. Rowmrrrooowww*. My imagination fixated on the pile of fish stashed in the trunk of the Taurus. Thirty cans. Enough for the rest of this horrible month-long experiment. And then some.

And soon enough I was at home. In the kitchen. With the can opener. With the bread. With the cheese. With the sandwich. That terrible sandwich. Dry tuna with no mayo. Soggy, cheap white bread. Bad cheese. The best thing I have ever eaten.

I'd like to say I ate it slowly. Savored it. But I didn't. And it might be more dramatic to detail how I devoured it. *Inhaled it*. But that's not true, either. I was ecstatic about the sandwich. I might even say that I loved it. But what I did was sit down and eat that sandwich in utterly undramatic fashion. Until it was gone.

And when it was gone I realized the obvious truth: Name-brand tuna tastes a hell of a lot better than crappy tuna that smells like metal. But it's not more filling.

I was still hungry. So I slouched over to the refrigerator, grabbed a container of lentils, and tried to get on with my life.

I had a problem. Several of them actually. Like the fact that I was constantly hungry. But that was nothing compared to the new scourge that was beginning to overwhelm me.

Boredom.

It's not like I was opposed to sitting in front of the television. I did it all the time. But it's different when you have to. When you don't even have the option of going to the movie or a coffee shop or, in my case, the bar.

I had read all my books and I couldn't afford more. The library? I didn't even know where it was. I couldn't pick up a hobby like cooking or woodwork because I couldn't afford food. Or wood.

As far as television goes, it was the worst time of year to become an Urban Hermit. Seasons were ending, which meant reruns. I'm not sure how many people know this, but Jaleel White, the actor who played Steve Urkel on *Family Matters*, had another sitcom called *Grown Ups*. How do I know? I saw the last few episodes of its one-season run. It was better than anything else on television at the time.

We owned three movies: *The Jerk*, *The Cannonball Run*, and *The Outlaw Josey Wales*. We had watched them so many times that I could recite them word for word. But watching them sober wasn't quite the same.

I spent some time talking to Skippy, but that was hit-and-miss because of his work schedule. Once upon a time, he had a job with real prospects at a truck-leasing company. He wore a suit and had a company car. But that went down the tubes in 1998 when they offered him a promotion and a move to corporate headquarters in Delaware. He turned it down. His reasoning, as I recall, went something like this: "Fuck it."

A few months later, no more suit. No more company car. No more job. I paid the rent and the bar tabs as long as I could, but eventually he started picking up hours at a fish warehouse. One of our drinking buddies ran the place. By mid-2000 Skippy was managing the warehouse and driving trucks filled with ten tons of fish to New York City. By the time I got home from Laurel, he was usually sleeping. Or at work. Or at the bar.

I was basically alone. So I just started walking.

I know. It sounds like some half-assed version of Forrest Gump. And kind of desperate. I was only ten days into the plan. But I couldn't take it. Sitting around the house listening to my stomach rumble. Dodging calls exhorting me to make plans for my fifth college reunion. (Only a month away!) Watching a mature, muscle-bound Urkel chat up the ladies. Ten days of that was more than enough.

Walking aimlessly can be tough, though, especially for a wildly irresponsible man on a budget. I couldn't go past Kisling's. Someone might spot me and lure me inside. Besides, everything reminded me of what I couldn't do. Hey, look over there. Another bar I can't drink at. The coffee shop. The lemonade stand. The kiosk that sells hot dogs wrapped in soft pretzels. Bad news. All of it.

That's why I tried to stick to the residential side streets. I walked up South Chapel, away from the harbor, then made a right on Gough. I passed the gleaming SUVs and BMWs parked in front of lovingly restored historic row houses. I passed old ladies sitting on stoops in front of row houses that no one had bothered to restore yet.

I walked past a bar called Butts and Betty's. We used to go there on Sunday mornings. They had happy hour at seven A.M. Or maybe it was six A.M. A lot of the old regulars spoke Polish. A lot of the newcomers spoke Spanish. The jukebox had a lot of Kenny Rogers. The draft beer was ice cold. And so were the cans of Genesee.

I wanted to stop for a few, but I kept walking up to Patterson Park. I kept my eye out for scary-looking hookers and stray pit bulls, then doubled back on Bank Street, toward my house. It was only eight o'clock when I got back to Chapel Street, so I doubled back again and walked down Eastern Avenue, past the old appliance shop. Past the duckpin bowling alley. Up toward Canton, a neighborhood that the yuppies were invading in droves.

Eventually I found myself down on Boston Street, by the Safeway and the American Can Company. Lots of young professionals hurrying, always hurrying. The kind of people who never drank Genesee at seven o'clock on Sunday morning. The kind of people who never mixed mustard with whiskey so their dogs would drink it. The kind of people who jogged with their dogs, and probably never drank with them at all. The sober-pet people. I neither despised them nor aspired to be them. I simply saw them as another species.

I was trying to ignore them when I saw the walkway along the water. I'd been living in the neighborhood for four years and I had never seen it. Maybe it was new. Maybe not.

The wide, wooded promenade hugged the manicured grounds of a high-end condo development. A marina bustled with sea kayaks, windsurfers, and other trappings of the active lifestyle; preppy-looking sailboats; catamarans; snow-white cabin cruisers with satellite dishes and darkened windows. All of them bobbed slowly in the water, raising a gentle ruckus as the ropes and canvas snapped lightly against the aluminum and fiberglass. More sober-pet people in well-pressed clothes milled back and forth between the boats and the condos. Everyone seemed quiet and polite. It was all so . . . khaki.

I kept walking. And walking. By the time I got back home it was nine-thirty. I had been wandering around for hours. How many miles had I covered? Two? Five? Twelve? There was no way to know.

It was the first of many such walks. And it was terrible.

Friday, May 5. I hadn't had a drink in almost two weeks.

I had always dismissed Cinco de Mayo as some kind of amateur hour. All the dickheads who needed an excuse crowding the bar, ordering stupid crap like B-52s and Blowjobs. Putting fruit in their stupid Corona. Challenging drunk chicks to do body shots. Forget it.

But Cinco de Mayo 2000 was different. Maybe I was feeling sorry for myself. I prefer to think that I wanted to get a more clear-eyed look at the amateurs. Either way, that night I took a risk and tried a different walking route. I headed down to Fell's Point because I knew it would be absurd.

What a madhouse. I could hear the girls hooting and the guys grunting and the sirens wailing. Every bar was packed with knuckleheads decked out in faux-Mexican attire—plastic sombreros and ponchos, all rendered in earthy-orange Dorito colors. The music sounded tinny from the outside.

I established a vantage point on the long pier and watched the debauchery unfold. Look at all those idiots over at the Horse You Came In On Saloon, where I used to work the door. The firefighters who drank in the back bar would not mix well with the amateurs, I figured. Fists would fly.

I was sitting a few yards away from three balding, overmuscled forty-somethings who were drinking beer on their twenty-foot ski boat. They had docked it right next to the tugboats. The biggest, baldest one of the bunch wore a tank top featuring Foghorn Leghorn's head and the words BIG PECKER'S BAR AND GRILL.

They were hammered, singing along to the Top Forty hits tinkling out of their little boombox, constantly trying to entice drunken twenty-something girls to join them. I chuckled at the futility of their efforts but soon got tired of watching. I was hungry. I was sober. And every fiber of my being wanted to join the idiots I was there to watch.

Damn, it looked like fun. I would have gladly climbed aboard that ski boat, guzzled a few beers, and shouted at the girls. I would have happily donned a Dorito-colored sombrero and stood in line for a B-52 and a Blowjob. But that wasn't possible.

I decided to walk up Broadway, past a dance club called 723. It was popular with the rowdy crowd, so there was a good chance there might be some people throwing punches out front. That was always fun to watch.

I didn't see any fights, though. I just went home and decided not to walk to Fell's Point anymore.

I didn't even bother with the TV when I got home. But I remembered the push-ups. Finally. I should have done them five days earlier, but things had gotten away from me. Better late than never, though. So I fell on my face and did as many as I could.

Thirty-five push-ups. Fifteen more than I did the night before I started the plan.

Weird. I was actually getting stronger. Or maybe just lighter. I reached down to my waist and tugged on my belt. It was loose again. I tightened it another notch. Two weeks. Two inches. Gone.

That seemed like an awful lot of weight to lose in twelve days. I thought about hopping on a scale, but we didn't own one. Besides, I didn't know how much I weighed to begin with.

I was hungry, poor, miserable, and alone—dissolving, maybe—but I didn't feel like I was dying. So the Urban Hermit Financial Emergency Rotgut Poverty Plan was still a go. Two more weeks. I could hold out two more weeks.

I was almost sure of it.

The trick was to stay busy. Fortunately, that was about to get easier, because there's nothing that will distract a man like a big fat pile of porn.

Once upon a time, Route 1 was a serious road. Stretching from Maine to Florida, it eventually became known as "America's Main Street" because it took drivers through so many little towns. Enterprising people built gas stations and diners and ice-cream shops along its entire length. It was a thriving interstate corridor—until someone decided to build Interstate 95.

Route 1 is still a busy road in Laurel, but it's a study in contrast. The old shopping center where George Wallace got shot is on Route 1. So is the new shopping center with the Lowe's and Best Buy, where nobody of any recognized import has been shot at all.

But the most important stretch sits on the line dividing Howard County from Prince George's County. That's where thousands of race fans go to bet on the ponies at Laurel Park, and where Route 1 north separates from Route 1 south, creating a divider strip about a hundred yards wide.

In April 2000, that divider strip was the most fascinating place in America. Or at least the most American place. From north to south, it included a McDonald's, a small Dodge dealership, a liquor store, a greenhouse, and a run-down trailer park complete with its own saloon. Then came a seafood restaurant–package store called the Bottom of the Bay, a small shopping center, and a hotel called the Valencia. Many of the immigrant track workers rented long-term rooms there for thirty dollars a night.

Civic leaders had been talking about adding slot machines to the racetrack for years. If that happened, the divider strip would become prime real estate. In the meantime, everything was falling apart. The trailer park looked like a war zone. Some of the trailers had deteriorated completely, crumbling into ridiculous piles of wires, broken siding, and busted plumbing.

And then there was the porn shop in the small shopping center behind the Bottom of the Bay. It had shut down in March. Or at least that's what everyone thought until my second week as an Urban Hermit. The owner of a pawnshop in the same shopping center called to tell me that the porn shop was up and running again. He said it wouldn't just be videos and dildos, either. He heard that the owner was installing coin-operated video booths in the back room. A whack shack for perverts and goons.

I knew I had to call John Stafford. Immediately.

I met John Stafford earlier that year when he was campaigning in the Republican primaries. He wanted to be a senator. Since he was local, I wrote a profile. And I will never forget it.

Stafford was a regular at the Bottom of the Bay and suggested we do the interview there. He said we could spend as much time as we wanted in the dining room prior to the evening rush.

We were not alone. Stafford, a stay-at-home dad, brought his three children along. The youngest was a toddler, a boy, barely able to walk. There was another boy, probably five years old, and a girl, about seven. They all seemed bright, well-dressed, and curious, but I wasn't sure what they were doing there.

The toddler sat on Stafford's lap. The older two chatted with us for a while, but eventually started darting in and out of the smoky, crowded barroom to play an old video game. Maybe it was Galaga. Or Dig Dug. They returned from time to time for more quarters, invariably getting tangled with the waitresses who were prepping the dining room. The waitresses kept asking when we were going to leave.

Stafford, fifty-nine, was a short, roundish man with thick glasses, slicked-down black hair, and a rumpled blue suit. He identified himself as the most reliably pro-life candidate in the race. He said he went to the Naval Academy with John McCain but later switched to the University of Maryland. He said he appeared in an Elvis movie. That he had been engaged to Mary Jo Kopechne (the woman Ted Kennedy drove off the bridge). And that he was good friends with many of the most influential politicians in America. His wife was a paralegal. They lived on Route 1, in the dilapidated trailer park adjacent to the restaurant. They cooked all their meals in the microwave. He home-schooled the kids. They heated their home with dozens of televisions tuned into various news stations twenty-four hours a day.

Strange as Stafford was, he was incredibly articulate. And many of his stories checked out. Congressman Steny Hoyer, a fixture in Maryland politics for decades, confirmed that he was Stafford's classmate at the University of Maryland. Hoyer recalled that the young Stafford was a brilliant sort of fellow, if a little quirky. No one could confirm the Mary Jo Kopechne story, but someone did remember Stafford doing a lot of political work in New England after graduation.

I liked John Stafford. Which was one of the reasons I took special interest in the story about the porn shop. I knew he would be fired up. Besides, pornography seemed like a good way to keep my mind off my hunger pains.

Stafford was irate. He complained that there ought to be a law against operating a porn shop so close to the trailer park. His neighborhood was run-down, he admitted, but old ladies lived there. And kids. He had a point. So I did a bit of digging and discovered that he was on to something. Almost.

There actually *was* a law forbidding "adult" businesses within five hundred feet of a residential area, but a county official pointed out that the trailer park wasn't zoned as residential. It was zoned for business. The trailer park didn't count, he said. Kids or no kids. But he added another interesting point: Viewing booths were illegal in Howard County.

So I put all my worries about money and lentils aside and drove to the porn shop. It was about half the size of a typical convenience store. A panel of white Styrofoam blocked the window to keep people from looking in. The inside was well lit and oddly sterile. Some cheap pink nighties were hanging limply on the walls. A few chest-high racks displayed movies, magazines, and butt plugs, all in garish packages referring to rock-hard this, Asian-teen that.

I looked around for about two minutes and peeked through an open doorway into the back room, which was completely empty. I asked the clerk if the store was installing booths.

"No," he said.

"What's the room for, then?" I asked.

"Storage."

It was just about the least titillating place I had ever been. It smelled like new carpet and cheap plastic, exhaust fumes and crab-shack Dumpster.

I knew I'd be back. And I knew that however I wrote the story, John Stafford would emerge as the hero.

Somehow.

6

Stop Your Bellyaching.

How to Shut the Hell Up and Mean It

I have never felt lonesome, or in the least oppressed by a sense of soli-tude, but once, and that was a few weeks after I came to the woods, when, for an hour, I doubted if the near neighborhood of man was not essential to a serene and healthy life. To be alone was something unpleasant. But I was at the same time conscious of a slight insanity in my mood, and seemed to foresee my recovery.

—Henry David Thoreau, *Walden*, 1854

I am not sure when it happened. It was gradual. Incremental. But it happened: Some time around the middle of May, I started get-ting tired of my own bullshit.

It wasn't supposed to be that way. I had promised myself that I wouldn't complain. No way. Not me. I had a long history of not com-plaining. I never bitched about being fat. I never moaned about be-ing broke. And I sure as hell wasn't going to groan about being an Urban Hermit.

And dammit, I held true to that pledge. I never cried on anyone's shoulder. I never told anyone at the office how the void in my stom-ach was beginning to overpower me. Be a man, and all that. You get what you deserve. Suffer in silence. *Suck it up*. I took great pride in my stoicism and fortitude. Quite a hero, no?

No.

Maybe I wasn't driving everyone else nuts, but the more time I spent alone, the more cuckoo I became. And the more cuckoo I became, the more I wondered: Have I always been such a pain in the ass?

The aimless walking amplified a few of my most annoying tendencies—weird little mental tics that I usually managed to control. One of the worst was a fascination with changing song lyrics. To be fair, I am really good at it. I can tamper with rhyme, cadence, and flow at astonishing speeds, unleashing a constant stream of hilarity, usually of the obscene variety.

I know it's annoying. So I try to keep my mouth shut, and I usually succeed. But the wheels in my head keep turning, churning, burning. Once, in college, I was incapacitated for days after an encounter with the chorus from Weezer's "Sweater Song": "If you want . . . to destroy my sweater." Something just clicked, and off I went, drowning in an ocean of grotesque nine-syllable ditties all ending in things like "heavy petter," "Irish setter," and "minister of exchequer." (You have to play with the meter, but it can work.) A similar crisis struck when I heard Madonna's cover of "Don't Cry for Me, Argentina." (Don't ask.)

Such flare-ups were rare. Largely because I—or somebody else—managed to keep me distracted. A movie. A case of beer. Anything to dilute the atmosphere, to cut back on the Sam MacDonald a little bit. At the very least, people around me could flee.

But walking those streets of Baltimore, utterly alone, I was defenseless against myself. And I started unloading. Anything—a song drifting out of a passing car, snippets of conversation—could set me off. Rhyming, chiming, all-the-timing with the obscene lyrical sliming. Griming. And occasional miming. (See?)

People like to think that, given some spare time, they'd do something useful or come up with solutions to important problems. And

maybe they would. But I suspect that most people have annoying inner voices like mine, whether they know it or not. Maybe theirs isn't
a sophomoric poet. Maybe it's a closet racist. A misogynist. A neat
freak. A weird sex freak. Whatever. Something they wouldn't neces-
sarily admire about themselves if they ever paused to think about it.
Especially if they got a huge dose, day after day. But that's all a hermit ever gets. Himself. All the time. Forever.

It was awful. I tried to clear my thoughts, but then I started
thinking about my aching belly, and that was even worse. So my
silly little mind started going a thousand miles an hour until I found
myself stuck in a different kind of rut. Like the lottery game. I'd
been playing it for years. Sometimes other people even joined in at
the bar. But without someone to pull me out of it, I just kept going
deeper and deeper:

Let's say I win the lottery, invest the winnings in high-tech
stocks, and become a billionaire. What would I do? More important, what could I do?

Could I get the president of Harvard to change his name to
"Craig" for a $50 billion donation? What about "Jerk"? Would
someone finally draw the line at something like "Fuckface J.
McAssBlast"? What if I threatened to give the money to Yale if
he wouldn't? What if I threatened to give it to the Ku Klux Klan?

If I went to a JC Penny and said, "I want to buy everything in
this whole damn store," would they ring it up and put it in bags
for me? How much would it cost? What would happen if I paid,
then came back the next day and said, "I want to return this"?

Could I sponsor my own NASCAR team and put a huge
picture of myself on the hood of the car? Would they let me
drive it in the Daytona 500? Could I buy each and every ad

slot at the Super Bowl and just show live footage of a chicken walking around a barnyard? What if I had a badger chasing the chicken?

What if I funded the construction of a supercomputer that generated every possible combination of words in the English language, 250 words at a time (a standard written page). When it was done, could I copyright the result? Would that mean I owned the rights to everything ever written after that?

Could I . . . Could I . . . Could I . . .

Yes. It's insufferable. Completely absurd. But reading what's written above only takes about twenty seconds. I stewed in it every day, from the moment I left work until the moment I went to bed. Living on eight hundred calories a day was nothing compared to that. I needed to limit my exposure, to cut back on my alone time.

The first strategy was simple: I stretched out my workday by taking long breaks, occasionally driving a few miles up the road to my sister's apartment in Savage, Maryland.

My sister, Grace. Skippy and I had crashed on her couch for about six months when we first got to Baltimore. She had since gotten married, had a baby, and moved to the suburbs. She was a public school teacher. English and drama. She was also five months pregnant with baby number two.

When I was out on assignment in the late afternoon I stopped by her place, ostensibly to chat or to visit with my little nephew, maybe ask about gossip from back home. Anything to keep my mind off the lentils and the hunger pains. Mostly I just sat on the couch for a while before heading back to work. Sometimes I fell asleep. Because I was tired.

Yeah. My sister had a full-time job, a toddler, a gestating baby, and a household to take care of. *And I went to her apartment in the middle of the day to fall asleep.*

What a jerk. And what a letdown. I was interesting when I was a big fat guy. Entertaining, even. Sure, I had been slipping deeper and deeper into debt, but it was my own debt. At least I could walk down the street without going insane. And I could stop by someone's house without passing out on the couch. Jesus. I was wallowing—that's right, wallowing—in my own misery. But did it even count as misery? For God's sake, my tummy hurt a little.

How embarrassing. It reminded me of those people who go on the Atkins Diet, then complain about not getting to eat any bread. Those people who major in psychology, then complain about their job prospects. Those people who drink all night, then complain about their hangover. Those people who buy forty-five-thousand-dollar SUVs, then complain about the monthly payment. Those people who . . . complain.

Maybe I wasn't bitching and moaning, but I was dangerously close.

By the second week of May I had to do something—anything—to get a grip on myself. So I developed a plan. A solution as simple as it was ridiculous. As elegant as it was absurd.

I would save myself from myself by tossing myself headlong into . . . fish.

And hippies.

Fish. That was the easy part. The seafood warehouse. The one our friend JJ managed, where Skippy worked. I had worked there part-time for drinking money in the past. It was perfect.

The warehouse was tucked away in a nondescript industrial park off of I-95. Tractor trailers arrived from New England carrying tons of lobsters, oysters, and other high-dollar stuff. But not many restaurants order a whole tractor-trailer load of lobsters, so our job was to unload that truck (and other trucks loaded with grouper from Florida, dolphin from Costa Rica, crab meat from Vietnam, etc.), break the cargo into smaller chunks, rearrange it, then put it back onto other trucks. All to be shipped off to smaller depots, retailers, and restaurants.

The depot got especially busy on Wednesday and Sunday nights. JJ relied on five or six part-timers to come in and pick up the slack. The place was usually full of clowns from the bar who needed a little extra cash. Friends of ours. We busted our asses when the trucks came, but it was actually kind of fun. We got to drive forklifts. Push things around on pallet jacks. Lift heavy shit. When it wasn't busy we kicked a Hacky Sack around. When a truck arrived . . . boom. Unload it. Rearrange it. Reload it. It was all about speed, really, because the warehouse wasn't refrigerated.

Almost all of the seafood was packed in ice. Small wooden boxes, about as big as a dresser drawer. Cardboard boxes as big as a coffin. Enormous crates big enough to fit a compact car. All crammed with shaved ice and sea creatures. All melting, dripping, sopping wet, revealing hidden flippers and eyeballs.

Occasionally the cardboard boxes would soak through and break, scattering hundreds of dollars' worth of mullet or sardines or haddock on our boots. And always the pink, stinky slush—icy blood and fish guts cascading onto the top of our heads as we tried to stack one soggy hundred-pound box on top of another until it was time to kick the Hacky Sack again.

I hadn't worked there in a while. But all of a sudden I was an Urban Hermit. I was bored. Broke. And the seafood looked an awful lot like salvation. So I pulled out a pair of cut-off jeans, selected a ratty old T-shirt that I was willing to sacrifice, and drove myself to the warehouse.

I knew it was going to be trouble. Most of the people on the crew were my drinking buddies. Now they had a chance to tell me what they thought of my hiatus from the bar, and they laid it on thick. So thick that I didn't even notice the fish stench when I walked through the door.

"Jesus Christ, look at this guy!"

"Who the hell is that?"

"Wait, can you work when you're on a lentil diet?"

"Hey, look. Someone invited Richard Simmons."

I tried to explain that I wasn't on a "diet." I promised them that it would all be over soon. They were not impressed.

"Pussy."

"Fag."

"Lentils?"

"Douche bag."

Finally, miraculously, I heard the rumble of an engine. A truck. I heard the rear door rattle open. I heard the high-pitched *beep-beep-beep* of forklifts in reverse. I was looking for a pair of heavy work gloves when one of the guys zipped past me on a forklift, then stopped. *Beep-beep-beep.*

"Hey, dickhead," he shouted above the din. "How much weight have you lost so far?"

"Hell if I know," I hollered. "I lost about two inches off my waist, though."

"Fucking-A," he said. Then he hit the throttle and raced into the icy mayhem.

The hippies are a different story. I had met thousands of them the previous summer. It was all part of my first-ever, honest-to-goodness freelance writing gig.

In June 1999, the Rainbow Family of Living Light announced that it would hold its annual gathering on the Allegheny National Forest near Ridgway, Pennsylvania. My hometown.

The Rainbow Gathering. Astonishing. Every Fourth of July, twenty thousand people gather for a week or so of peace and love. I heard there would be lots of drugs. And lots of naked people. The local police were already on alert. People were locking up their daughters. I had just quit my job at the financial newsletter, so I thought, "I have some free time. Why not go write about the Rainbows?" I had no real journalism experience. But I had an angle. I knew the police. I knew the daughters.

I pitched the story to the editor of the *Baltimore City Paper*. He said no. But he did know the guy at the *Pittsburgh City Paper*, and he might be interested.

So I covered the 1999 Rainbow Gathering for the *Pittsburgh City Paper*. I was there a few days, and I was off my ass the entire time. Marijuana. Ecstasy. Mushrooms. One night I got lost in the woods. It was raining. I didn't have a flashlight. I eventually stumbled across a yurt full of Hare Krishnas. At least a hundred of them. They were dancing and singing and having a wonderful time. They invited me in. They made me fried cakes covered with cinnamon and honey. They took care of me until some dude with a flashlight came along and led me back to my tent.

But the story turned out pretty good. The whole thing made the cover. I got paid five hundred dollars. Things were going well. I had about fifteen hundred in the bank. But then things really went to hell.

The week after the gathering I went to a buddy's wedding in Boston. An Amtrak ticket. Two nights in the Copley Plaza Hotel. A tuxedo. A $160 bottle of Johnny Walker, which I drank at the reception. A swim in the Copley Square fountain, which resulted in a ruined tuxedo, one lost shoe, and one lost pair of glasses. An Amtrak ticket back to Baltimore. I had eight dollars to my name when I got home.

Joe Murchison called me from the *Laurel Leader* the next day. He had an opening for a reporter. I didn't even remember sending him my résumé, but I guess I must have. Skippy had to drive me to the interview. I didn't have any glasses.

Maybe I got the job because of the Rainbow story. (It was the only clip I had.) Maybe I got the job despite the Rainbow story. Looking back, I am open to either interpretation. But at the time, I was sure that my connection to the Rainbows was important. I figured it was a perfect story for a big national publication—a magazine that would give me a huge budget for first-class travel and potent narcotics.

So once I got a few months under my belt at the newspaper, I wrote a ridiculous proposal letter for a Rainbow story and sent it off to *GQ* and *Esquire*. I didn't bother learning how to write such a letter, or who would want to read one. I sent one to *Rolling Stone*, attention Jann Wenner, the editor who had worked with Hunter S. Thompson in the 1970s. I didn't even know if he was still alive.

And sure enough, nothing happened. I didn't even get a rejection letter. From anybody.

"Fucking journalism," I told myself. "Jann Wenner, my ass. If you don't have connections, you don't have shit." I made a note to check the magazines the following summer to see if any of them had stolen my story idea.

My attitude had softened by mid-May. The fish warehouse was only two nights a week and I was desperate for something to do. So one day, on my nightly walk, I wandered into the bookstore next to the Safeway. Ignoring all the pretty people who were there to actually buy things, I idled over to the reference section, sat down in a plush chair, and started flipping through a huge book called *The Writer's Market*.

That's how I learned to write a query letter. How I learned that, given my experience, I was unlikely to command a sizable narcotics budget. That Jann Wenner is not the proper point of contact at *Rolling Stone*. It's how I discovered the names of other editors at other magazines who might be interested in a story about hippies.

And I went to work.

So some nights I tossed fish. Some nights I wrote query letters. And some nights I just walked around. But at least I had a few things to think about when my belly started aching.

· 7 ·

The Urban Hermit Lives
Combat Zones, Communes and the
Liquidity of Starvation

Besides casual onlookers there were also relays of permanent watchers selected by the public, usually butchers, strangely enough, and it was their task to watch the hunger artist day and night, three of them at a time, in case he should have some secret recourse to nourishment. This was nothing but a formality, instituted to reassure the masses, for the initiates knew well enough that during his fast the artist would never in any circumstances, not even under forcible compulsion, swallow the smallest morsel of food; the honor of his profession forbade it.

—Franz Kafka, "A Hunger Artist," 1922,
translated by Lolla and Edean Muir

Then, suddenly, everything started to pay. And not just the hunger. I mean everything. Stuff I didn't even know about. Investments I never made.

The first hint came in my paycheck. Well, not in the paycheck, exactly. That hadn't changed. But something had.

I normally had zero dollars in my account by the time I got paid, but May 2000 was different. When I got paid two weeks into the Urban Hermit experiment, I still had three hundred dollars left in the bank.

Despite the fact that I had paid most of my bills. Even rent. *On time.* And I hadn't parked a single penny on my credit cards.

Strange how that works.

Developments were afoot, however, and they promised to make my three-hundred-dollar windfall look like chump change.

I never knew anything about the stock market. Even in the late 1990s, when I was the managing editor of a financial newsletter that specialized in investments. I didn't make the picks. I proofread them.

I wasn't completely unaware of the boom times. I saw people getting ahead. The guys who owned Kisling's were branching out into real estate. The resident Ecstasy dealer drove a Mercedes. But in May 2000 I woke up and discovered that I was a player. Not in Amazon or eBay or any of that high-tech nonsense. My money—I guess you could call it my money—was tied up in a dinosaur industry known as Big Media.

See, way back in March 2000, a huge corporation called the Tribune Company announced that it was buying the Times-Mirror Company. The blockbuster $8 billion deal was the kind of news that I took special care to not give a shit about. And I didn't. Until someone at work mentioned that Times-Mirror owned *The Baltimore Sun.* Which apparently owned a group of community newspapers called Patuxent Publishing. And one of those community papers was the *Laurel Leader.*

I was getting taken over. Bought out. Merged. And almost certainly screwed, I remember thinking. There were sure to be layoffs. As a twenty-seven-year-old entry-level reporter at a minor paper in the company's portfolio, I'd be first on the chopping block. Damn the luck.

But then some specifics began to emerge, and we started hearing that the merger might be a sweet deal. It was the 1990s, dammit! Or at least it was close enough! People were talking about something called "stock options." Someone said that a five-year Times-Mirror employee stood to collect twenty-three thousand dollars. More than four thousand dollars per year on the job. There was some griping about journalistic integrity and all that, but most people focused on the money.

I had a hard time doing that, though. I never bought any stock options. All my earnings were tied up in the Ecstasy dealer's Mercedes. It looked like I had missed the boat. Or gone down with it.

Then someone explained to me that I was an idiot. Of course I had stock options. One hundred of them. The company distributed them at the beginning of every year, even to people who had only been working there for a few months. Or maybe I got them as part of the buyout. I never really did figure it out. All I know is that sometime in May I realized I was sitting on a stock market bonanza. A font of wealth and plenty. At least by my standards.

Times-Mirror shareholders would convene a special meeting on June 12 to approve or reject the merger proposal, which called for buying all the options. Even from clowns like me. If that deal went through, I'd make something like $4,800 after taxes. For doing absolutely nothing. Four thousand eight hundred dollars. Enough for forty-eight hundred Rolling Rocks at Kisling's. About a year's worth, I figured. Or six hundred weeks of Urban Hermit supplies.

I needed the money. Immediately. But the deal was still up in the air. If the money ever did materialize, it would be months in coming. For the moment, I had the same amount tied up in the stock market as I always had: none. Only now there was more upside.

Unfortunately, my creditors were not willing to accept "upside."

With my luck, some jerk with an agenda would botch the merger, and the precious options I had done so little to accumulate would come to nothing. I couldn't risk it. I was still way behind on my bills. And my taxes. And my student loans. And the car repairs.

What the hell. I was more than halfway done with the Urban Hermit experiment already. I figured I might as well finish it.

That was a good decision. For once.

I don't remember what I was doing. Probably writing a story about a city council meeting. Or maybe I was putting the police blotter together. Either way, I was working quietly in my cubicle when I heard my editor's voice.

"Sam," he said.

"Yeah, Joe?"

"Can I talk to you for a minute?"

"Sure."

I stood up, walked five feet to his office, and poked my head in. He was sitting at his desk, his back to the door. "Yeah, Joe?" I asked.

"You've been doing good work," he said as he spun around in his chair and faced me.

"Thanks," I said, a little perplexed. Joe was a nice guy and a good boss. But he was a serious fellow, and it seemed like he was building up to something. There was an awkward pause. Then he smiled.

"What would you think about going to Bosnia?" he asked.

"Bosnia?"

"Bosnia," he said. "The National Guard unit from Laurel is over there."

"I know. I covered their send-off back in February."

"The Air National Guard has some spots on a plane," he said. "They're taking some reporters over. Someone from *The Washington Post* is going. A few local TV stations are sending people. You interested?"

"Sure," I said. "When?"

"Late June."

"Wow," I said. "An international assignment."

"I don't have all the details yet," he said. "But you should probably start getting ready."

It took a few days to nail everything down. The higher-ups talked about sending a different reporter. Maybe someone with more experience. Maybe someone from one of the other papers. But in the end, I was the guy. And I was clueless.

I had a few weeks to prepare, but time was tight. I got my picture taken. I filled out some paperwork. I went to Washington, D.C., where they can process a passport application in one day. I got mine on May 16, 2000.

But that was only the beginning. And of all the places I was about to go, Bosnia was the least bizarre.

The last two weeks of May were a lot like the first two. At least in terms of the Urban Hermit plan. I was still hungry as hell. I was still bored stiff.

I missed the series finale of *Beverly Hills 90210*—the last episode ever—because it aired on May 17. A Wednesday. I tossed fish on Wednesday nights.

I also missed two Modest Mouse shows—May 23 and 24—at the Black Cat in Washington, D.C. They were out supporting a new album called *The Moon & Antarctica*, their major-label debut. I had been listening to them for a few years, so under normal circumstances I would have gone to those shows. I would have missed work. It would have been a three-day drunk. Easy.

But Urban Hermits don't go to concerts. And they don't go on three-day drunks. Especially when they are confused.

The new wrinkle was the Bosnia deal. How was I supposed to pay for that? The National Guard was paying for the flight, but the trip required a few stopovers. One night in Newfoundland. One in Germany. Maybe more. The paper would give me some spending money for meals and reimburse me for hotels, but I would have to pay for a lot of stuff up front, then present receipts when I got back. Besides, I would need some pocket money, right? For emergencies? I had no idea.

I only knew one thing for sure: I was flat broke. And getting flatter.

People at work had become accustomed to the smell of microwaved lentils. Most of them were kind enough to avoid the subject entirely. Hardly anybody offered me money or cake anymore. But they did notice that things were changing, and Joe started asking questions during the third week of the Urban Hermit plan.

"So how are you doing, Sam?" he said.

"I'm doing okay," I said. "I saved three hundred dollars so far. I sent it out to the credit cards. I should have another three hundred after the next paycheck, but I think I might have to save some of it for the trip."

"Good thing you've been saving money."

"Yeah," I said. "I guess the timing was pretty good."

"But do you feel all right?" he asked. "Is it still eight hundred calories a day?"

"Yeah. Eight hundred."

"You haven't cheated?"

"No," I said. "I just try to keep busy. Keep my mind off it."

"That's really impressive," he said. "You ought to write it up."

"What do you mean?"

"For the paper. You should write a column about it. People love that kind of stuff."

"What kind of stuff?"

"Weight loss," he said. "Diets. Everyone's on a diet. How much weight have you lost?"

"I have no idea," I said.

"Well, you look great. I bet you've lost twenty-five pounds."

Really? Twenty-five pounds? I'd been so focused on the money that I never thought about it in terms of pounds. Not that I hadn't noticed some differences. I just saw them in terms of belt notches and push-ups. And mostly they made me worry. If I wasted away too fast and started getting weak, I'd have to abandon the plan before I saved enough money.

Besides, it's not like I was etching a six-pack. I started out as an enormously fat bastard. So now I was just a little less fat. My passport photo was proof positive: double chin, thin sheen of fat-guy sweat on the brow, a double-XL oxford shirt from Sears that was two inches too small in the neck. My pants weren't even loose. They had just started fitting again—I could actually pull them up to where they belonged.

But sure. Come to think of it, I probably had lost quite a few pounds.

"I guess it could be twenty-five," I said.

Stephanie, another reporter at the paper, was walking past and overheard our conversation. "Yeah, I was going to say something," she chimed in. "I would say twenty-five pounds. At least."

"I don't know about that," I said. "But I just pulled my belt another notch tighter the other day. That makes three inches in about three weeks."

"That's thirty pounds, then," Stephanie said. "It's a rule of thumb: One inch equals ten pounds."

"Okay, then," I said. "Thirty pounds."

"Maybe even forty," she said.

"So you interested?" Joe asked.

"Interested?"

"In writing a column."

I wasn't sure. Did I really want to be a columnist on top of everything else? Expose my personal life in the paper? Would anyone really care? On the other hand, it would be extra work, and that would keep me busy.

"Do we have space for it?" I asked.

"Sure."

"Okay," I said. "I'll write something up for you."

The column laid out my financial crisis, detailed the food I was eating, and explained how I had diverted about six hundred dollars to creditors and the upcoming Bosnia trip. I also included some predictable rubbish about "learning from my mistakes." It ended like this:

When I finally emerge from the shadow of my recent fiscal crises, I have promised myself that I will pay closer attention to my financial well-being, and that I will at least attempt to stem the flow of superfluous spending that got me in this mess. While that might be easier said than done, it can't be any worse than life as an Urban Hermit, an experiment that I'd rather not be forced to repeat.

I probably meant it. After all, I had been wasting a lot of money. Why not try to spend less? Seven or ten bucks on lunch every workday adds up to $150 or $200 a month. And why not be reasonable at the grocery store? I was even willing to cut back at Kisling's. For heaven's sake, a pint of Rolling Rock was only a dollar. Skippy and I had no business running up a $175 bar tab on Friday night, another $200 on Saturday.

But ultimately I viewed that column as a celebration. A victory lap. An obituary for the Urban Hermit. I *hated* the Urban Hermit. It was a damn painful way to earn six hundred dollars. It'll do if you really need the money, which I did, but apart from that it sucked.

Besides, it was a terrible way to live. Being careful with money is one thing, but a man ought to be able to catch a movie. Buy a cup of coffee. And, yes, a man ought to be able to have a few beers with his pals. Or a lot of beers. Nothing wrong with that. Especially if the beers cost a dollar.

To hell with it. I had done my penance. I had put a little sunlight between me and the creditors. And I had put together some money for the trip. I was proud of myself. I owed a few dues, and I paid them. Now it was back to the bar stool for me. Chastened, perhaps, and a little thinner. Maybe even wiser. But this bullshit was almost over.

The column was set to appear in the paper on May 25. Two days later, May 27, would mark a full month of lentils and tuna fish. The

end of the Urban Hermit. It would be a Saturday. Which seemed for-
tuitous, because I deserved at least one night of celebration. I told
the people at Kisling's to reserve my regular bar stool in the corner.
Skippy was polishing up his drinking shoes and patching the holes
in his big-boy pants. The guys at the fish warehouse were shivering
in their stinky little boots because they knew that vengeance was in
the air. Lock up the flammables. Tell the women to avert their eyes.
Someone distract the local constabulary. It was going to be epic. My
return from the dark side: May 27, 2000.

Only it never happened.

Urban Hermits, I discovered, are hard to kill.

I got the news via e-mail. His name was Jesse Walker. He was an
editor at *Reason* magazine. He had just received my letter about the
Rainbow Gathering. He wanted to talk.

Holy balls.

I was familiar with *Reason*. Free minds, free markets. Guns are
good. Taxes are bad. Legalize drugs. I liked all that libertarian stuff.
And it was a national magazine. A good one.

I had pitched a story about "spontaneous order." How do thousands
of disorganized hippies manage to change the event's location every
summer but still show up in the right spot on the right day? How do all
these people—supposedly drug-addled to the last man—get fed? How
do they all manage to piss and shit in the right ditch, despite the fact
that nobody tells anybody what to do? And did I mention the drugs? It
was equal parts *Economist* and *High Times*. Milton Friedman meets
Hunter S. Thompson. And Jesse Walker from *Reason* wanted to talk to
me about it.

I stopped planning my trip to Bosnia. I stopped plotting my

return to Kisling's and I gave him a call. He asked a few questions. I answered them.

He bought the story. I couldn't believe it.

I would be heading to Montana to live with the Rainbows for a while. I needed to be there by July 2. At the latest. But I wouldn't be getting back from Bosnia until June 28. At the earliest.

I put together a list of things I was going to need. It must have included at least a hundred million items for the Rainbow trip alone. The first 99 million of which were: drugs.

Unfortunately, drugs cost money. So does airfare to Montana. Or bus fare. Or gas money. (Would my car even make it?) What about food? Supplies? How was I going to pay for all of that, especially after fronting all that money for Bosnia? The stock options windfall was still months away. I would need hundreds of dollars, all told. Maybe thousands. There was no way in hell I could come up with that kind of money. Unless . . .

Hold on a second. I know one way to save money. It's a crappy, ridiculous way, sure. But unless someone can come up with a better idea . . .

On Wednesday May 24, 2000, the day before my obituary for the Urban Hermit appeared in the *Laurel Leader*, two days before my much-anticipated return to Kisling's, I walked through the automatic door of the Boston Street Safeway and made my way to the dry-goods aisle. To the lentils.

The Urban Hermit.

Stick around, jackass.

· 8 ·

Oops, I Did It Again

Maybe you've hit bottom. But I haven't hit bottom yet. I got a long way to go. And I'm gonna bounce back. And when I do, I'm gonna buy you a diamond so big it's gonna make you puke.
—Navin R. Johnson in *The Jerk*, 1979

May 26, 2000. Friday evening. Skippy and I were sitting side by side in our recliners. I was eating a tuna fish sandwich. He had just gotten home from work and smelled like rotten mackerel. I told him I would not be going to the bar as planned.

"What do you mean?" he said.

"I can't," I said. "I don't have the money."

"But you've been saving money."

"Yeah, but I've been sending it all out for the bills," I said. "Now I'm saving it up for Bosnia and Montana. I have to have cash."

"The guys at the bar are going to be pissed."

"I know," I said. "Tell them I'll be at the warehouse on Sunday night."

"So what's the deal?" he asked. "You're going to eat lentils forever?"

"Just another month," I said. "Three weeks, really. I'll be heading to Bosnia around the twentieth."

"When are you getting back?"

"The end of June. At least I hope so."

"And when are going to Montana?"

"I'll probably head out the same day I get back from Bosnia. I already told Joe I was taking some time off. Maybe a week or ten days."

"So how are you getting there?" Skippy asked.

"I don't know. Flying might be tough. I can't be sure when I'll get back from Bosnia. Besides, the gathering is way out in the woods. I'd have to fly into Bozeman or Billings, then rent a car. I can't afford all that."

"So you're going to drive?"

"I guess," I said. "But it'll take a few days, and I need to be there by July second to get settled in. The main day is the fourth."

"Dude," he said, "are you going to make it?"

"I have to."

Skippy paused for a minute. Then an idea seemed to strike him. "You said the Rainbow thing is a good time, right?"

"It's pretty weird," I said. "But, yeah, it's a blast."

"And you're heading out at the end of June?"

"Yeah. Hopefully the twenty-eighth."

"You need another driver?"

"Huh?"

"Maybe I'll go."

"What about work?" I asked.

"Fuck it," he said. "I'll tell JJ tonight when he's drunk. What's he going to do, fire me?"

"You know, it might actually be a good idea. Maybe we could take your car. How many miles are left on your lease?"

"I already blew way past that," he said. "I'm going to have to buy the damn thing anyway."

"But wait a minute," I said. "Shit."

"What?"

"I can't drive a stick."

"You're an asshole," he said.

I didn't disagree.

"We'll figure something out," Skippy said. "It'll be just like *Fear and Loathing in Las Vegas*. I can pose as your Samoan attorney. We'll eat a whole bunch of mescaline."

"Do you even know what mescaline is?"

"No," he said. "What is it?"

"I have no idea."

"Either way, I get to be the attorney."

If I had been paying attention, I might have noticed that it was an interesting time to be alive in America. There was an election in the works, and it was sizing up to be a real humdinger. It was the year 2000. Peacetime. Boom time. An era of big ideas.

And not just in politics. Things were *happening*. On May 16, Britney Spears released her second LP, *Oops! . . . I Did It Again.* It sold 1.3 million copies in a single week. On May 23, a rapper named Eminem released an album called *The Marshall Mathers LP.* It sold 1.76 million albums in a single week. On May 31, CBS introduced America to a television show called *Survivor.*

I couldn't afford to buy albums, though. I missed the *Survivor* debut, too. I was at the fish warehouse that night.

That's how the month went. I missed things. And I worried about money. My creditors were still harassing me, but I kept about half the money I saved up in the second half of May. I needed it.

The weight loss continued unabated. In early June I tightened my belt another notch. The pants I had been wearing finally started to sag, even when I dried them on "hot." That amounted to a real crisis. The last thing I could afford was a new wardrobe. So I dove into a pile of old clothes crumpled up on the floor in my bedroom and found a pair of jeans I hadn't worn in years. Size 40. A pair of Dockers. Some shorts. Good thing I was so lazy. Otherwise I would have gotten rid of all that crap.

I was a little worried, though. That was a lot of weight to lose, and I couldn't afford to be getting weak. Especially with the Rainbow Gathering on the horizon. I'd be walking all over the place. I remembered the first weekend of the Urban Hermit plan, when I went camping. I could only make it about a quarter of a mile with a full pack. That wouldn't do.

So I did a test run. I packed my camping gear, strapped it on, and started walking. My normal route. It took me about an hour. Then I walked from Butcher's Hill to Greektown, straight up Eastern Avenue. About two miles, most of it on a gentle uphill grade. The pack was heavy. And it was hot outside. But I made it. No problem. I could have kept going, but I saw no point in that.

I turned around and walked back. Downhill. When I got home I flopped on the floor to max out on push-ups. I did fifty of them. Thirty more than I could do six weeks earlier.

Screw the health concerns. I was still hungry and miserable, but I sure as hell wasn't weak. Besides, I didn't have the time or energy to worry about it.

Same with the stock options. Stockholders approved the Tribune/Times-Mirror merger on June 12. I stood to make $4,800. Ordinarily, that would have been big news. I probably would have spent it before I ever saw a penny. But I had no idea when I would get the money. I knew it would never show up before I took off for Bosnia, so it just didn't matter.

It would someday. But someday was a long way off. I could only deal with what was directly in front of my face. Forget the hunger. Forget the boredom. It's almost over. Just stay busy. Which meant one thing.

Work.

"Damn," I thought to myself. "This place is creepy."

It was dark. Warm. Claustrophobic. And busy. I could hear quarter after quarter dropping in the hollow metallic abyss, followed by the muffled squeals and grunts of hardcore porn. There were ten viewing booths in total, maybe fifteen. Brand spanking new, all of them. I reached down and felt the bulge in my pocket. Three dollars in change. Still there. Here goes.

It was nerve-racking. How do you know if a booth is occupied? Knock? That had to be a breach of etiquette. I noticed that the doors didn't go all the way to the floor, kind of like the stalls in a public bathroom, but there was no way to peer underneath without looking suspicious. Besides, what would I see? A pair of dirty shoes? Pants around ankles? And what if someone caught me looking?

I stood there for a few seconds and gave a good listen. I eyed the booth to my right. I gave the door a nudge. It opened.

Empty. Thank God.

It was quite a setup. A small room, maybe three and a half feet by three and a half feet, painted red from floor to ceiling. There was a small seat attached to the wall and a small television screen, maybe fifteen inches, sunk into the opposite side. Next to that was a complicated vending system: a slot for coins, a series of buttons, and a schedule of viewing material. A few channels for oral. A few for gay. More for lesbian action, Asians, and amateurs. And then the hybrids like "Asian teen lesbians."

"Geez," I thought. "You kind of have to know what you're doing."

Then there was the "buddy button." One wall of the room contained a large window. Directly behind that was some kind of opaque barrier. I thought maybe it was something that let people pay to watch a live dancer. But no. The instructions said that if I inserted coins and pushed the buddy button, it would send a signal to the adjacent booth. If that customer was in the mood for a buddy, he could hit his button, too. Which would remove the opaque barrier between the windows. There would still be a glass barrier, but I would be able to see into my buddy's booth.

"What good would that do?" I thought. But then I thought about it a little more and . . . "Oh."

I looked back at the door and noticed a lock. I slid it shut. I reached into my pocket, grabbed a quarter, raised it to the slot, and tried to drop it in.

It didn't fit. Then I noticed the sign: TOKENS ONLY. AVAILABLE AT THE FRONT DESK.

Good grief. I unlocked the booth and headed back to the counter. I approached the front desk with four quarters. "Could I get some tokens?" I said.

The clerk, a nondescript guy about my age, didn't seem to notice my nervous twitching. Nor did he comment on the reporter's notebook I was carrying. I guess he had seen stranger things, because all he said was, "Two-dollar minimum."

"Okay," I said. "Two dollars." He took my quarters and handed me the small gold tokens without looking me in the eye. Quite a discreet fellow. The right man for the job. Good show.

And soon enough I was watching porn, taking notes about the room and the available material. But then I heard the booth next to mine open and close. I heard tokens clanging into position. I heard someone shifting around. I heard the porn. Then I looked at the buddy button. Jesus H. Christ. What if that son of a bitch lights up?

I got the hell out of there, blowing past the clerk on my way out. I didn't bother to ask any questions. The clerk I interviewed a few weeks earlier was obviously wrong about the back room being used for storage. Or he had lied to me.

The pawnshop owner was right. Someone had gone and installed a whack shack about fifty feet from John Stafford's trailer park. And now I had to write a story about it.

"This is a strange way to make a living," I thought as I drove back to the office.

But I didn't care. I kind of enjoyed it, actually. Deadlines meant structure. Peace of mind. A break from all the noise. Which was getting louder and weirder as the month went on.

I needed a photographer.

Reason hadn't requested one, but I convinced them that the Rainbow Gathering was pretty damn shocking from a visual point of view. They agreed to throw in a bit of extra money if I could find someone willing to snap photos. Which was awesome. Because Skippy and I needed another driver.

I asked people I knew at Patuxent Publishing. No takers. I asked a freelancer I knew. No dice. No one could take that much time off for a few hundred bucks. I was at a loss until I talked to my mother on the phone a few days later.

"What about Aaron?" she said after listening to my conundrum.

"Aaron?"

"Aaron Ross."

Aaron Ross. My cousin. Actually, his mother, Sally, was my cousin. Which I guess makes him my first cousin once removed, or some such. He was a year or two younger than me. He grew up an hour away from Ridgway in a little town called Clearfield. He, Skippy, and I had formed a strange sort of bond, probably because we started sneaking beers and cigarettes around the same time. He had gone to college, but I heard he dropped out. Then went back. I hadn't seen him in a few years.

"I'm sure Aaron would love to go hang out with the Rainbows," I said. "But I need a photographer."

"He is a photographer," my mom said.

"He is?"

"I think so," she said. "He moved out West awhile ago. He took some classes."

"Some classes?"

"I think he does weddings," she said. "He traveled to Europe last year. Sally showed us the pictures. They were good."

"Where is he now?" I asked.

"Last I heard he was living out in Oregon," she said. "Sally said he's living in a commune or something weird like that. He has a beard."

"Wait a minute," I said. "A commune? You mean he's a hippie?"

"I don't know," she said. "But Sally says he's a photographer."

Interesting. A third family member on the trip? Why not? Only he was already in Oregon, so he wouldn't be able to help drive. Unless another preposterous bit of serendipity were to intercede.

My mom got Aaron's number from Sally. He was living in Portland. I called from work and left him a message.

He called me back that night, and he was already on board. He knew all about the Rainbows. He knew a bunch of people who would be at the gathering. I mean, this guy was enthused. So enthused that I was a little worried.

"It'll probably be good for your résumé," I said. "It's a national magazine. But it doesn't pay much."

"That's cool," he said. "I'm in."

"And you have to have your own gear. I don't have shit."

"No problem," he said. "I have all my own stuff. Besides, I want to try out some new equipment I got last time I was in Clearfield."

"You bought a camera in Clearfield?"

"No," he said. "I went drinking at the Knights of Columbus with my grandpa. We were talking with some old guy. He said he had a kit of Russian cameras and lenses from like 1950. He gave me the whole thing."

"Why?"

"I don't know," he said. "That's just Clearfield, I guess."

"So you're going to take pictures with fifty-year-old Russian cameras?"

"Cool, huh?"

"Why not?" I said, fully aware that things were getting strange. "The problem is going to be getting there. Think you could hitch a ride with someone from Portland?"

"Screw that," he said. "I'm going with you."

"Portland isn't on the way to Montana," I said. "Is it?"

"No," he said. "I'll be in Clearfield at the end of June. You can pick me up there."

"Jesus, that's perfect. You can be our third driver."

This was excellent news. Aaron's dad had owned a Buick dealership for years, and Aaron had always been pretty handy around a car. Unlike Skippy and me, who could barely operate a gas pump.

"You might have some work to do," I said. "My car's a piece of shit, so we'll probably limp all the way to Montana."

"We could take mine," he said.

"Really?"

"Yeah. It's at my grandma's in Clearfield. That's why I'm heading home. To do some work on it."

"What kind of car is it?"

"It's a 1969 Volkswagen bus," he said. "Well, they call it a bus. But it's really a van."

"Wait a minute. You mean like the Grateful Dead kind of van? The thing in *Scooby-Doo*?"

"Yeah," he said.

"A hippie van?" I said.

"Yeah," he said.

"Oh boy," I said.

I had saved up about six hundred dollars. But there was no way six hundred dollars was going to cut it. I would get paid again in early July, but I would be on the road.

My only hope was direct deposit, so I filled out the paperwork. And not a minute too soon: The first paycheck was scheduled to hit my account sometime during the Rainbow trip. I was cutting it close, but there was no use worrying about it.

Besides, I was amazed that I had saved up what I did. Thank God for the Urban Hermit. He made it all possible. As for my creditors . . . they would have to wait.

It was time. I took fifteen crisp twenty-dollar bills, put them in an envelope, and handed it to Skippy. "Get us some drugs," I said. "I know it's not a lot. But pitch in what you can and try to get a good deal."

"What kind of drugs?" he said.

"No coke," I said. "Too expensive. Plus the Rainbows don't like that shit. Stick with pot. Good stuff, if you can get it. And shrooms."

"Mescaline?" he said.

"No mescaline," I said.

"All right," he said. "I'm just saying."

"Just make sure you get it done," I said. "You know who to call."

"Yeah," he said. "No problem."

"I mean it."

"Relax. I'll take care of it."

"Okay," I said as I grabbed my enormous backpack and heaved it into place. "I'm off to Bosnia."

9

Crisis

There Are No Lentils in Newfoundland

In December, I first reviewed Iron Chef—*the weirdest cooking show since the classic* Twilight Zone *episode entitled "To Serve Man."*

I described Iron Chef *as a cooking show about "an eccentric millionaire with a frightening dye job, and what looks like the stolen wardrobes of Siegfried and Roy, who has a sick obsession. Each week, he makes the best chefs in Japan fight each other in a vicious cook-off that would give Betty Crocker a breakdown."*

And now, in that short time, it's become the Food Network's second-highest-rated show. Too bad it got canned in Japan. (I know that sounds like a tuna fish joke; it's not.)

—Linda Stasi, "NYC's Best Food Fight,"
New York Post, June 22, 2000

The trip got off to a bad start.

I expected Andrews Air Force Base to be an epic place—to stand out a bit more. It's the president's airport, after all. I thought there would be some kind of hoopla. Nope. There was just an exit.

I didn't realize I missed it until I had driven almost halfway around the Washington Beltway. Which was bad. Because if there is one thing the United States military will not tolerate, it's tardiness. I checked the clock in my car. I still had two hours. I reversed course.

I didn't miss the exit again, although I thought I must have as

I eased off the Beltway. There were no tanks. No commandos rappelling off cliffs. It was just a road. There were a few gas stations. Some restaurants. Then the guardhouse, staffed by a polite young man who waved me through after I told him who I was.

The squat cinder-block building I drove up to was even less remarkable. It looked like a standard commuter terminal. I parked, grabbed my stuff, and walked through the door into a bland waiting room. I saw a few people in civilian clothes milling around with a few people in camouflage. I introduced myself to a lanky red-haired guy with a goatee, about my age. His name was Jeff. He was my photographer from Patuxent Publishing. We had spoken on the phone but had never met in person. We exchanged pleasantries.

Jeff had been there for a while. He introduced me to an older reporter, maybe fifty years old, from *Army Times*. A TV reporter from one of the D.C. stations. She was pretty, in a TV-reporter sort of way, maybe a year or two younger than I was. Maybe a year or two older. Her cameraman was busy arranging all of his equipment. A younger reporter from one of the other D.C. stations was carrying her own stuff because her boss hadn't sprung for a cameraman. She was pretty hot, though, and it seemed like the other reporter's cameraman might be willing to help her out.

Then there was the old man and his wife. They were probably seventy-five years old. They looked like they were going on vacation. Because they were. The old man explained that former military personnel can travel on cargo planes when there's room. Free of charge. It's called flying "space A," or "space available."

"I'm retired Army," the old man told me. "We travel all over. Germany. Alaska. You name it."

"That seems like quite a deal," I said.

"You have to be flexible, though," he said. "Sometimes there's no space. It helps if you don't care where you're going. Just get on the first plane that has room."

"Sounds adventurous."

"It can be tough getting back home," he said. "One time we got stuck for a week in Alaska waiting for a flight."

"So where are you going now?" I asked. "You're not going to Bosnia for vacation, are you?"

"Germany, hopefully," he said. "We're scheduled for a stopover. But I hear we might end up going through England. Which would be fine."

Yes. Military travel. The first leg of our trip would take us to St. John's, Newfoundland. From there we would fly either to England or Germany, and from there on to Bosnia. The trip would take two full days.

We chatted for a while until two guys dressed in camo approached. One introduced himself as Capt. Drew Sullins, the National Guard public relations officer in charge of the trip. I recognized him. He had filled in as a sports reporter on one of the local TV stations, which was pretty cool. He seemed like a hard charger, not your typical PR flack. He told us he had been to Bosnia before—when he was in a tank brigade. He was short, powerfully built. He looked like he was leaning forward, no matter how he stood. I kept expecting him to stumble, but he never did.

He was probably blond, but his impossibly precise high-and-tight made it hard to know for sure. His eyes were pressed into a permanent squint. He *looked* like a tank commander. Maybe even like a tank. I don't know why, but that made me like him.

As Captain Sullins talked, however, my eyes kept drifting to the guy standing next to him. The army fatigues threw me for a minute, but I knew him from somewhere. Mid-thirties. Black glasses. Dark hair, heavy eyebrows. He occasionally chimed in with a few details about our schedule. I knew his voice, too. I looked at his name tag.

Gould.

Holy shit. Rob Gould. The CSX spokesman who got his ass kicked by the mob of angry commuters on that first day of the Urban Hermit plan.

I approached him as our briefing came to an end. "Rob Gould?" I said, extending my hand.

He gave me a quick, quizzical look.

"Sam MacDonald," I said. "From the *Laurel Leader*. I was at that CSX meeting a few months back."

"Oh, yeah," he said. "Good to see you."

"That was a pretty rough meeting."

"It was terrible," he said, laughing.

"What'd you do, quit and join the Army?"

"No," he said. "I've been in the Guard for a few years."

We joked around about the thrashing he took, how going to Bosnia would be like a vacation for him. But eventually he had to go deal with some paperwork.

"Sorry I didn't recognize you," he said. "I'm usually pretty good with faces. Did you lose some weight or something?"

"Long story," I said.

The C-130 Hercules was squatting on the runway a few hundred yards away. Its ass-end was wide open. A crew of workers pushed pallets up the loading ramp, into the belly of the beast. The four turbo-props began coughing. Spitting. Spinning. They were loud. Even from a distance. Even though I was looking through a thick plate-glass window, I could almost *see* the noise. I was so transfixed that I didn't notice Captain Sullins until he was standing shoulder to shoulder with me. He was looking at the plane, too.

"Seems kind of old," I said.

"The C-130 is a workhorse," Captain Sullins said. "It's been in service for decades. There are faster planes. Newer planes. Planes that can carry more. But nothing's as reliable as the C-130."

Sullins was giving me the company line. But he couldn't keep it up for long.

"It's a beautiful plane," he said. "Just look at it."

I looked.

"Let me tell you something," he said. "The son of a bitch floats. If we go down in the ocean, as long as we don't break up, we'll float around until someone comes and gets us."

"Really?"

"That's what I hear," he said. "But we won't go down in the ocean. It's a beautiful plane. Just *look* at it."

It did exude a certain workmanlike charm. A goofy, pragmatic sort of appeal. It didn't have the sexy lines of a fighter plane or the imposing gravity of a bomber. But if you want to drop a tank and a few airborne ass-kickers on top of someone you don't like, and you want to drop them there on time, the C-130 gets the job done.

"So what are they loading on there now?" I asked.

"Instruments," Sullins said.

Instruments of death and destruction? Flamethrowers? Grenades? Machine guns? Survival knives? Cudgels of some sort? Brass knuckles? A reporter needs to know such things. "What kind of instruments?" I asked.

"Instruments for a band," he said. "Tubas. Clarinets. Stuff like that."

Instruments? For a band?

"Why in the hell are we taking clarinets to Bosnia?" I asked.

"The Army band is putting on a concert."

"Really?"

"It's not much of a load for a C-130," he said. "That's why we had extra room for you guys. By the way," he added, "how much do you weigh?"

"I have no idea," I said. "Why?"

"You and your stuff," he said. "We have to document how much weight we're putting on the plane. We're not even close to maxing out. But regulations, you know."

He was holding a clipboard to record the information. I paused for a second. The last time I hopped on a scale was right before football season in 1990, when I weighed 215. It had been six weeks since I started the Urban Hermit scheme. How much did I weigh when I started? Three hundred? Three-twenty? Three-forty? How much had I lost? Thirty pounds? Fifty?

"I don't know," I said. "Maybe two-seventy-five?"

"Okay," he said.

"Or two-eighty?" I said.

"Okay," he said.

"And my stuff," I said. "I have some clothes. The office gave me an old laptop to bring along. I'd say maybe sixty pounds total. So three hundred and fifty total. At most."

"All right," he said. "I'll put you down for four hundred. Like I said, we're not even close."

"You say that bastard floats?" I asked, giving the plane another look.

"That's what I hear," he said, smiling. I couldn't tell if he was serious.

"Put me down for four hundred and fifty," I said.

I thought we would get to walk up the rear cargo ramp, like the paratroopers do in all those movies. So I was disappointed when we went up some stairs and entered the plane through a small side door.

The interior was dark and hollow. Cavernous. A few guys in green jumpsuits were strapping things down and yelling into the mouthpieces attached to their earphones. I couldn't hear anything except a dull, heavy drone filtered through the foam earplugs Captain Sullins handed me earlier. The back half of the plane was filled with huge pallets, almost the width of the entire plane, covered in cargo netting.

The front half of the cargo area was divided in half along the length of the plane. There were no seats. No trays to set in their upright position prior to takeoff. No headphones for an in-flight movie. It was all straps and levers and knots and buckles. Green things I couldn't identify. We would be sitting in cargo nets. A series of them were attached to each interior wall of the plane. Another series ran down the center. Four rows of seating, paratrooper style.

Cool. Only the guy next to me didn't look like a paratrooper. It was the old man and his wife. As we settled in and the plane lurched forward, he leaned over to me, cupped his hands over his mouth, and screamed in my ear.

"Have you ever flown on a C-130?" he hollered.

"No!"

"It's going to get cold!" he said as he leaned back toward his wife and smiled.

The engines roared louder as we sped down the runway, louder still as we leaned into a steep incline. It made me queasy. There were no windows for reference, just the loose cargo netting drooping at odd angles. And sure enough, the higher we got, the colder it got. Once we leveled off I reached into the backpack that I had tucked between my legs and pulled out an old sweatshirt. I put it on and pulled up the hood. I was glad to be sandwiched so tightly and warmly between the old man and the reporter from *Army Times*.

It dawned on me that I would have been a terrible paratrooper.

A few reporters went forward to sit in the cockpit for a spell. A few others went toward the back, past the band equipment, to piss in a little basin that served as the bathroom. At some stage Rob Gould distributed some boxed lunches. I didn't take one, though. I was trying to get some work done. I dug the company laptop out of my bag and tried to turn it on. It wouldn't cooperate. To hell with it. I'd figure it out later. I jotted down a few notes in a pad.

The engines eventually quieted a bit. Or maybe we just got used to them. Either way, we could chat with people if we were willing to shout and read lips. So I shouted with the old man for a while. Then I turned and shouted with the guy from *Army Times*.

"Ever been to St. John's?" he shouted.

"No," I shouted back.

"I'll show you around," he shouted. "Nice place."

We landed in the early afternoon and checked into a hotel. Then people started peeling off. A few guys decided to check out one of the local strip clubs. That was the last thing I needed. And it wasn't exactly the kind of thing a guy can expense. So I didn't get into that cab. I was just about to head back to my room when I saw *Army Times* standing around with another photographer I had met briefly at Andrews.

"You heading into town?" *Army Times* said.

"I guess. Any ideas?"

"We'll figure something out," he said.

And the stuff we did. I mean . . . The three of us walked up a huge hill and toured a tiny castle. At least it looked like a castle. Some guy sent the first transatlantic telegram from there. Or received it there. Or something like that. I stood in the actual room where it happened. From way up there we could see the entire harbor, which had been protecting ships from cataclysmic storms for centuries. A tour guide explained how the fishing industry had collapsed, how oil had replaced it, and what the airbase meant to the local economy. Later we went to a watch store. It was fascinating shit.

Okay. I admit it. I wasn't in the best position to judge. I had spent the previous seven weeks staring at my own walls and wandering around Baltimore. I would have had a ball in Toledo, Ohio. Duluth, Minnesota, would have seemed like Paris, France. But what did I care? St. John's kind of rocked, as far as I was concerned. There was a college, an aquarium, and a hopping bar-and-restaurant district to serve the students, oil workers, and military personnel. It reminded me of Fell's Point.

I strolled through the streets with *Army Times* and the photographer. They said they were hungry. We ended up at a sports bar, which looked like any other sports bar. Two or three big-screen televisions, a bunch of smaller ones. Most of them were tuned into cable news stations. The walls were plastered with garish advertisements for Budweiser and Goldschlaeger.

And then it hit me.

Holy crap. I'm going to have to eat something.

The place was empty except for us. We sat by a large window look-ing out onto the street. A young waitress approached and asked if we wanted anything to drink. My companions ordered. I think they asked for beers.

"And can I get you something?" she asked, turning to me.

I sat there. Paralyzed. A deer in the headlights? No. I was more like a dead-drunk truck driver behind the wheel of a rickety old semi with bad brakes, going 137 miles an hour down a steep grade that leads straight into the heart of Shitbag Village, the meanest, mangiest town in all of Cocksucker County. Completely confused. Careening. Out of control.

How did I get here? How do I stop this thing?

I guess I knew this was coming. But seriously. Would I like something to drink? I mean, that's what this lunatic just asked me, right? What kind of question is that? Do you mean do I *want* a drink? Do you mean *should* I have a drink? And by "drink," do you mean *drink*? Or do you mean DRINK? Great Christ, woman! What sort of torture chamber are you operating here? Because if you want to see someone drink, I can show you a thing or two. Oh, yes. Make that three. Make it a triple. Make it . . .

"An iced tea," I said.

"Sweetened or unsweetened?"

Sweetened or unsweetened? Are you serious, you ignorant skank? Can't you see I'm dying here? If you knew the shitstorm of drunken debauchery that I'm capable of unleashing on this dive, you'd know that I like my iced tea served with tequila and gin and some sort of apertif, whatever that is, whatever you got, hold the iced tea, of course. And throw in about thirty-eight beers of the high-powered Canadian variety and . . .

"Unsweetened."

Then she put a menu in front of me and things got strange. The whole place went in and out of focus. I couldn't pay attention to anything my companions were saying. I just kept staring at the menu. A cheeseburger? Potato skins? French *fucking* fries? I had put all that crap out of my mind a long time ago. Pushed them outside the realm of possibilities. There were no decisions to make. Just the sad, simple life of an Urban Hermit. But now, without warning, here it is: the ear-splitting noise of this goddamn menu and all of its choices and possibilities and delicious fried this and scrumptious broiled that and the liquor. Oh, the liquor!

But I was done being an Urban Hermit. Right?

Right?

Sort of. There was still that problem with the money, but there was no way I could find a place to eat lentils in St. John's, Newfoundland. Even if I did, would lentils be cheaper than a burger and fries? So get it over with and order a burger and fries. But could my stomach handle a burger and fries after two months of nothing? Jesus, I didn't even know how the iced tea was going to sit in my belly. What if I just—

"Sir?"

It was the waitress again. She was back. She had already taken orders from *Army Times* and the photographer. I was on the spot.

"Huh?" I asked.

"Do you know what you'd like?"

"Umm . . ."

"Do you need a minute?"

"Uhh . . ."

"We do have some specials today," she said.

"Okay," I said, trying to buy some time, trying to get a grip. "What are the specials?"

"We have a grilled tuna with—"

"What's that?" I said.

"It's a grilled tuna with—"

"Yes," I said.

"Sir?"

"Tuna," I said. "I'll take the tuna."

· **10** ·

Combat Descent

You are not the sort of person . . . who would watch Survivor. *It's not just the larvae-eating contest. . . . It's the gladiatorial concept: stranding sixteen people on a tropical desert island to scrabble for food and shelter, all for the delectation of sluggards licking Cheetos dust off their fingers in their air-conditioned living rooms. It's the Machiavellian twist: having the contestants vote one another off the island until there is a single million-dollar winner and fifteen rejects. It's the suffering, the mean-spiritedness, the humiliation.*

—Time, June 26, 2000

W e landed at Ramstein Air Base in the early afternoon, collected ourselves on a blue bus, and headed to the PX—a carefully crafted outpost of American consumer capitalism.

Fast food out the wazoo. Ice cream. VCRs and stereos. Cars, even. Brand-new ones on display in a roped-off area right outside the front door. Not just minivans and station wagons, either. I'm talking about cars that appeal to young servicemen with fat wallets and no discretion. Fast cars. Ford Mustangs, candy-apple red.

"What kind of clown would buy a Mustang in Germany?" I asked as we stopped to admire the muscle cars. "What do you do with it when they send you back to the States?"

"Take it with you," one of the crew members from the plane said. "Have it shipped back over."

"The Army pays for that?"

"Hell, no," he said. "It costs. But you get things tax-free at the PX. Shipping it from here costs less than paying sales tax back home."

"Crafty."

"Hell, yeah," he said.

We eventually made our way to the bank. They used German currency in Bosnia, so I needed enough for about a week. I decided to get two hundred dollars' worth.

People had already started to make plans by the time I walked out into the afternoon sun. We weren't scheduled to leave until morning, and a few of my fellow travelers were heading out to see some castles in Heidelberg.

"How are you getting to Heidelberg?" I asked.

"Train," someone said. "It leaves in about an hour."

"How much does that cost?"

"Not much," someone said. "It's Europe. Trains are cheap."

"And the castle?"

"Not sure. But it can't be much."

No. Absolutely not. Every penny in my pocket had cost me dearly. The last thing I was going to spend money on was a tour of some stupid castle.

I wasn't alone. *Army Times* passed on the castles, too. So did my photographer and a few other guys. So after checking into our hotel, we took a cab into Kaiserslautern. The soldiers called it K-Town. There was a university, a football stadium, a dinosaur park. But I didn't see any of that. I saw gift shops that sold T-shirts and snow globes. And restaurants, none of which seemed particularly "German." There were pizza joints, burger stands, burrito huts, and bars. Lots of bars. Which would have been great under different circumstances, because I would have gotten drunk. But I couldn't afford it. So we ended up in some strange place getting something to eat.

There was no drama. No wild rambling, like when I ordered that tuna in St. John's. That was the first real meal I had eaten in months, and it was good. Delicious even. But not in any life-changing way. It didn't lead to any collapse. I didn't end up spending $150 at the bar and missing the plane. I survived.

Something must have clicked because, to be honest, I can't remember what I got to eat at that restaurant in Kaiserslautern. I remember ordering at a counter, kind of like a Chinese place. But I don't think it was Chinese. Indian, maybe? We ate outside in a little café. I remember that I didn't eat very much. Not because I didn't like it. It was just . . . food.

I remember talking most of the time. About lentils. And Rainbows. Word had started to spread about the Urban Hermit scheme and my Montana plans. And pretty soon I emerged as the Weird Guy on the trip. The other reporters laughed at me. Not in a mean-spirited way, though. They asked the same questions everybody asked. Why lentils? For how long? How much weight have you lost?

Then they laughed at me some more. But eventually we headed back to the hotel. Which was good. I wanted to type some background notes into the laptop. Finally. I needed to stay ahead of the game.

We parted ways in the lobby and I went to my room. I cracked open the computer and pressed the power button, but I still couldn't make it work. It seemed like the battery was dead. I tried the backup. That didn't work, either. I tried to plug it in, but I didn't have an outlet converter.

Dammit.

I made a note to ask one of the photographers to help me the next day. They were pretty good with high-tech stuff. I jotted down a few things in my notebook. Then, with nothing left to do, I went to bed.

Despite the computer hassle, I was proud of myself for being so diligent. Or at least trying to be. And for not spending the money on the Heidelberg trip.

And for not getting drunk.

Then the plane started to crash. I swear.

The C-130 lurched forward violently. There were no windows to look out, but I could *feel* it. Then—good Lord!—everything that wasn't strapped down started tumbling. Empty water bottles, oranges from the boxed lunches, backpacks. Even with my earplugs firmly in place, I could tell that the engines were struggling. Straining. Whining. What the fuck! Had they actually reversed the propellers? Would that help? If we were in some sort of nose-down death spiral, could they actually slow this bastard down enough to make a difference? Good God, of course not! Jesus, we were going faster by the second! We weren't just falling out of the sky, we were driving ourselves into the ground. I could feel it, and the faster we went, the louder it got inside that hideous death trap. Pull out of it, man! Pull out!

And then I heard a voice screaming. I could barely make it out in the chaos. But there it was again. And it was saying: "What?"

It was shouting directly into my ear. Again. Only now it was shouting, "Did you say something?"

It was *Army Times*. He was sitting in the cargo netting just to my right. He was holding a book open. Perfectly calm.

"What the fuck is going on?" I screamed as an apple core bounced off my foot and skipped toward the cockpit.

"Combat descent," he screamed.

"What?"

"They didn't tell you?" he screamed.

"What?"

He stopped screaming. Started laughing. My notebook and pencil bounced off my lap.

"Combat descent," he screamed into my ear once he collected himself. "They get the plane in and out of hostile areas as fast as they can."

"What?"

"Straight down, unload the cargo, then straight up. Lowers exposure to anti-aircraft fire."

Then my eardrums started pounding and I couldn't hear anything. I looked up and saw Captain Sullins screaming in Rob Gould's ear. They were laughing, too. Probably at me. These crazy fuckers are actually doing this on purpose? Son of a bitch. Was this really necessary? Or was it some kind of show for reporters? Because if it's a show, that seems . . .

Then Sullins's face did a strange contortion, shifting from smile to smirk to grimace in quick succession. He looked like he was in pain. Oh God, I thought. Something is wrong.

Yes. Something was wrong. But not with the plane.

After about two more minutes of high-speed drama, we were safely on the ground, coasting to a slow roll on the runway as the crew prepared to unload the tubas, clarinets, and reporters before the locals realized we were in their midst. I wiped the sweat off my brow and tried to get my bearings. We were intact.

Except for Captain Sullins, who was still grimacing, his eyes clenched, his palm pressed firmly against his jaw. One of his molars cracked due to the extreme pressure change brought on by the combat descent.

Our first casualty.

Bosnia was torn by a vicious civil war in the nineties. There was genocide. There was ethnic cleansing. In Tuzla, more than seventy children were killed when a single artillery shell burst in their midst. The violence culminated in a massacre of eight thousand in the city of Srebrenica, a UN-established safe-zone, while Dutch peacekeepers in goofy blue helmets looked on.

Like most Americans, I didn't know anything about any of it. It's easy to criticize us for being so self-absorbed, for being so preoccupied with our Internets and our Boy Bands and our bar stools. But as far as wars go, this one was confusing. There were Serbians. And Bosnians. And Bosnian Serbs. And Croats, some of whom lived in Croatia, some of whom did not. Some of the people were Muslim. And it all had something to do with Albania. Or Kosovo. Or Albanian people who lived in Kosovo. Or vice versa. I knew a very nice Serbian guy in college. He tried to explain it to me. But I think *he* was confused.

Still, President Bill Clinton picked sides and unleashed air assaults. Republicans blasted him for meddling in foreign affairs, but the shooting stopped in 1995. By the time I got there in June 2000, it would have been an exaggeration to call the place "hostile." In five years, only one American had been killed—while trying to defuse a land mine.

The land mines. They were scattered all over the countryside, obliterating children and livestock from time to time. Soldiers used wooden boardwalks through certain sections of Eagle Base, where we were staying. They hadn't even managed to clear the mines off a major military installation yet. So nobody ever stepped off the boardwalk.

But it wasn't all bad. Eagle Base was a claptrap collection of tents and trailers in the mid-nineties, but the military had added some amenities over the years. A movie theater. A computer lab. A huge gym. A running track. A coffee shop. There was even a nightclub where soldiers could get drunk.

As long as they weren't American. Unlike other members of the UN task force, American servicemen were not allowed to drink. They could only order Borsodi—a heinous nonalcoholic selection. But it kept people from staggering off the boardwalk.

These might seem like trivial observations, but I wasn't in Bosnia as a war correspondent. There was no war going on. I was a community journalist working for a community weekly. Members of that community were serving overseas, and I was there to write about what they were doing. Was it a fluff piece? Maybe. The *Washington Post* reporter had backed out at the last minute. But it was important enough for the *Laurel Leader*. And rightly so. I wasn't going to win any Pulitzer Prizes, but it was a big deal for the people who read our newspaper. So I gave it a shot.

On our first day in country, my photographer, an interpreter, and I got into a convoy of armored Humvees and rode to a village called Grbska. It had been home to about nine hundred before the war, but it was mostly rubble when I got there. I spoke with an ancient-looking Muslim man who had recently returned to his home after living as a refugee for years. His house had no roof. A wall was missing. But he had nowhere else to go, so he and his wife were living in the basement. They had a few chickens. His youngest son had been killed in the war.

Down the road we encountered a man whose home had been reduced to a bare concrete slab. There was still a fruit tree in the front yard, though. He saw me eyeing it, smiled, and started hollering. His wife came out of nowhere carrying a bowl full of tiny pears. He insisted that I take one. When I did, one of the soldiers warned me not to eat it. Not because it was poisoned or anything. He said it might give me the shits.

The man invited me into another bombed-out building. My interpreter told me to take off my shoes. It was the village mosque. There was no light. The floor was covered in old blankets. There was a copy of the Koran on top of a box, tucked into a corner to keep it away from the water dripping through a gaping hole in the roof.

The Laurel soldiers were in military intelligence. Part of their job was talking with people in town to monitor ethnic tensions. The man in the mosque said that when the Muslim villagers returned to Grbska a few months earlier, residents of a neighboring village had pelted their buses with rocks.

But not every inch of Bosnia looked like Grbska. The next day, we went to a small city called Doboj. (The soldiers pronounced it DOUGH-boy.) It was 70 percent Muslim and Croat prior to the war, but the Muslims and Croats left when the Serbs threatened to kill them. Then Serbs ousted from other cities started moving into the empty homes. Doboj was 99 percent Serbian when I got there.

Ethnic cleansing.

Now that the war had been over for five years, some of the Muslims and Croats wanted to move back. But the displaced Serbs living in Doboj wanted people out of *their* homes first. Or complained that their homes were destroyed. Or that if they went back to where they came from, people would start killing them again. Which seemed extremely primitive and intractable. Because it was.

The thing that stood out to me about Doboj was . . . well . . . What stood out was the fact that the city looked pretty good. There were a lot of bombed-out buildings, and the ones left standing had a lot of bullet holes, but I saw stores selling fashionable clothes. Sidewalk cafés. There were parks and trees. And for a small city, it was a happening place. There was a parade. People were everywhere, walking and talking and enjoying themselves.

Which brought me to my second observation: The chicks in Doboj were hot as balls. Seriously. On a per-capita basis, I saw more beautiful women in that obscure little town than I have ever seen anywhere in the United States. College campuses? Beaches in Florida? They had nothing on Doboj. These were not the refugees I was used to seeing on television. They were tall. Lanky. Fit. And they were dressed exactly like fashionable women in America. They wore sunglasses. Miniskirts. Halter tops, even. The soldiers laughed when they saw me staring, because they had noticed the same thing months earlier.

"Ever see all them supermodels with weird names?" the young soldier driving our Humvee asked. "You know, like Paulina Porizkova?"

"Sure," I said.

"Well, this is where they're from."

I seemed to recall that Paulina Porizkova was from Czechoslovakia. But I knew what he meant.

Going to the city was good duty. It was reasonably safe. And it was almost like being a tourist, if you let yourself get lost in the moment. Which was easy for me, because I wasn't in charge of security. We went to a café, had a cup of coffee, and chatted with the local men. Some of them were drinking beer. All of them were watching the girls walk by. They were nice to us. The soldiers clearly had a good rapport with them.

Later I went with soldiers to deliver food to needy families. Then I joined a convoy that delivered supplies to a smaller base out in the hinterlands. Back at Eagle Base, I checked out the movie theater and the gym and the cramped barracks. I asked where people were from. If they were from Maryland, I talked to them for as long as possible. I met a mother of three from Laurel. A father of two from Columbia. I met a man who decided to join the National Guard on a whim at age thirty-five, never dreaming that he would ever be deployed.

Then I met a guy, about my age, whose wife had just given birth. He had been a nuclear engineer in the Navy before switching to the Army National Guard. I told him I knew a really sharp guy in high school who had skipped college in favor of that same nuclear engineering program.

"What was his name?" he asked me.

"Denny McNutt," I said.

"You have to be kidding me," he said. "I went through training with Denny McNutt. I was in his wedding."

Small world.

We slept on military-issue cots in a large dormitory-style room. We got up at five-thirty to shower and get squared away. We had full access to the mess hall, but I can't recall going there for breakfast. I don't remember going there for lunch, either. I probably ended up eating less in Bosnia than I did as a stateside Urban Hermit. I was always interviewing soldiers, organizing my notes, hassling Captain

Sullins to find me more people from Maryland. I didn't have time to eat. So my recently acquired ability to go long stretches without food was a real asset.

I do remember one meal, though. It was probably our second day. I noticed that I was hungry. So hungry that the familiar pit in my stomach had become even emptier. So hungry that I was getting a little woozy. I realized I had to eat something. So I strolled over to the mess hall for dinner with a bunch of reporters.

No lentils. No tuna. But I didn't care. It was free, and it looked good. I got rigatoni and meatballs. Wow. That was excellent stuff. Maybe a little overcooked, but what's the difference? The roll with butter was even better. I think I had some broccoli and some iced tea. I could have eaten more. I could have gone up for another round. But I didn't. We had more work to do. So we went and did it.

I felt better. Strong, even. And my stomach wasn't growling anymore. So I just kept walking and talking and scribbling. At some stage, maybe the next day, maybe the day after that, I tightened my belt another notch.

There were no more notches left.

For once I had a strategy. One that seemed like it might actually work.

I had planned to type all of my interviews into the laptop every night, then write the story on the way home, cutting and pasting the notes as needed. But I was working late every day, and I was taking a ton of notes. There was no way I could type everything into the laptop. Besides, I still couldn't get the laptop to work. One of the photographers assured me that the batteries just needed charging, so I plugged them up that first night in Bosnia and forgot about it.

And I changed my strategy. We were supposed to land in England or Germany on the trip home, stay over one night, then spend a final night back in Newfoundland. Forget about typing all the notes. I would review them and select quotes on the first leg of the trip, then write the story in whatever hotel we stayed at. That would leave me a full day in Newfoundland to pretty it up. I would do final edits on the flight back to Andrews, and file the story as soon as I got back to the office.

Genius. It would have been pure genius. If it hadn't been for the shocking blunder I was about to make.

Damn. I was *so close*.

The Fat Bastard's Revenge

"There are going to be times," says Kesey, *"when we can't wait for somebody. Now, you're either on the bus or off the bus. If you're on the bus, and you get left behind, then you'll find it again. If you're off the bus in the first place—then it won't make a damn."*

—Ken Kesey, as quoted by Tom Wolfe in
The Electric Kool-Aid Acid Test, 1968

Yeah, I think they really wanted me to be on the bus. In fact, I never was.

—Tom Wolfe, *Rolling Stone* interview, August 21, 1980

> *Get on to the bus*
> *That's gonna take you back to Beelzebub*
> *Get on to the bus*
> *That's gonna make you stop going rub-a-dub . . .*
> *I'll scratch you raw*
> *L'etat c'est moi*
> *I drink the drink*
> *And I'm wall to wall*
> —Soul Coughing, *"Bus to Beelzebub,"* 1994

I wasn't on the bus. But it didn't make a damn. At least at first. Because I didn't even know it. The only thing penetrating the fog was that earsplitting noise. Again and again.

BAM! BAM! BAM! BAM! BAM! BAM! BAM! BAM! BAM!
BAM!

[rattle rattle]

BAM! BAM! BAM! BAM! BAM! BAM! BAM! BAM! BAM!
BAM!

What *is* that? It's so angry. So painful. Can't a guy get some rest? But am I resting? What is that on my head? Is it a pillow? Am I sleeping? Where am I? Why am I so sweaty?

And suddenly the noise has a voice. A muffled one. Screaming.

"SAM MACDONALD!"

[rattle]

[WHAM!]

"SAM MACDONALD!"

Sam MacDonald. That's me, right? Oh my . . . What happened?

My senses come back to me in waves. Jesus, my head. My stomach. And the taste in my mouth. Battery acid? Sour milk? And then my eyes rattle open and the cold hard facts start pouring in.

First, the ceiling of the hotel room. Then the bed, still made. Me on it, fully clothed. All my shit scattered across the floor. Then the clock. Where's the clock? Is there a clock?

Oh, no. Fuck, no. Don't tell me . . .

I roll off the bed, take a knee like I'm praying. But no time for that. I stand. I cringe. I stumble toward the door. It senses me coming. It chides me. "SAM MACDONALD!" it hollers. BAM! BAM! BAM! BAM! BAM! BAM! BAM! BAM! BAM!

I open it. And I see him. Wide-eyed. Crazed. Sweat rolling down his neck onto the collar of his camo. Rob Gould.

"Oh my God!" he shouts. "What happened to you?"

I stare at him. I think about responding. But it's all a haze and I know I won't have a reasonable answer any time soon. He can't wait. He has to tell me the score. To confirm my worst fears.

"The bus!" he shouts.

I gather myself as best I can. Square my shoulders. Get a grip. This is bad. So first things first. Figure out what's going on.

"What's going on?" I ask.

"The bus!" he shouts. "It's leaving without you!"

"Okay," I say. "How long do I have?"

"You don't get it!" he shouts. "It's leaving right now! I've been trying to get you up for an hour! The bus is moving through the parking lot *right now!*"

And then I hear it. A low rumble. Some gears. Motion! I race over to the window and heave the heavy red curtain to the side. The bright light of morning nearly blinds me, but I can see the blue bus start to roll through the parking lot, maybe twenty yards away.

"Holy shit!" I shout at the window. "Stop that fucking bus!"

I turn around to say it again, but Rob Gould is already sprinting down the hallway to the exit. "Rob!" I shout down the hall. "Stop that bus!"

I grab my stuff in a frenzy. My bag. My notebooks. And that goddamn laptop that caused this whole disaster in the first place.

Okay. The laptop only kind of caused it. But whatever. I don't have time for this shit. If there is one thing the American military won't tolerate, it's tardiness. I don't have time to go to the bathroom. Or get my stuff. Razor. Deodorant. Toothbrush. To hell with it. To the bus!

I race down the hallway with a half-empty backpack, a laptop bag with cables and papers trailing behind me. An armful of shirts and underwear. I toss my key at the front desk, make my way down another hall, and burst into the sunlight, my head aching, my stomach churning. Undone zippers and untied straps. An idiot on a mission. On fire. If I miss that bus, I miss that plane. And if I miss that plane, I'm doomed. Run, fucker! Run!

I try not to think about my throbbing head and I try not to shit my pants, but all that's beside the point because there's only one thing to do.

Run!

Missing that bus is out of the question. *Unacceptable.*

Faster!

I can see them. The reporters. There's *Army Times*. There's Jeff, my photographer. Captain Sullins. Rob Gould. He made it. He's safe. They are all on the bus with their faces pressed to the glass. Watching me. Gauging my speed. Look at him go! Look at him suffer!

Run!

And as I storm across the hot asphalt, a clear picture of him flashes in my mind. That fat bastard. Oh, that fat bastard. He's watching me, too. And laughing.

But now I'm getting ahead of myself. Because for this to make any sense, I need to explain a few things. Like why you should never, under any circumstances, tip a bartender with coins when you're in a foreign country.

Balls.

I was optimistic when the return trip got under way the previous day. I had a ton of notes. I had some good stories. And I still had most of my money. I bought three packs of Croatian cigarettes, which I thought would be a hit at the Rainbow Gathering. Plus I dropped about twenty dollars at the PX on a camo Army coat with a lot of pockets. It was an extra-large, marking the first time I had bought something other than an XXL in years. It would serve me well during the cold nights in Montana. I figured I deserved it.

And then the flight. Without the band equipment, the plane was nearly empty. That made it even colder and noisier, but it did give us room to spread out. Once we got to altitude, I scoured my notes for good quotes and anecdotes. There was a lot of material to organize, but we had time. We were bypassing Germany and landing at Milden-hall, in England.

I got a lot of work done, and I was pretty squared away by the time we landed. I traded in my deutsche marks and got two hundred dollars' worth of pounds, just in case my credit card wouldn't work at the hotel. It's like I was a real person. An efficient one, even. A professional.

I was still on the straight and narrow when we got to the squat Tudor inn. It was called the Smoke House. The literature in the lobby insisted that it was historic, but that didn't matter to me. I wanted to get to my room, fire up the laptop, and start writing. So I paid for the room with my credit card—still working!—and got on with my plan.

Nothing could stop me. Not even the strongest temptations. Almost all of the people in our group decided to hop a train, go to Cambridge, and do some drinking. It was only twenty-five miles away and we'd be back before midnight. Ha! Not for me. I had plans. Gosh, I was a *rock*. I gathered up my gear, carried it to my room, and plunked it all down. I got settled. I showered. I pulled out the laptop. I pushed the power button and . . .

Nothing. Not even a flicker.

Shit shit shit shit shit.

I should have made sure the laptop worked. And if I couldn't make it work I should have borrowed someone else's. Or something. Instead, I was stuck in Mildenhall with nothing to do, no way to get my work done. I never should have let that happen. I was frantic. And pissed off at myself. Another plan up in smoke.

But then I pulled myself together. It was a glitch, to be sure. But that's why you stay ahead of the game, see? That's why you build some slack into the plan. Wow. This whole responsibility thing. Incredible. Is this how normal people live? It's not a whole lot of fun, but it sure as hell makes things more manageable.

Someone had to be able to figure out this laptop once and for all. Maybe I could catch one of the photographers before they all headed off for Cambridge. I left the computer on the bed, opened the door, and walked into the hallway.

The hotel seemed abandoned. Even the front desk. I figured I had missed everybody, but then I heard some chatter. Some clinking and clattering. Some people. I followed the noise, wandering through the hotel's empty restaurant until I happened upon . . .

The hotel bar.

And there they were. Jeff. *Army Times*. Maybe one or two others. But it's hard to say. Because that's when things start to get a little fuzzy.

"Hey, there he is!" I think one of them shouted.

They were having a beer.

"You out looking for dinner?" one of them asked.

"No," I said. "I'm looking for someone to fix my laptop."

"That thing still acting up?" *Army Times* asked. "I thought you charged the batteries in Bosnia."

"I thought so, too," I said.

"It might be the cold."

"What?"

"On the plane," he said. "I think the cold might be bad for batteries. Especially if they're old."

"I am guessing these are old," I said. "Piece of shit."

"Can't you just plug it in?" he asked.

"Plug it in?"

"To the wall," he said.

Just plug the damn thing into the wall. It was so simple. So elegant. So . . . obvious. I was almost embarrassed.

"Do I need an outlet converter?" I asked.

"I don't know," *Army Times* said. "If you do, I bet they have one at the front desk. Lots of Americans staying here."

You know, I thought, he's probably right. Just settle down. This doesn't need to be a disaster. Just plug the computer in and get to work, knucklehead. Perfect.

"Good idea," I said. "I'll go find somebody and ask."

And then it happened. For the life of me, I can't remember who said it. But someone said, "Might as well join us for dinner."

"What?"

"We're going to grab something to eat."

"The restaurant's closed," I said.

"They probably have a bar menu," someone said. "Or we might go into town."

I thought about it. Hey, it's not such a bad idea. I'm going to have to eat sooner or later. Besides, I could use a breather. I need to settle down. I'm all worked up and there's no way I can get any writing done now. I can't even think straight enough to plug in my laptop. I've been staring at those notes for hours and . . .

"Grab a seat," someone said.

So I did.

Ooooohhhhhh, it felt good to . . . just sit there. To slide up next to the bar. To lean into it. To rest my feet on the rail. To feel my forearms on the tacky wood. To feel them stick a little. To stop thinking about wars and hippies and lentils and money and starvation and deadlines. To just *relax* for a damn second.

To come home.

"I earned this," I remember thinking.

We chatted for a minute or two. Straight-up bullshit. We probably talked about the Rainbows. About filing our stories. About . . .

"What can I get you?"

It was the bartender. A big guy, barrel-chested. About my age. He had an accent. I looked at him for a second.

"Huh?"

"Can I get you something to drink?" he asked.

Wow. What a thing to say. I had heard it a million times. But suddenly it had real weight. Real meaning. It was like a prayer, a promise, and an indecent proposal, all mashed together and sung to a catchy little tune: "Can I get you something to drink? Tra-la-la! Tra-la-la!"

What a stupendous, earth-shattering question. I knew the answer immediately.

"To hell with it," I said. "Give me a beer."

"There you go!" someone in my group shouted.

"What kind of beer?" the bartender asked.

"I don't care," I said. "What do people around here drink?"

"Newcastle."

"Then a Newcastle."

He poured it. He put it in front of me. An impossibly tall glass, impossibly brown.

I reached into my pocket, pulled out some English money, and put it on the bar. Then I looked at the glass again. I touched it, felt the familiar wetness. I picked it up.

And then, out of nowhere, there he was.

The Fat Bastard.

Tra-la-fucking-la!

I was just going to have one. Or maybe two. Or however many a normal person has while getting ready to have a normal dinner. But the Fat Bastard was back. And he wasn't normal at all.

I had a good time with the original crew. Sure, the bar was supposed to be an authentic English pub. And it probably wasn't. But who cares? We were having beers. It worked for me. And dammit, it kept working.

A few guys peeled off to town for dinner, but a few of us stayed behind. Then someone else went to do some work, and I was there by myself. If I had left at that moment, I would have been fine. But I didn't leave. Because that's not what Fat Bastards do.

I stayed. Long enough for the original bartender's shift to end. His replacement was a young girl. I don't recall what she looked like, but I suspect I thought her quite attractive. So I kept drinking and talking and making jokes about England and America and Benny Hill. She kept laughing. I kept putting money on the bar and she kept filling my glass.

Then a group of American bikers showed up. I kept trying to figure out what they were doing in Mildenhall. They kept explaining, but I kept not understanding. I drank with them anyway. Until they left.

Then a bunch of Japanese people showed up. They didn't speak English. I bought them a drink. They smiled at me. I smiled back at them and kept trying to tell them things about Benny Hill, louder and louder, until they left.

I was hammered. Completely rocked. The room was spinning and my stomach was churning and my words were slurring and I *loved it*.

Bartender! A round for the bar!

Shots!

And then, suddenly, people I knew. The plane's loadmaster—a large round man in his forties—and a thin redheaded crew member a few years younger. The redhead smoked like a chimney. They had been drinking in town, but not nearly enough, I figured, so I tried to get them up to speed. We had some beer. Then some shots. Then the red-haired guy laughed at me when I tossed the bartender a few coins.

"What are you doing?" he asked.

"Tipping," I said.

He laughed again. "How much do you think you just gave her?"

"I dunno," I said, looking at the coins on the bar. They were blurry. "Maybe a buck?"

"More like five bucks," he said.

I just stared at him.

This sent them into a fit of drunken laughter. When they were done, they tried to explain about conversion rates and coins. They said some coins are worth more than a dollar. And that when you tip with a handful of coins, sometimes you're tipping three dollars. Or eight dollars. Or more. Depending on the coins.

I was too drunk to figure it out. So I pulled all the cash out of my pocket and tried to calculate how much I had left, in dollars. They helped me.

I had about fifty bucks. Meaning I had already spent about a hundred and fifty. No wonder the bartender liked me.

I ordered another round.

And then, eventually, I left. I have no idea what time that was. I am not sure if the guys from the plane crew were still at the bar. For all I know, I shut the place down. Either way, I ended up staggering outside, stomping through the carefully manicured flowerbeds. I think I was looking for a convenience store or a gas station or a fast-food place. But there was nothing. So I stumbled around in front of the hotel until I came across the sign, about half my height and twice as wide, stuck in the ground along the side of the road. It had the name of the bar on it and a big arrow pointing toward the door.

It was made of metal, and it sounded like a goddamn bomb went off when my foot hit it.

Maybe I tripped over it. Maybe I was kicking it. Either way, I hightailed it back into the hotel when I heard it. The last thing I needed was to get arrested in this shithole of a place, and where's my room and where's my key and what's all this shit all over my bed and this piece-of-shit laptop and BAM! BAM! BAM! and what is that pounding on my fucking door and Rob Gould says the bus is leaving!

Fat Bastard!

Rob Gould.

Thank God for Rob Gould. Not only had he spent an hour trying to wake my dead ass up, he also convinced the bus driver to slow down. And I made it.

I stumbled onto the bus, stinky and stuttering, my eyes swelled almost shut. Unshowered. I hadn't had a thing to eat in two days, and I had about two hundred gallons of British beer sloshing around in my bowels. Maybe I should have stayed in bed.

The bus ride was horrible. A few people were chuckling at my plight, but some of them were giving me the stink eye. I swear they were. They had been sitting on that bus waiting for me for forty-five minutes, and they didn't need that kind of drama.

Fair enough. But screw them. I made it.

I reached into my pocket, pulled out my money, and did the painful calculations. I had the equivalent of about $30 left. I had spent $170 at the bar.

Oops.

And then the devastating plane ride. For the first five minutes I thought I might be a hard-ass. I thought I might force myself to do some work. But, no. Hell, no. I couldn't even stand the noise of the air conditioner on the bus. The C-130's four supercharged engines destroyed me.

I was out of practice. I hadn't had a drink in two months, and I failed to make the necessary adjustments. I went out drinking like a 340-pound boozehound. Because that's how I drank. But I wasn't a 340-pound boozehound anymore. I was a 260-pound pansy. Or maybe a 270-pound pie-ass. Either way, there's a huge difference. And I was feeling it.

It was like having a stomach virus. Bad. In a car. And the nearest rest stop—the nearest bathroom—is five exits away. And it rumbles. Oooooohhhhhhhhh noooooooooooooo. The pressure. Bear down. Ignore it. I can make it. Can I make it? Then the rumble again. The burn. The panic.

Only I wasn't in a car. And the next bathroom wasn't five exits away. The next bathroom was on another continent. And we wouldn't be landing there for another eight hours. Throw in the headache and the money problems. And the fact that I hadn't done a lick of work. And the fact that the plane was so cold, so unbelievably cold. And I was sweating and shivering and my eyes were almost swelled shut and I smelled so bad and . . . my teeth. If I had just been able to brush my teeth.

I couldn't take it. Once the plane leveled off I undid my straps, rooted through my gear, and pulled out my sleeping bag. I staggered toward the back of the plane and found a level spot where the band instruments had been just a few days earlier. It was an impossibly uncomfortable place. Metal floor. Vibrations. Noise. But it was the best I could do.

Just as I was about to bed down, I noticed the heavy-smoking redhead I had been drinking with the night before. He was leaning against the wall of the plane. I could smell the stale whiskey and to-bacco on him. He looked bad, but not nearly as bad as I did. He smiled when I caught his eye. He shouted something. I couldn't hear him over the engines, but I think he asked how I was doing. I shrugged my shoulders. He laughed, approached, and hollered into my ear: "Rough night!"

"Yeah," I said. He couldn't hear me. But he understood.

Then I noticed that he was chewing something. Emphatically. I couldn't scream anymore. But I gave him a curious glance and he knew what I meant. He offered a huge, exaggerated grin. His teeth were stained black with . . . what was it? It looked like coffee grounds.

I gave him another curious look.

He held up a cigarette. Or half of one. And then it sunk in, forcing me to holler one last time: "Are you eating a fucking cigarette?"

"Long flight," he screamed. "Eight hours. I'd never make it."

Then he took another bite. Right down to the filter. And he smiled.

I didn't even try to muster a response. I just turned away. I got onto the floor. I crawled into my sleeping bag and zipped it up. All the way. It was a mummy bag. So the only thing showing was my mouth and nose.

Then I started shivering. Then I started sweating. Then shivering again. I tried to ignore my headache. To fight off the rumble in my stomach. To forget all the work I didn't have nearly enough time to complete, and forget about whether I had enough gas money to get to Montana.

It went on for hours.

And then somewhere over the North Atlantic, as I was ignoring everything I could think of, it occurred to me that I was in the sleeping bag. I mean actually *in it*. The same sleeping bag from that first weekend as an Urban Hermit, when I went camping in the mountains of western Maryland. The sleeping bag I didn't fit into because my belly was too big.

Well, I sure as hell fit into it now.

But it didn't matter. I was on the plane. And I was going back to America. Back to Baltimore. Back to Beelzebub. I had no choice.

And then I went to sleep, never even considering the possibility that maybe, just maybe, the starvation had only just begun.

PART II

●

And here we must recite the iron law which nature thunders in these northern climates. First she requires that each man should feed himself. If happily his fathers have left him no inheritance, he must go to work, and by making his wants less or his gains more, he must draw himself out of that state of pain and insult in which she forces the beggar to lie. She gives him no rest until this is done; she starves, taunts and torments him, takes away warmth, laughter, sleep, friends and daylight, until he has fought his way to his own loaf. Then, less peremptorily, but still with sting enough, . . . she urges him to the acquisition of such things as belong to him. Every warehouse and shop-window, every fruit-tree, every thought of every hour opens a new want to him which it concerns his power and dignity to gratify. It is of no use to argue the wants down: the philosophers have laid the greatness of man in making his wants few, but will a man content himself with a hut and a handful of dried pease? He is born to be rich.

—Ralph Waldo Emerson,
The Conduct of Life, 1860

· 12 ·

The Savage Journey
Underway

*When scenes of death and carnage are every day before his eyes,
how is it possible that a man should not acquire a contempt of
death . . . especially if life is made a burden by continual creation
and mortification? The love of poverty is a fictitious virtue that
never existed.*

—John Adams,
a letter to Dr. Richard Price, 1794

Ever notice the awl on a Swiss Army knife? It's that short, pointy thing designed to punch holes in leather. At least that's what my dad told me when I got my first Swiss Army knife. I was eight years old. Or maybe ten. And ever since then, I've wondered: Who needs to punch holes in leather? And what kind of idiot needs to do that so often that he has to have an awl on hand at all times?

Then, when I was twenty-seven, I met an idiot of that exact sort. And he was me.

That's right. I needed an awl. More than once. And it was all because of the Rainbows. God bless their souls.

But that's what everybody always wants to talk about. The awl. And the numbers. Always the numbers. Well, I don't want to talk about that yet. I'm sick of it. So I'm going to talk about something else for once.

But I'll get back to the awl. I promise.

There is not much to say about the rest of the trip home from Bosnia, except that it was horrible. I didn't shit my pants on the transatlantic flight, though, so I guess it could have been worse.

I didn't wake up until we hit Newfoundland. I checked into my hotel and started writing. Without the laptop. I wrote in longhand, on paper. I ignored the headache and the stomach rumble and the debilitating fatigue and kept scribbling through the night. The following morning, I got on the plane and kept scribbling until we landed at Andrews Air Force Base. Then I got in my car and drove a half hour to the *Laurel Leader* office.

It was late in the afternoon. Nobody was there, so I just sat down and started typing what I had written. I suck at typing, but I got it done and I filed the story. It made me nervous. What if Joe had questions? Or complaints? He wasn't going to be able to reach me where I was heading.

Then I put it out of my mind. Because it was out of my hands.

Taptaptaptaptap

I was trying to be careful. I didn't want to wake Joseph, who was fifteen months old at the time. I shouldn't have worried. Gracie was holding him when she opened the door. He was still awake.

"Oh my gosh," she said. "You made it."

"Just barely," I said.

I followed my sister into the apartment and gave her some basic details about Bosnia. As I rambled on, I noticed how pregnant she was. I had only been gone about ten days, but it looked like she had doubled in size. "Geez," I said as she collapsed in a rocking chair with Joseph. "How much longer do you have?"

"Two months," she said. "I know. I'm huge. And it's so hot. I'm miserable."

"It looks it."

"Yeah," she said. "But what about you? How much weight have you lost? I told Mom. She's worried."

"I don't know," I said. "It's not a big deal."

"I bet you've lost another ten pounds since you've been gone. I think it's dangerous."

"I feel fine. Really."

"Come on," she said. "I'll make you some dinner."

"Don't worry about it. I don't have time."

Which was true. It was seven-thirty. I called the fish warehouse, but Skippy was already gone. I was expecting him any minute. I grabbed all the camping gear I had stashed at Gracie's before heading off to Bosnia and jammed it into my backpack. I put a load of laundry in the washer. I hopped in the shower, hoping to scrub the Mildenhall funk from my mood. (It didn't work.) Then, when I got out of the shower, I saw it.

On the floor. A bathroom scale.

I was curious. So without thinking too much about it, I eased over and stepped on it. It creaked. The numbers whirred. Then stopped: 255 pounds.

What did it mean? How much had I lost? Fifty pounds? Seventy pounds? Eighty? In two months? That was a lot. Too much? Too fast? I didn't have time for that, either, so I got dressed and decided not to worry about it until I got back from Montana.

The atmosphere had changed dramatically by the time I got back to the living room. Gracie's husband had just gotten home from work. Little Joseph was screaming. And Skippy . . . I couldn't see him, but I knew he was there from the smell of rotten fish. He was in the other bathroom taking a shower.

Then he emerged. Not sparkling, exactly, but as clean as he could make himself. He looked sheepish, though, which made me nervous. So while Gracie and her husband worked on putting Joseph to bed, I got Skippy's attention.

"So," I said. "Did you get it?"

"Get what?"

"You know."

"Oh," he said, lowering his voice to a whisper. "The drugs?"

"Yeah," I said. "The drugs."

"That didn't work out."

That was a terrible answer. Going to the Rainbow Gathering without drugs? I hadn't done something that stupid since . . . going to Bosnia without a functioning laptop. And it wasn't just about the recreational value. The Rainbows operate a cashless society. Money means nothing. It's all about "trade." And the one thing that's always good for trade is marijuana. Even people who don't smoke it take it as payment because they know they can trade it for something else.

But we didn't have any.

"What do you mean it didn't work out?"

"I got skunked," Skippy said. "Sorry." He handed me the money envelope I had given him. And he smiled, despite the fact that he was trying not to.

I pulled the cash out. "What the . . ."

I counted out two hundred dollars in twenties. I had given him three hundred dollars.

He didn't wait for me to ask. "I went to the bar to find the drugs," he said. "I went down two nights in a row. And . . . you know."

He spent a hundred dollars at the bar. And I was pissed. What kind of jackass uses the drug money for . . . Then I remembered the hundred and seventy dollars I blew at the bar in Mildenhall.

"We're in trouble," I said.

"Take it easy," he said. "It'll be all right."

It'll be all right? We had $250—about $270 less than we should have because the two of us had spent it on beer. We had no visible way to turn any of our money into the drugs we needed, and quite possibly not enough gas money to get to Montana. We didn't even have any food. I could charge things, but I had no idea how much credit I had left after charging all those hotel rooms. And I hadn't made a payment since May.

"We're in trouble," I said again.

"Take it easy," Skippy said again.

And he was right. There was nothing left to do but go. I would keep charging at the gas pump until that stopped working. Then I would dip into the cash and hope it lasted until my paycheck came through in direct deposit. And if it didn't?

It was out of my hands.

I pulled the Taurus into Clearfield sometime around midnight. The town was empty. I stopped at a convenience store, located a pay phone, and called my Aunt Virginia's number. Her grandson—my cousin Aaron—answered.

"We're here," I said.

About two minutes later we heard a humongous racket in the distance, like someone was dragging 150 trash cans behind a

Sherman tank. The sound ricocheted through the abandoned streets until . . . suddenly . . . from the darkness . . . there it was.

Aaron's 1969 Volkswagen van came careening around the corner and screeched to a halt directly in front of us. It was tan on the bottom, white on the top. And it was *clean*. Sparkling. You could tell he babied it. But all that noise made me wonder.

Then we noticed Aaron behind the wheel. My mom was right. He was a hippie. Not an annoying tie-dye hippie, but definitely a back-to-nature type. He was twenty-five. Wiry. He was wearing a brown T-shirt with no logos, a well-worn brown cowboy hat over short-cropped brown hair, and a big brown beard that did nothing to hide the broad, innocent grin beaming out from underneath. If it hadn't been for the facial hair, he could have passed for seventeen.

I have never seen a man as happy as Aaron was at that very moment. He knew that this preposterous monster of a vehicle was the only thing in the whole damn world that could have made the journey any more ridiculous, and he had delivered it to us. He just sat there grinning. And blinking. Slowly.

Which seemed just about right. Aaron did a lot of things slowly. He could walk right beside someone and keep up. But to anyone watching, it would look like Aaron was falling behind. Like he was floating or wandering around. He could tell a story—about anything—but it always ended up sounding like an epic poem or a profound treatise on the Good Life.

Skippy and I stood in the headlights looking at Aaron, then back at the van, which seemed to make even more noise when it wasn't moving.

"Is that thing going to make it to Montana?" I asked.

"I guess we're about to find out," Skippy said.

. . .

We followed Aaron back to the house to transfer all our stuff to the van. Aunt Virginia was waiting for us.

I couldn't believe she was still up. She must have been in her eighties. But there she was, a tiny red-haired lady in her proper white nightgown, leaning against the doorframe smoking her cigarette. I had never seen her without one, except maybe in church. And it was always a Carlton 120, a smoke so long that I never thought she would be able to light it with her tiny little arm. But she always managed.

She waved us into the house as soon as we pulled in, and I could see her eyeing me as I came into the light of the kitchen. "Sam," she said as she yanked the Carlton from her lips. "What happened?"

And she said it so theatrically, with one hand resting on her hip, the other waving the Carlton in the air. Which was her way. She was a longtime member of the local Footlighters, and every word she said tumbled out as if intended for an audience. Or maybe she was just pissed off that we showed up in the middle of the night.

"Sorry for being so late," I said. "But I had to finish writing a story and then get my stuff together and—"

"No," she said. "What happened to *you*?"

"Huh?"

"My God," she said. "You must have lost a hundred pounds!"

"Oh, yeah," I said. "I guess I might have lost a little weight. I just got back from Bosnia and—"

"A *little* weight? My God! The last time I saw you . . ."

It went on like that the whole time we were grabbing Aaron's things out of the basement. Which didn't take very long because

Aaron was the real deal: a full-blown tree hugger. Not like me and Skippy. We both had tents and sleeping bags and pots and pans and knives and pillows and enough clothes for just about any climate. I even had the water purifier. Aaron had a plastic tarp, some underwear, a thermos, and some tea.

"What the hell are you going to sleep in?" I asked.

"That's what the tarp's for," Aaron said slowly, with a huge grin.

"We're going to be there for a while," I said. "What are you going to do if it rains?"

"The tarp," he said again, smiling.

"Are you high?" I asked as Aunt Virginia lit another cigarette and waved it around while interrogating Skippy about my weight loss.

"A little," he said.

"Aaron, I thought you were going to drive the first leg of—"

And then it dawned on me.

"Wait," I said. "How much do you have?"

"How much what?"

"Pot."

He reached into his pocket and pulled out what looked like a dime bag, maybe a little more.

"Can you get more of that?" I asked.

"Maybe tomorrow," he said. "I might know a guy. I don't even live here . . . but, yeah, I could probably get something tomorrow."

Damn. We couldn't wait another day. Besides, how much could we afford?

"To hell with it," I said. "We'll figure something out. Just don't smoke it all. We might need that shit in Montana."

"Okay, yeah," he said. "Oh . . . and did I show you this?"

He held up a serious-looking sepia-toned cylinder—the decorative packaging for an enormously expensive bottle of single-malt scotch. Glen-something-or-other, aged thirty-one years. I grabbed it from him. It was heavy. He hadn't even opened it yet.

"Where the hell did you get this?" I asked.

"Scotland," he said.

"Wow. That's sweet."

"Yeah. I thought we'd hit it from time to time. Maybe stop some-place cool along the way. Maybe the Badlands. Or just on the side of the road somewhere."

I didn't know how much stopping we'd be doing along the way. But I'd sure as hell be happy to take a pull. Huzzah! Things were looking up. At least a little. We were broke. And we were stupid. And we didn't know where we were going or if we would get there. But suddenly we had a little marijuana, a bottle of high-dollar scotch, and a gen-u-ine, tree-hugging, van-driving hippie leading the charge.

Excellent.

We packed it all into this 1969 Volkswagen van, which Aaron insisted on calling the Bus. It had a full bed in the back. For sleeping and for storing our stuff. Which seemed perfect. So when Aaron jumped in and fired that mother up, we were in good spirits

It was time.

"My God, Sam!" I heard Aunt Virginia holler as I gave the sliding door a long, lazy tug. "A hundred pounds, I bet!"

And we were off.

There was no way the pot was going to last until Montana. That became clear before we got off Aunt Virginia's street. Because Aaron, who was driving, was rolling a joint on the steering wheel. "We have to start this trip out right," he said.

Skippy agreed.

I was the lone dissenter. "Seriously, guys," I said. "We probably ought to save some of that for later."

That must have been a really shitty argument, because by the time we were on Interstate 80 five minutes later, the joint was gone.

I had abstained. Maybe as a protest. Or maybe I didn't want any. All I remember is that my brief encounter with optimism was dwindling faster than our drug stash. The more I thought things through, the more I got this nagging sense of . . . doubt. Are we going to *make* it? Even if we had unlimited cash and a thoroughly reliable vehicle, could the three of us get anywhere?

Probably not. We were like the Three Stooges. Only Skippy and Aaron were both Curly: happy, sort of carefree. I was the guy who was doing this as a *job*. The curmudgeon. The killjoy. So I guess I could have been Moe. But nobody feared me. I was more like Larry. Or worse, a half-ass Shemp.

There was no leader. There were no followers. Just a loose kind of meandering. Which is probably why our first trip on the interstate lasted about thirty seconds.

I was riding shotgun, staring at the lines on the road, when I felt Aaron looking at me. I glanced over at him. He was smiling. Slowly.

"Uh-oh," he said.

"What's wrong?" I asked. "Did you forget something?"

"Yeah," he said. "Gas."

I looked at the gauge. We were bone-dry.

Miraculously, we were just coming up to a truck stop. Aaron steered onto the exit ramp and eased up to the pumps. We were the only people in sight.

We all stumbled out of the Bus. Skippy and Aaron wandered into the convenience store. I approached the pump, grabbed my wallet, and fumbled through it for my credit card. Here goes nothing, I thought as I rammed it into the slot. The machine pondered my request for a few seconds, then . . . score!

I knew I was going to regret traveling on credit. But it was better than getting stranded halfway. So I put it out of my mind and stuffed the hose into the tank. As I pulled the trigger, I saw Skippy and Aaron exit the store. Skippy was carrying a Gatorade and a fistful of Slim Jims. He had already eaten a few—I could see a few pieces of red and yellow plastic fluttering from underneath his fingers.

"Dude," I said. "How much money do you have?"

"I don't know," he said. "Maybe eighty bucks. Or a hundred and twenty. Want a Slim Jim?"

"Just be careful," I said. "I don't know how long my credit is going to hold out."

"Take it easy," he said. "Have a Slim Jim."

Oh, God, I thought. If I'm the voice of reason, we're finished.

"No," I said. "I don't want a Slim Jim. Just pay attention to what you're spending and—"

A copper-colored Eagle Talon pulled up to the gas pump next to ours just as I began unloading my crappy sermon. It had Massachusetts plates. The backseat was full of junk, packed all the way to the ceiling. The driver and the passenger were both white guys, in their late teens or early twenties. Both were wearing sunglasses and long dreadlocks. The windows were shut tight, but we could hear Bob Marley playing at top volume until the driver turned off the ignition and stepped out into the late-night air.

He took one look at us and he smiled.

"You guys headed to the gathering?" he said.

No shit. That's exactly what he said. We were two thousand miles from Dillon, Montana, but this guy could tell. Maybe it was the Bus. Maybe it was the Slim Jims. Maybe it was our bizarre

Curly/Curly/Shemp routine. Maybe it was some combination. But it was obvious to him.

"Yeah," I said. "You?"

"Most definitely," he said.

Skippy and Aaron thought the exchange was hilarious. An excellent omen. Proof that we were the right men for the job. They laughed while the guy turned his attention to our vehicle.

"Man," he said. "Looks like you guys are going in *style*."

The grin on Aaron's face got even bigger.

"That's right," I said. "The only way to travel."

"I did that last year," he said. "But Montana's too far, man. This year it's all about *speed*."

"You in a hurry?" I said.

"Oh, yeah," he said. "I got to *get* there."

His finished filling his tank before I did. He gave me a nod and climbed into his car. Then the passenger-side window came down. The driver leaned across his buddy and shouted, "Yo! See you there!"

The buddy shot us a peace sign. And then they were gone, peeling out of the parking lot, vectoring to warp speed before they even hit the merge lane.

See you there? I could only hope so as I hung the hose back on the pump and climbed into the Bus, where Skippy and Aaron were waiting. And laughing.

I never expected the Bus to approach warp speed. But the speed limit would have been nice. After about five miles I leaned over to check our progess: forty miles per hour.

"Aaron," I said.

"Yeah?"

"Are you okay?"

"Sure," he said. "Why?"

"Why are we going so slow?"

"We're doing fine."

"We're only going forty."

"Yeah," he said. "This thing is temperamental. It'll overheat if you push it. Especially in the mountains. You kind of have to baby it, or you'll blow the engine . . . wait . . . see?"

He pointed at the temperature gauge below the speedometer. A red warning light was blinking at us.

"Holy shit," I said. "You're telling me this thing's top speed is forty miles an hour?"

"The problem is, there's no radiator."

"What the hell are you talking about?"

He tried to explain. Something about this being an air-cooled engine, but the engine is in the back, so it's hard to get air. It's the same engine they put in the Beetle, he said, but the Beetle is pretty small. The van is too heavy. A lot of people cut scoops in the side to direct more airflow to the engine, but when it comes right down to it, the whole idea is knowing the engine and getting the most out of—

"Listen," I said. "I don't understand a word you're saying. How fast will it go?"

"You just have to baby it a little," he said.

I could hear Skippy laughing.

Then things got tense. I said I wanted to turn around and switch to the Taurus. Aaron almost collapsed. He said it's supposed to be about the journey, dude, and what's the rush? I disagreed. I said it was about getting our sorry asses to Montana. On time.

But the Taurus wasn't in much better shape. And the Bus definitely had more room. And we had already dumped a whole tank of gas into the thing. Skippy declared that things would work out either way. So we decided to stick it out in the Bus.

A few things had changed, though. There was no way I could drive. Initially, we figured I could at least take the wheel in the flat country. I could drive a stick well enough to get it going, and once we were in fifth gear, there wasn't a lot of shifting to do. But this thing . . . no way. Aaron didn't trust me not to grind the gears into dust, which was only a few bad shifts away. My new role was to stay awake for as long as possible, navigate, and keep the drivers awake. Curly and Curly would drive the whole way. Skippy was a master, after all. He worked for a truck-leasing company for two years, and he drove a twenty-four-foot fish truck for a living. He said he could shift without the clutch.

Aaron made him promise never to do that. In fact, there were all sorts of rules. The most important of which were . . . watch the temperature gauge! And baby it!

The tension eased once we settled on the plan. The cool night air seemed to agree with the Bus and we made decent headway. We even caught up a little. Aaron told us about dropping out of college. About moving to Oregon and starting school again. About picking up photography. About living in the commune. About traveling in Europe. About his Russian girlfriend. About how this was his third trip across country in the Bus.

I mellowed. The Bus was slow, but it was pretty damn stylish. Not to mention spacious. Besides, without saying a word, I knew that Skippy and I had a plan.

We stopped for gas when it started getting light out, somewhere in Ohio. Skippy and Aaron got something to eat at McDonald's. I played the heavy again and warned them about money. Then Aaron gave Skippy a final rundown on how to operate the Bus and handed over the keys.

Once we were on the road, Aaron read us some poems out of a notebook. Aaron is the kind of guy who can get away with that sort of thing. So we listened until he settled down on the mattress and fell asleep.

I looked at Skippy. He looked at me. It was time to move.

"Kick it in the tits," I said.

Skippy nodded, looked back at the road, and stomped on the gas. I mean, he really ripped it. And the Bus gave out a tremendous howl.

BBBBWWWWAAAAAAHHHHHH!

A shout of protest? A cry of liberation? Hell if I know. But sure enough, it responded. Faster, faster, faster, and then we were keeping up with the motor homes. And then with the cars. And then we were passing people. And then . . .

"Whoa! Whoa! Whoa! What the hell's going on?"

It was Aaron. He was awake. He had one hand on the back of Skippy's seat, one on the back of mine, his head directly between ours.

"Look at the engine light!" he shouted. "Look at the engine light!"

The engine light was glowing red, telling a terrible tale of heat and woe.

"You're going to blow it up!"

"Oh, sorry, dude," Skippy stammered. "I guess I wasn't paying attention. I didn't even notice—"

"You have to pay attention," Aaron hollered as we coasted back down to forty-five miles per hour and the traffic started passing us again.

"Yeah," Skippy said. "Sorry."

The engine light finally went off when we dipped below forty. Aaron calmed down and went over the instructions again. He was still pissed, but Skippy talked him out of it. I went to work on him, too.

"Listen, Aaron," I said. "You have to get some sleep."

"I know," he said, "but we can't blow up the engine."

"Don't worry," Skippy said. "It'll be all right."

"Any of that pot left?" I asked.

"Good idea," Aaron said.

And pretty soon he was dead asleep. And Skippy punched it. And we were passing cars like crazy. Until we hit the traffic jam in Chicago.

The awl? The Swiss Army knife? Take it easy. I'm getting to it.

Peace, Love, and Scotch

The Transaction

> *There is no official mechanism or policy of enforcement if individu-*
> *als refuse to comply with the guidelines. This is not viewed as a prob-*
> *lem but as an acceptable risk since individual freedom is the key*
> *feature of the gathering. Each participant is autonomous and re-*
> *sponsible for controlling their own behavior. (This freedom is prized*
> *for its entertainment value as well as for its ideological appeal.)*
>
> —Rap on Rainbow Disorganization,
>
> www.welcomehome.org

The traffic jam nearly killed us. We were on the verge of over-heating the entire time. Then we almost ran out of gas. Then we got lost.

But we made it, and a few hours later we were outside Madison, Wisconsin. It should have taken us ten hours to get that far. It took us sixteen. And we were only a third of the way to the gathering. Those guys in the Eagle Talon were probably in Wyoming.

I was getting frustrated, but we had to stop for gas. My credit card still worked, so I charged it. Then we headed into a grocery store next door. I bought a bag of oranges, which I planned to save for the gathering, and a few bottles of water. But that was all. My Urban Hermit training was standing me in good stead.

I headed outside and sat down in a grassy area separating the gas station from the grocery store. Skippy came out next with a few bottles of Gatorade, more Slim Jims, and some other food-type things. "How's that going to work on your stomach?" I asked, a little worried about his Crohn's disease.

He was working on an answer when Aaron appeared and set some bags down in front of us. He smiled broadly, then reached in and pulled out four six-packs of high-end beer. Some Hefeweizen. Some imported stout. Pale ale. Something with blueberries in it.

"Sweet!" Skippy said.

"Aaron!" I shouted.

"Nice, huh?" he said.

"Aaron," I said, "how much did that cost?"

His smile disappeared. "I don't know," he said. "It seemed pretty reasonable."

"Jesus," I said. "We're already a half a day behind. And we're completely broke."

"Don't worry," Skippy said as he twisted the cap off a pale ale. "It'll be all right."

"We just need to go," I said. "Can we just go?"

"But that's why I got the beer," Aaron said.

"What are you talking about?" I asked.

"We need to change the oil."

"Why?" I said. "We've only gone a few hundred miles."

"These engines don't have oil filters," he said. "And we've been driving it hard."

"So what are we going to do? Find a Jiffy Lube?"

"No," he said, pointing to five bottles of oil in a shopping bag. "I'm going to change it right here."

"In the grocery store parking lot?" I asked.

"Sure."

"Oh my God," I said. "How long is that going to take?"

"Changing it won't take long at all."

"Good."

"We have to wait for the engine to cool, though."

"Are you serious?"

"That's why I got the beer."

Unbelievable. I grabbed one, cracked it open, and joined Skippy in the shade under a little tree. We drank beer and watched families head in and out of the grocery store. I thought we'd get arrested for sure, but we didn't. Aaron sat with us for about an hour in silence, then moseyed over to the Bus and got to work.

I hadn't slept or eaten since Newfoundland. Maybe thirty-six hours. So I broke down and busted out a can of mixed nuts I found in the van. Which helped. So did shooting the shit with Skippy. It was only Thursday evening. June 29. It was slow going, but we could still make it. The main day of the gathering wasn't until the Fourth of July. I wanted to get there a few days before that. But we still had time.

What the hell. No reason to be a dick about it. Aaron was trying. And damn, look at his fingers fly. He was good with an engine. Skippy and I wandered over and offered to help, but everyone knew we'd just get in the way.

Aaron finished on his own and put everything back together. He was a mess. There was oil on his hands. On his face. On his clothes. He had drained the rest into a bunch of paper cups he had salvaged from a nearby trash can. He seemed happy as ever.

"What are you going to do with that?" I asked, pointing to the dirty rags and filthy cups.

He smiled, shrugged, and gathered everything in his arms. Then he walked across the parking lot and tossed the whole mess, including five quarts of dirty oil, into the trash.

I looked over at Skippy. He was laughing.

"You don't see many hippies do *that*," he said.

Then things got even slower and my surly mood returned. Forty-five miles an hour through the heart of America. We needed to go faster. No matter what. Aaron suggested a side trip to the Badlands to drink the scotch. I vetoed the idea.

Skippy and I tried to force the issue. Our most ambitious maneuver came in South Dakota in the middle of the night. Aaron had just fallen into a heap on the bed. But Skippy had been driving for hours. He was on his last legs.

"All right," I said. "Let's do it. But keep it quiet."

He knew what I had in mind. So we danced.

It was an intricate maneuver. We had to switch positions without slowing down too much. Otherwise we'd stall, and there was no way I'd get it going again. So he stomped on the gas and stood up while I slid underneath him and got my foot on the pedal. We were all over the road but it didn't matter. There wasn't anyone else for miles.

And then I was driving, pressing as hard as I could on the gas, ignoring the red engine light. "I don't even think that light means anything," I said to Skippy as the Bus began to scream.

"I don't think so either," he said. "This thing'll rip."

I pushed it harder and harder, past fifty-five, past sixty, past sixty-five. "Look at it go," I said.

"Like a raped ape," Skippy agreed. "Keep it up."

I never let off the gas and I never shifted. Not even once. I just raced toward the horizon, as fast as the Bus would take us.

Aaron woke up eventually. I laid off the accelerator before he came to his senses. And he was cool with me driving. At least on level ground. But then we hit a wall. In Wyoming.

The Bus hated the mountains. Aaron was driving by that time, and he was terrified that the engine was going to blow. We slowed to forty miles an hour. Then thirty-five. We went through a seventeen-mile stretch of construction. The highway was down to one lane, and cars lined up behind us as far as I could see. People were honking. Flipping us off. I thought we were dead.

Then the construction ended and the traffic blasted past us. We were alone again, limping along at thirty-five miles an hour until Aaron let out a yelp, slammed on the brakes in the middle of the empty highway, and put the Bus in reverse.

"What the hell?" I said.

"See that?" Aaron pointed to a hillside in the distance.

"What?"

"It's another Bus," he said.

And he was right. Somehow, incredibly, he had spotted a Volkswagen van parked in a field on the hillside. It must have been a mile away. He backed up about a tenth of a mile to an exit and took us off the highway.

"Where are we going?" I asked.

"I need to talk to the guy who owns that Bus," he said. "He can probably help us with the overheating."

"You have to be fucking kidding me," I said.

He wasn't kidding. Aaron had brought along an extra exhaust system for the Bus. It was a bunch of weird-looking pipes in a large cardboard box stashed in the back with the rest of our stuff. He was convinced that it would solve the overheating problem, maybe even add some much-needed horsepower. Every time we stopped for gas or to let the engine cool, he suggested taking a break to do the work. Only he wasn't sure if he had all the parts. Or how long it might take. Or if he knew how to do it.

"No," I said, every time.

But now, in the hills of Wyoming, he had a plan. Which involved that van he spotted. We drove around for half an hour looking for the thing. I bitched the entire time.

"Come on, this is ridiculous." . . . "Seriously. We need to go." . . . "Aaron, we need to *go!*"

But then we found it, somehow, in the middle of a field at the end of a crap-ass road. It was an old rust bucket of a van. We couldn't even tell what color it was supposed to be. The tires were flat and there were weeds growing up all around it. The only thing near it was an old trailer that looked like something out of *Deliverance*. I figured it was abandoned. Or worse. But Aaron took one look at all the old car parts and appliances in the yard and decided that this was where we needed to be.

"Skippy," he said, pointing to the trailer. "Go knock on the door."

"My ass," Skippy said.

So Aaron went and knocked. Nobody answered. He knocked again. Still no answer. He stood there looking at the door. And he knocked again.

We sat there in silence for about fifteen minutes. Aaron occasionally walked over to the old van and looked at it. Then he walked up the road a bit. Then walked back. Then knocked on the door. I started to feel bad for him. I could tell he wanted to *fix* it. Everything. But he couldn't.

"Aaron," I said. "I really think we need to go."

He climbed back into the Bus without saying a word. We drove back down the hillside to a gas station. I filled the tank while Aaron went inside to get something to eat. But he wasn't carrying anything when he came back out, and he was excited. The cashier knew the guy who owned the beat-up old van. Aaron wanted to call him.

"He might have some manuals I'm looking for," Aaron said. "If I can get the exhaust system . . ."

We were already eighteen hours behind schedule, and we weren't even in Montana yet. We still hadn't seen the worst of the mountains, and I was starting to think we weren't going to make it.

"I think I'm going to hitchhike," I said.

"Come on," Aaron said. "It won't take that long."

"I know," I said. "And I'm not pissed. But I really need to get there. It's getting dark. I'll have a better chance of getting picked up if I start hitching now. You guys stay here and work on the Bus, then get there as soon as you can. I'll meet up with you."

That looked like it was going to be the plan.

I started collecting all my stuff while Aaron looked the guy's name up in the gas station's phone book. He called. No answer. Every few minutes Aaron went to the pay phone and called again. We sat under a tree for another hour. No one ever picked up. We knew it was never going to work, so we all got back into the van.

We staggered through the mountains, into Montana. Past Bozeman, where we stopped to let the engine cool again. Up into Butte, where, against my advice, Skippy bought a case of cheap beer. (We still had about half of Aaron's fancy beer left. But it was warm. And no one was in the mood for fancy beer.)

The sun was rising when we got to Dillon. It was completely up by the time we found the old road leading us past the ranches, into the national forest, past the enormous banner at the entrance of the Rainbow Gathering. It said, WELCOME HOME.

The trip should have taken us about thirty-six hours. It took fifty-seven. But we made it. And I'd be lying if I didn't admit that we made a grand entrance. It never hurts to show up to the gathering a little dirtier and a little later than expected. And it sure as hell doesn't hurt to show up in a 1969 Volkswagen van that smells like it has a few miles on it.

"Aaron," I said as he guided the Bus up the final hill and I finished the last of Skippy's cheap beer.

"Yeah?" he said.

"Thanks."

"Yeah," he said. "This is pretty cool."

Then Skippy weighed in from the backseat: "I told you it'd be all right."

There wasn't much time to celebrate. We had work to do. Lucky for us, we were coming up on A-Camp.

There is very little that Rainbows won't tolerate. Especially in terms of mind-altering substances. A lot of people get mean when they drink, though, so the Rainbows, in their collective wisdom, came up with the idea of A-Camp. Or Alcohol Camp. It's the one place at the gathering where drinking is "permitted." It's not a real rule. No one enforces it. Just like no one tells you where to shit and piss, and no one is in charge of ferrying out people who get bit by rattlesnakes. But generally speaking, the collaborative vibe prevails. People shit in the right place. No one gets killed by vipers. And for the most part, people keep the liquor in A-Camp.

A-Camp is always at the head of the main trail, right next to a field where people can park. Which means that the job of organizing the parking usually falls to the A-Campers. Who are, by and large, completely fucking hammered.

When we arrived, the guy tasked with guiding newcomers into their spots was lying flat on his back in a pile of sage brush. He was probably twenty-five. He wasn't wearing shoes. Or a shirt. Just a pair of dirty cutoff jeans. He was lean and fit. Blond. Painfully sunburned. Like a surfer. A drunk one.

He finally came to his senses, leaped to his feet, and started waving his arms when he heard the Bus approach. He could barely stand. He could barely keep his eyes open. But dammit, he picked out a spot and directed us into it. Perfectly.

"Well done, dude," I said out the window as Aaron cut off the engine.

"Welcome home," the Surfer said.

He gave me a hug when I got out of the Bus. I hugged him back. Then I pulled out one of my Croatian cigarettes and gave it to him.

"Cool," he said, staring at it like it was some kind of exotic animal. "Thank you, brother."

I saw an angle. A-Camp is a place of commerce. It's where the real economy and the Rainbow economy collide. It's where you can still get things for money. Sort of. So when the Surfer lit his cigarette, I handed him another.

"Thank you, brother," he said again.

"No problem," I said. "By the way, I have a question."

I asked the question. He answered it. And a few minutes later, we got exactly what we deserved.

We saw the huge blue tarp drooped between a series of trees at the top of the hill, just where the Surfer said it would be.

It was early morning, still cool and crisp. There were campfires everywhere. Some had just gone out. Some appeared to have been freshly lit. Most were surrounded by ragtag groups of people who looked like they had come from . . . Where? It's not like there was a *type*. Hippies. Bums. Teenage beauty queens. Whatever. Most of them were already drunk. Or still drunk. There were RVs, pop-ups, sports cars, pickup trucks, you name it. Some of the vehicles were pulling in. Some were pulling out. But it was hard to tell. Mostly because of the fight.

A young guy in a fringed leather cowboy jacket was sitting on a log, staring into a smoldering fire pit. He was dead silent until he noticed us passing by. That's when he sprang to life, jumped into the air, and shouted, "It's Guatemala Day!"

He must have been gooned up on something good, because he was ecstatic, spinning and staggering dangerously close to the embers. "Guatemala Day!" he screamed again. "It's . . . Guatemala . . . Day!"

It was the kind of drug-induced non sequitur that most Rainbows are accustomed to. But for some reason it didn't go over that morning. Maybe it was too early. Or maybe the guy had been shouting for hours. Either way, a tall, thin middle-aged man at another fire—mustache, red bandanna, can of Budweiser in hand—didn't want to hear it.

"Shut up!" he shouted.

"But it's Guatemala Day," the young cowboy sang, laughing and spinning.

"You don't know shit about Guatemala!" the other guy screamed as he threw his empty beer can into his fire. "Shut your fucking mouth!"

Maybe he wasn't pissed off about the noise at all. Maybe he was more concerned about the accuracy of the statement. Maybe this was a standoff about Guatemala knowledge. If so, the cowboy was sticking to his guns.

"But it's Guatemala—"

The guy by the fire didn't wait for him to finish. He untied his pit bull. And the pit bull knew exactly what to do. It took off after the cowboy, who let out a pathetic yelp and started stumbling away from the dog. It was useless. He was too slow.

But the dog never reached him. Because someone—presumably an ally of the cowboy, or perhaps a Guatemalan—responded to the attack by loosing another pit bull, which immediately attacked the first one. So there was a lot of barking and biting and snarling and ripping flesh while the cowboy staggered away in a daze.

I looked at Skippy. He looked at me.

"Holy shit," he said.

We were in way over our heads. It was too early to be at A-Camp. Or maybe too late. Either way, we knew it was time to get the hell out of there. But Aaron didn't notice. He just kept walking toward the tarp.

"Aaron," I hissed.

He didn't even flinch.

"Aaron!"

Too late. He had already found a guy.

"Hey," Aaron said. "We're looking for Punch."

The guy looked us over, looked back at the tarp, then waved us on.

Okay. Here we go.

The camp was pretty tidy, considering. Someone had piled rocks around the fire pit to support a wire grill, maybe three feet by three feet. On top of that was an old cast-iron coffeepot, alive with black boiling liquid. The fire was smoking heavily, like someone had just tossed a pile of green wood on it.

A red-haired lady, maybe in her fifties, was sleeping in a collapsible chair. I was checking out the tattoos on her leathery arm when she stirred a little. I hurried to look away, but there was no safe line of sight: the old man hacking up a lung over by the woodpile; a guy in a doo-rag complaining that he had to take a shit but couldn't find a shovel. All of them were staring us down. And then . . .

Punch.

He must have been a biker. But to be honest, I never saw a bike. I just assumed that the sleeping woman belonged to him, and that he was in charge of the whole gang. He was short and thick. Greasy. Maybe fifty years old. Or forty. He had a Fu Manchu mustache with about five days of growth coming up underneath it. He was wearing a vest of some sort. No shirt. Dirty jeans.

He didn't look happy. For a second, I thought he was going to eat us. But he didn't. He just stood there, about five feet away from me. I had no idea what to say.

He finally broke the silence with his thick, raspy voice.

"What?" he said.

"Uhh," I said, looking back at Skippy. "The guy in the parking lot sent us up here."

"For what?"

"Well," I said, lowering my voice to a ridiculous whisper. "We heard you might have some pot."

"Yeah?" he said. "So?"

"Well, we want some."

"Okay," he said. "What you got?"

Excellent. A businessman. I was carrying a bag that contained about half the oranges I bought in Wisconsin. Skippy rolled up beside me and put the remaining twelve-pack of fancy beer next to them. And Aaron . . . no Aaron. Where was Aaron?

"We have these oranges and this beer and, uh"—I put my hand into my front pocket and pulled out the cash I had carefully counted out—"and thirty-four dollars."

"Is that it?" he said.

Yeah. It was a shitty offer. Oranges? Like this guy eats oranges. And the beer with blueberries in it? If we wouldn't drink it, why would he?

"Well," I said, looking around for Aaron. "I guess . . ."

Then we saw him. He was standing over the fire, holding the coffeepot—Punch's coffeepot—sniffing it. Scowling. "This coffee *sucks*," he said to no one in particular. Then, noticing that everybody in the camp was staring at him, he added, "Do you guys have any more coffee?"

I thought Skippy was going to have a stroke. I am pretty sure I did.

"Aaron!" I said. "Put that shit down."

"I'm just saying," he said.

"Just bring me the booze," I said.

Which he did. The thirty-one-year-old Glen-whatever that he had been saving for a special moment. Well, this was as special as it got. And that bottle was something strange. Something these people didn't see everyday. Even Punch realized it. I could tell by the way he looked at it.

Success.

"Hold one second," Punch said, eyeing up the bottle. "Let me see what I can do."

Thank God for brown liquor.

But before Punch could head off to wherever he kept his stash, the Big Drunk Indian spotted the bottle.

This sounds like racial stereotyping of the worst sort. So horribly callous and mean. But I don't know how else to describe the guy who was making a beeline right for Aaron, waving his arms and chattering, " Punch! Punch!"

He was definitely big. That bastard must have been six and a half feet tall. Or maybe nine thousand feet. Every inch of it *focused* on the bottle. At least 240 pounds—250 if you counted the jeans and the huge leather duster he was wearing. And drunk? Good grief. The man was devastated.

As for "Indian," I'm no expert, but he sure looked like a Native American to me. And I wasn't the only one, apparently. Punch saw him coming and hollered, "Would someone tell that big drunk Indian to shut the fuck up!"

I was sure another pit bull fight was on the way. Or a stabbing. Only we didn't have any dogs. And we didn't have any knives. Just a couple college degrees between us, and some oranges.

The Indian was gaining speed, bearing down with a horrifying, thirsty look in his eyes. Aaron probably should have tossed the scotch into the weeds and bolted, but he didn't. He didn't even seem to notice. He was looking toward the fire again, saying to no one in particular, "Does anybody have any coffee?"

I could have jumped into the breach to slow the Indian down. To save Aaron, and maybe even the bottle. But I was frozen. And it's a damn good thing. Because I didn't know the rules. And as it turns out, everything was completely under control.

The Indian stopped short, just inches away from Aaron, and turned to the man in charge. "Come on, Punch," he said. "It's my birthday."

"Shut up," Punch said. "I know."

"But, Punch. It's my birthday!"

"Shut up, Chief!" Punch said. "You're drunk already."

Another crony showed up and handed Punch a big plastic bag full of marijuana. It looked mottled. Kind of brown. Kind of green. But it was a lot. I think it was probably a freezer bag. One of those one-gallon jobs. Punch looked at it for a second, then took two strides toward me and put it in my hand.

"How's that?" he asked.

I didn't understand the question, exactly. Was he asking me if the quality was up to snuff? I had been party to a few drug transactions over the years, but never in a situation like this. And never with this much pot. Did he expect me to smell it? Taste it? How much was I supposed to take? I looked at Skippy. He looked at me.

"Okay," I said, unsure what I had just agreed to.

"Okay, then." Punch snatched the thirty-four dollars out of my hand and the scotch out of Aaron's, ignoring the oranges and the beer entirely. "Nice doing business with you."

The whole bag was ours.

Punch turned around and began walking away from the tarp, bottle in hand, with the Indian in hot pursuit. "Give it to me now, Punch. Give it to me now."

"Shut up," Punch said. "You can have it later."

"But it's my birthday."

It was touching, in a weird sort of way. I might have even teared up, but Aaron was paying attention all of a sudden and he had other ideas. He grabbed the huge sack of weed out of my hand. He opened it, stuck his nose in, and gave it a good whiff. Then he held it up to his face and started rolling the contents through his fingers. "I don't know," he said. "There's a lot of shake in there."

"Shut up," I said.

"Seriously," he said. "Look at all that shake."

The Indian stopped in his tracks. Punch spun around on his heel. "Problem?" he asked.

"No," I said. *"Shut up, Aaron."*

"Okay," Punch said.

"I don't know," Aaron said.

"Shut up," Skippy said, grabbing the bag and shoving it into his backpack.

Punch looked us over one last time. Considered his options. And then went back to arguing with the Indian about the scotch as he walked away.

"But, *Punch* . . ."

By the time Skippy and I gathered ourselves, Aaron was back at campfire. He had taken the coffeepot out of the old lady's hand and was lecturing her about technique. "You're doing it all wrong," he said. "You're boiling it too hard. First thing you do is fill it with water."

Everyone in the camp was looking at him like he was nuts.

"Oh, no," Skippy said.

"Aaron," I said, "we have to go."

"Let's stay here and have some coffee," he said.

The fact that I still had about two hundred dollars in my pocket was making me extremely nervous. I estimated we had about fifteen seconds to live. "No way," I said. "We have to go."

"No," Aaron said. "We need some coffee."

He wasn't going to budge. We couldn't leave him there, so Skippy and I slinked off to a corner by the woodpile. We stood there and watched the pit bulls go at it while Aaron berated Punch's woman about her coffee skills and showed her a better way, the right way, to make coffee on a campfire.

She didn't kill him, though.

It seemed like she kind of liked him, actually.

· 14 ·

Awls and Exhaust Systems
Adventures in Simple Living

Americans, however, should find it difficult to expect that an effective moral order will originate in a recondite communism of spirit in a people without leaders. We have been operating on some such basis for a number of years, and if ever a nation needed "geniuses," "heroes," or "divine leaders" it is America now.

—Lyle H. Lanier, "A Critique of the Philosophy of Progress,"
in *I'll Take My Stand*, 1930

Our huge sack of marijuana came in handy as soon as we got on the path to the main meadow. Aaron was sitting in the sage grass rolling a joint, still griping about the shake and the seeds, when a skittish-looking dude in shorts and a tie-dye T-shirt spotted us. He was maybe eighteen or twenty. Paranoia—the worst kind— had already seized him.

"Dude," he whispered. "Can I get some of that shit?"

He was sweating. His eyes were bloodshot. He kept looking over his shoulder. Maybe a toke was exactly what he needed. Maybe not.

"Let me finish rolling it," Aaron said.

"No," the guy hissed. "I don't mean a hit. I mean a *trade*."

Interesting.

"Okay," Skippy said. "What you got?"

"I got this sweet shit," he said, looking around nervously before pulling a Baggie out of his shorts pocket. "It's hydroponic."

It sure as hell was. Purple. Fuzzy. A fat log of extremely high-grade marijuana. Maybe a quarter ounce.

"Jesus," Skippy said.

I was a little confused, though. And as messed up as the kid was, he could tell.

"Your shit looks like homegrown," he said. "I've been smoking the hydro for days. It's fucking me up. I just need to get straight, man."

"Are you serious?" I asked.

"Absolutely."

Skippy didn't waste any time. He snatched a handful of pot out of our bag and extended his arm to the guy, who nearly collapsed.

"Are you fucking crazy!" he gasped. "Not out here!"

The path was humming like a busy city sidewalk, and half of the people on it were smoking joints. Two law-enforcement officers from the Forest Service were mounted on horseback about a quarter mile away, but they didn't seem to mind. What were they going to do? Arrest everybody? Our new friend was in a bad way, though, so we followed him into the woods to make the transaction: his high-octane purple marijuana for an equal amount of our mediocre brown schwag. We gave him a hit off our first joint for good measure.

"That's the stuff right there," he said as he exhaled, visibly calmer. "Where'd you get that shit?"

"A-Camp," I said.

"Oh, shit," he said. "You have to be careful up there, man."

Then I got to work. If you can call it that.

No point looking for leaders or planners. There weren't any. I just stopped and talked to anyone who looked interesting. Offered them some pot. Smoked it with them. Not so much that I couldn't write, usually. But you have to fit in as best you can.

There was Mad Mike, the guitar-playing teenager from New Orleans who made up songs in exchange for pot. There were the Hare Krishnas, who never touched the stuff but kept themselves busy chopping wood and baking sweets. The aging flower children in the teepees who had been to every gathering since the first one in the early seventies. The sanitation engineer who volunteered to design and locate all the trenches everybody was shitting in.

Walk, talk, smoke. Walk, talk, smoke. Take a few notes. Smoke. Smoke. Smoke. Walk. Smoke. Notes. Talk a little. Smoke a little. Not-a-little-notes-a-little. Sit down. Get up. Repeat.

It was a lot like Bosnia. Except for the drugs.

Montana was hot, at least during the day. It was also dry as a bone, so there weren't any showers. Everyone just agreed to be dirty. Walking the paths, kicking up dust, watching it stick to sweaty skin, watching it dry out and crust up as the cool nights rolled in. Everyone stank. But when everyone stinks, it's kind of like nobody does. Filth is relative.

And so is hunger. There are no vendors at the Rainbow Gathering. People eat what they bring or rely on the volunteer "kitchens." They prepare food for the asking all day. Late in the afternoon, all twenty thousand people gather in the main meadow for dinner, sitting in enormous concentric circles, waiting for people from the kitchens to bring food around. Sometimes it works. Sometimes it doesn't.

Skippy and I were in the outer circle on the second day. The hydro was kicking our ass, and we were hungry. We were sitting Indian-style, shoulder-to-shoulder with a bunch of street kids from Seattle, and we were all watching some guy lumber toward us, dragging a cooler behind him. It was full of thick brown mush, which he doled out with a huge a ladle. Everybody who was hungry extended a dish for him to fill.

Plop. "Thank you, brother."

Plop. "Thank you, brother."

Plop. "I love you, brother."

People who didn't have dishes just stuck out their hands, and the *plop* would sound more like a *splat.*

"Look at that," I said to Skippy as the food guy approached. "I think it's some kind of lentil concoction, dude."

"Sweet," Skippy said as we both cupped our hands together and extended them. But the cooler went empty right before it got to us. Skippy looked at me and smiled.

The guy apologized and promised to return. We just kept smiling, occasionally talking nonsense until he came back with a full cooler five minutes later. But we forgot to stick our hands out, and he started distributing the food about three people beyond us. Or maybe he started in the wrong circle. Either way, we got screwed.

"Wow," Skippy said, smiling.

"I know," I said, smiling back.

"We missed dinner."

"I know. That's okay, though."

"I know," he said. "It'll be all right."

It wasn't the only meal we missed. Aaron had donated the rest of our oranges to a kitchen near our camping spot. We were surviving on some Slim Jims Skippy had squirreled away. We were having a good time, though. And I was doing good work.

We walked up huge hills. Back down. Back up. Back down. Walking. Talking. Smoking. Laughing. Smiling. I hardly noticed the hunger. Maybe it was all those months of self-induced privation. Maybe I was just high. Either way, there I was, walking, talking, laughing, ignoring the stink and the dust and the hunger, when I recognized that familiar sag. The looseness around my waist. My pants were falling down.

"Hold on," I said to Skippy.

I stopped in the middle of the path and reached across my body with my right hand. I grabbed the end of my belt and tightened it with a solid yank. I pressed on the buckle's metal spar, right below my belly button, then I released the tension, waiting for the spar to catch the next notch. It missed. I tried it again. Missed.

Then I remembered. And I looked down to confirm it.

I was out of notches.

I tried to figure out what to do. I couldn't walk around like that for another three days. Then the answer washed over me. The Swiss Army knife. It was in a leather case attached to my belt. I pulled it out. I fumbled with it. Blade . . . blade . . . can opener . . . screwdriver . . . toothpick . . . saw . . . coarse file . . . fine file . . . Where the hell is it? . . . Wait a minute . . . there.

The awl.

Punching a hole in leather isn't easy. Even with an awl. I tried to do it standing up, with my belt still on. No way. The point kept slipping, making little scratch marks in the warm, sweaty leather. So I took the belt off and laid it on the ground. I measured out the right spot, put the point of the awl in place, and leaned on it.

Kerdunk!

The leather surrendered and the point of the awl plunged into the dirt below—one inch closer to the center of the earth.

Then we lost Aaron.

Skippy and I hadn't seen him all day. We decided to run the A-Camp gauntlet and check back at the Bus. When we got there, the Bus was gone.

"Holy shit," I said.

Thank goodness the Surfer was still on the job—drunker, higher, and more sunburned than ever, but still remarkably helpful.

"You looking for your buddy?" he asked. "The guy with the van? And the beard?"

"You seen him?"

"He came up last night and said he needed to do some work on the van," the Surfer said. "He took it down to Bus Village."

"Bus Village?" I said.

He pointed down the hill to another pasture filled with vehicles, maybe a quarter mile away. I gave him three more Croatian cigarettes. He gave me a hug, then sat down in the sage brush and lit one.

We found Aaron standing next to a pile of pipes behind the Bus. He was beaming. He didn't even ask where we'd been. "Check it out," he said.

"What's that?" I asked.

"I met a guy," he said. "He has a Bus. I think it's a 'sixty-seven. Dude knows everything. I told him about the overheating."

"Great," I said. "But what's all this?"

"I think I'm going to put it on," he said.

"Okay," I said. "But what is it?"

"The exhaust system," he said.

Oh, shit.

"You're going to put on a new exhaust system?" I asked. "Right here?"

"Sure," he said. "Why not?"

"Do you know what you're doing?"

"I talked to that guy," Aaron said. "I think we figured it out."

"I thought you needed some parts."

"Yeah," he said. "That guy had the parts. It was just a couple of brackets."

"He just gave them to you?"

"I told you, he's cool," Aaron said. "I loaned him a couple tools. Smoked him out."

"Goofy bastard," Skippy said.

Aaron just smiled.

"Fine," I said. "But remember. You're here to take pictures. You're taking pictures, right?"

"Oh, yeah," he said. "Probably about three rolls so far."

Wow. I never saw that coming.

"What'd you get?" I said.

"Come on," he said, smiling again. "I'll show you."

Then he introduced us to his neighbors. All of them.

Aaron was on a first-name basis with everybody in Bus Village. Most of them were driving Volkswagens or old International Harvester school buses. Or weird combinations, like the van that had the sailboat welded on top as a second story. Some of them were falling apart. Others looked like they had just come off the showroom floor. Aaron knew the story behind every one. I followed him around and took notes while he took more pictures—young stoners, old gay couples, middle-aged families with little kids, all of them his new Rainbow Family.

While I had been wandering around playing Rainbow, Aaron was busy being one. I could do my best to fit in. Or at least not stand out too much. But Aaron could just go with it. And he did.

He disappeared from time to time, but he always showed up someplace even stranger and better. Once we found him in a dark blue van where some guy was doling liquid acid out of an eyedropper. Things got hazy for a while after that and we lost him again.

Later we were looking for him when we stumbled across a scraggly kitchen just down the hill from A-Camp. It was called Merry Sunshine. A huge sign advertised free showers to any and all takers. Grungy Rainbows were lined up ten deep while a naked guy stood under a tree, scrubbing himself clean. When he gave the word, water came cascading out of a large plastic bladder hanging off a limb.

But there wasn't enough water for showers. The kitchen was pretty close to the parking lots, so I figured they were trucking it in. Then I saw a tiny stream winding through the camp. A tiny watering hole, maybe four feet across, held back by a makeshift dam. And a young man, calf-deep in the water, tending to the barricade.

It was Aaron.

Talk about outcasts. Merry Sunshine was the only kitchen at the entire gathering that served meat. It was close to the parking lot because a lot of the people running the kitchen were in wheelchairs. A few of them were Vietnam vets. Others were ex-bikers who had been injured in accidents. It also attracted people who didn't feel like hiking to the main meadow, so it was packed with local kids looking to get high, A-Campers taking a break from the pit bull attacks, and hobos.

Real hobos. We met one guy who had been hopping boxcars for decades. Tweed pants and an old blazer, all patched together. A scratchy beard. Skin like burlap. A red bulbous nose. He treated us to a convincing treatise on America's best Dumpsters.

"College towns are the best," he declared. "You wouldn't believe the shit they throw out."

"That's right," another hobo said. "I was just in Michigan—"

"Ann Arbor?" Hobo Number One asked.

"Yeah, Ann Arbor," Hobo Number Two said.

"You talking about the Arby's?" Hobo Number One asked.

"Yeah. The Arby's in Ann Arbor," Hobo Number Two said.

"Oh, yeah," Hobo Number One said. "The Arby's in Ann Arbor has the best damn Dumpster in America. I think people order shit there just to throw it away."

I looked at Skippy, who was listening so intently that I half expected him to suggest stopping in Ann Arbor on the way home. But he just smiled and shook his head. I turned to my left and saw a guy named NZANE sitting in his wheelchair. He had a long, flowing white beard and a denim vest. I think he was missing a leg. I was about to ask him if the hobos were bullshitting when I saw Aaron. He was cleaning dishes at a makeshift workstation by the kitchen; then tending to the dam; then fetching water to heat for the shower. He was running the whole damn show. Slowly. But he was running it. NZANE saw what I was looking at.

"Your buddy," he said. "He's a hard worker."

"Yeah," I said. "He is."

We slept in the bus that night. When we woke up, we started getting ready to go. I wanted to hit the road by noon. Skippy and I trekked back to our original camping spot and packed the gear while Aaron made some final adjustments to the Bus.

At least that's what I thought he was doing. The van was in pieces when we got back to Bus Village. The exhaust system. I forgot about the exhaust system.

Aaron said it would take only an hour or two. So Skippy and I walked and talked and smoked for a while. Shot the shit with NZANE and the hobos. Then we headed back to Bus Village to get ready for departure. The Bus was still a wreck. So we left and came back an hour later. It was still a wreck. Aaron was missing some parts. He wandered through Bus Village to trade for them.

I was almost getting ornery again, but the right parts materialized. And as we watched Aaron work, the true enormity of his efforts became clear: The Bus was getting more preposterous by the minute. The new exhaust system included a three-foot-long "stinger" pipe jutting out the back of the Volkswagen—an oddly sinister touch to the otherwise jolly-looking vehicle.

The concept was simple. The stinger was a big hunk of metal. It would draw a lot of the heat off the engine. Aaron said the pipe would get so hot it might even glow at night.

When he finished, we thought it good. A few hours late again, but what can you do? We loaded up the Bus with tents, backpacks, clothes, little souvenirs we had gathered. And then we were done. Except for one last thing.

Before jumping in, I took off my belt and laid it on the ground. I fetched my Swiss Army knife out of its case. I unfolded the awl and punched another hole in the leather, one inch away from the previous one.

Then Aaron fired up the Bus. Wow. We thought it was loud

before, but the stinger pipe changed everything. Now, instead of a Sherman tank dragging trash cans, it sounded like a Sherman tank dragging lawn mowers, all of them running at full throttle. Rainbows and A-Campers and Bus Villagers came from all around. They had never heard anything like it.

"WAPWAPWAPWAPWAPWAP!"

All the way down the dusty road. All the way out of the national forest. All the way back to Dillon, Montana, and beyond.

Our first stop was all business. A grammar school. Or maybe it was a middle school. It was closed for the summer, but Forest Service officials had set up a temporary headquarters there to monitor the Rainbows.

I needed quotes from some official sources, so I strolled through the front door. Someone eventually agreed to talk to me. I'm not sure why. I hadn't taken a shower in seven or eight days. I smelled awful. But they played along and I got what I needed.

Next stop, Nirvana.

We were rolling along at a decent clip, watching the temperature gauge to see if the new exhaust system made a difference, when we saw the sign: PIZZA HUT. ALL YOU CAN EAT BUFFET. $4.99.

We hadn't eaten much of anything in days. Hell, I hadn't eaten anything in months. And suddenly . . . Pepperoni pizza. White pizza. Pizza with ham and pineapple. Meat Lovers pizza. Cheese Lovers. Veggie Lovers. Plus all the Pepsi we could guzzle. We sat there for hours, stuffing our faces and stinking up the joint while the workers, the old ladies, and the young mothers gave us strange looks. They didn't know us. But they knew what we were all about.

We were with those hippies.

. . .

The rest of the trip was easy. We went across North Dakota instead of South Dakota, so it was a little cooler. The stinger pipe helped, too. It was heavy, and it drew a lot of heat off the engine. Aaron forgot once and walked right into it when we stopped for gas. It burned his shin. We heard it sizzle. We laughed.

Later, battling some kind of stomach virus, Aaron shit his pants. Which Skippy and I also thought was hilarious. Aaron said there was no need to stop, though. He was in the back of the Bus, so he took care of business with our last roll of toilet paper. Then, joking around like guys do, he tossed the whole mess—underwear, toilet paper, turd, and all—right past my head. It was a great shot, sailing straight out the passenger window. But when I turned to congratulate him, I saw the nasty little bundle unravel in the wind and blow right back into the Bus through the window of the sliding door, little by little, as Aaron struggled in vain to block the window with his hands.

Yes. It was a much easier trip. I got my paycheck via direct deposit. God bless direct deposit. We had gas money. I even treated us all to Egg McMuffins, hash browns, and real coffee. It was spectacular. But it was over soon enough. The drive took two days—a bit longer than it should have, but a half day faster than the way out.

We parted ways with Aaron at Aunt Virginia's. I told him how to submit the pictures. We transferred our junk to the Taurus. Said our good-byes. We even hugged, like good Rainbows do. And then we were gone.

· **15** ·

Dead Again

Two Bills and a Quarter

Leasing spectacular crewed yachts to the very rich at an average price of $40,000 a week has proved to be an excellent venture for Paul Madden. Yachtstore Ltd., his online business, has grown steadily in the past five years. But nothing quite prepared him for this year: Orders for charters are up 400 percent. . . .

After a period of phenomenal economic growth, consumer spending in many areas has slowed as investors watched interest rates rise and their worth on paper decline along with the stock market over the past six months. . . . But one segment of the economy that is still on fire is luxury goods. . . .

"The people who are buying luxuries have had the biggest gains," said Jason Trennert, managing director and economist at International Strategy & Investment, a brokerage firm specializing in economic research. "The wealthy are still ridiculously wealthy."

—The Washington Post, July 7, 2000

July 7, 2000. Early evening. We walked through our front door and collapsed into our recliners, side by side. We turned on the television. Ignored it for an hour or so.

Skippy broke first. "Dude," he said. "I'm going to go take a shower."

"Yeah," I said. "Don't use all the hot water."

I turned my attention to the mountain of newspapers that had ac-
cumulated on the floor in my absence.

While I was in Bosnia, dozens of ornate tall ships docked in Baltimore as part of an international sailing festival. More than two
hundred thousand tourists flocked to see them every day. The day
we left for Montana, Elián González got on a plane and flew back to
Cuba. Later, two students at the U.S. Naval Academy were accused
of raping a female midshipman. They were already back in Annapolis for football practice.

But none of that was making headlines anymore. Newspaper and
television reporters were chasing a mob of wild preteens who were
marauding through the streets because, at the stroke of midnight,
bookstores would begin selling *Harry Potter and the Goblet of Fire*.
I watched it unfold on live television. Little boys in round glasses.
Little girls in tears. I was mesmerized. Until I heard Skippy holler
from upstairs.

"You're up!" he shouted.

Shower time. Finally.

We passed on the stairs.

"Dude," he said, stopping midstride.

"What?"

"You stink."

So I went to the bathroom and scrubbed the Rainbow off myself—
watched it gather in a long brown streak, slide across the tub, and spiral down the drain.

The next day I drove Skippy to my sister's apartment to get his car.
He climbed in and drove off to the fish warehouse. I walked over
and knocked on the door. Gracie opened it.

"We made it," I said.

She looked at me like she had opened the door to a ghost.

"Oh my gosh," she said.

"What's wrong?"

"Have you looked at yourself in the mirror?"

"No," I said. I thought I had missed a filthy spot, or maybe I had a huge Montana tick hanging off my ear. "What?"

"How much weight have you lost?" she asked.

Then I was in her bathroom, stepping on the scale, listening to the squeaking metal, watching the digits on the wheel blur past the tiny plastic window. They slowed to a stop, then reversed course, teetering. Then stillness. And the numbers.

225

Two hundred and twenty-five pounds. Two bills and a quarter. Thirty pounds less than I weighed the day I got back from Bosnia eleven days earlier.

And I had lost a lot of weight in Bosnia.

I had lost something like fifty pounds. *In nineteen days.* And that wasn't counting any of the weight I had lost leading up to Bosnia. I was looking at something like eighty pounds total. Maybe a hundred, actually. Or more. I could have easily weighed 340 pounds when I started this whole scheme. If that was the case, I had lost 115 pounds since Easter Sunday. In ten weeks.

"My gosh," Gracie said again.

I guess I should have noticed what was happening. Especially in Montana. Punching the holes in the belt and all the rest. But I never thought about it. Maybe I was too busy. Buried too deep in the Rainbow haze. But the night before, when we got back, I should have noticed something in the shower, right? It had been ten days and thirty pounds since I had seen myself naked. But it didn't register. Maybe I was too intent on the strange sensation of hygiene. Or maybe I didn't look at myself in the shower. It's not something Fat Bastards do.

But the Fat Bastard was nowhere to be seen. My God. I killed the Fat Bastard. Without even knowing it. He had shown up in Mildenhall, then . . . *Wham!*

"I don't think I've weighed two hundred and twenty-five pounds since high school," I said.

Gracie just kept staring at me.

"Do I look bad?" I asked. "Do I look sick?"

"No," she said, finally snapping out of it. "I don't think so. Maybe a little tired. But . . . no."

"You sure?"

"Listen," she said. "This is weird. You need to eat something."

"I've been eating," I said. "We had some pizza on the way home. We even stopped at McDonald's."

"Good," she said. "So you're done with this lentil nonsense?"

"I—"

I stopped. Because I didn't know the answer. I hadn't thought about it. Thinking about it was hard. There was too much going on.

"What did you eat this morning?" she asked.

"Nothing," I said. "I guess I forgot."

"I'll make you something."

"No, I don't have time. I need to get this story written."

She stared me down as I collected the clothes I had left in her apartment after the Bosnia trip. She had folded them all in a neat little pile.

"Don't worry," I said as I headed out the door. "It'll be all right."
But I wasn't so sure.

There was no time to think about the Urban Hermit scheme. It was
Saturday. I had to be at work on Monday, and I would be busy once
I got there. The Bosnia story hadn't gone to press yet. For all I knew,
I had to rewrite the whole thing.

So I needed to write the Rainbow story. Immediately. *Reason*
wanted about four thousand words. They were being cool about it.
There was no rush. But sooner was better than later. Especially for
me, because I wouldn't get paid until they accepted it for publication. And I needed the money. Worse than ever.

Unbelievable. Two and a half months of starvation to straighten
out my finances—ten weeks of hunger and pain—and I was worse
off than when I started. I realized it when I got back from Gracie's
and started wading through the pile of angry new bills on the floor,
listening to the angry new messages on the machine.

> Mr. MacDonald, we are calling to thank you for the payment
> of a hundred dollars we received on May 18, and to remind you
> that another minimum payment of at least fifty dollars is due no
> later than June 5. . . .

> Mr. MacDonald, we are calling to inform you that we have
> not received your minimum payment. Please call us to make a
> payment over the phone or to make other arrangements as soon
> as possible. . . .

> Mr. MacDonald, we are calling to inform you that your
> account is once again in arrears. We have already applied all

applicable late fees. If you do not call immediately to make arrangements to pay your balance in full, we will be forced to send your account to a collection agency. . . .

Balls.

Fifty dollars would have been bad enough. But the minimum payment would hardly get them off my back now. And that was only one credit card company. The other one was just as pissed. It probably had something to do with the fact that I had just charged hundreds of dollars at European hotels, then hundreds more at gas stations across America while ignoring their calls. The student-loan people? My landlord? I was probably two months behind on both counts.

I had to do something, but I didn't stand a chance against them on the phone. So I wrote a few checks to the people who sounded the meanest. Stuffed a few envelopes. Tracked down some stamps. I hoped there was enough in my account to cover what was going out the door. Probably not, but it would have to do. At least Punch and the bartenders in Mildenhall got paid.

For now, I had four thousand words to write. There was still a bag of lentils and about ten cans of tuna in the kitchen. Hell, a little tuna and a handful of lentils would be a feast compared to what I had been eating in Montana. I could make it through the weekend. Easy. I'd worry about the rest of it later.

"Look at his belt!"

It didn't matter who was saying it. Because everybody said it sooner or later.

"Seriously. Did he show you the belt?"

I came back to the *Laurel Leader* a little battered, a little bruised, and frantic about my finances. I was upbeat, though. Proud of myself. I had managed to get a few things done. And I had some good stories to tell. The bombed-out mosque in Bosnia. The Bus. Punch. I figured I had enough material to keep the conversation going for weeks. The weight loss was only the *means*. And for me, it was the shitty part. The painful part. The stuff I had to get past to do the good stuff.

But the weight loss was the only thing anybody wanted to talk about. That and the belt. Which was the same thing.

"Did you see it? He had to punch holes in it. With his knife!"

I understood. It was weird. But the questions wouldn't stop. I would explain the whole thing to a group of four or five people, who would go tell four or five people, who would all come to see for themselves.

"Come on. Show us the belt. I heard you had to poke a hole in it with a *stick*. How much weight did you lose?"

"Uh, actually, it was an awl. But like I was saying, so then this big drunk Indian sees the scotch and comes stumbling over and—"

"Wait. Was this before or after you poked a hole in the belt?"

Joe was probably my best audience. He had been a reporter for years, so he was interested in hearing about the journalism stuff, and he had a vested interest in the Bosnia story. As for the Rainbows, he was a pretty straitlaced guy, so some of the hippie shenanigans struck him as fascinating. But even he was curious about my weight loss.

"I can't believe you lost that much weight that fast," he said. "But you can't do that forever. Are you done with the lentils?"

"I'm flat broke right now," I said. "We get paid next week. I'll look at my bills and decide what to do once I'm done with the Rainbow story."

But then everything got turned upside-down.

In between comments about the belt and the lentils and all the rest, someone slipped a big fat bomb into the conversation.

"Did you hear?"

"Hear what?"

"You didn't hear? They told us while you were gone."

"Told us what?"

"We're getting the merger money next week."

It was coming. Finally. For sure. Four thousand eight hundred dollars. And that changed everything.

I should have done some kind of jig. A victory dance. I actually *made it*. Financially. I was out of the hole. I should have let out a scream. I should have called Skippy. I should have headed straight to Kisling's. I should have gone bat-shit crazy.

I didn't.

The information didn't compute. What the hell does it all mean? I started unraveling. Thinking too much. Getting way ahead of myself. I still had the writing to deal with, and the credit cards and the landlord and the student loans. Gracie kept calling me to see what I was eating, and now this check was coming out of nowhere and . . .

"Just get through the week," I told myself. "Don't think. Just ignore it and get through the week."

Focus. If there is one thing an Urban Hermit can do, it's focus. Forget about the hunger and the stomach growling and the pain and all the noise. The lentils actually helped. They made things simple. No decisions. No hand-wringing. Just work.

I pounded out a draft of the Rainbow story in the evenings. At the office, I followed Joe's lead and nailed down the rest of the Bosnia stuff. He asked me to write a little column detailing the combat descent and Captain Sullins's broken molar. So I wrote it. I wrote it all. I e-mailed the Rainbow story to *Reason*. I met my deadlines at the *Leader*. And then—nothing.

No more international assignments. No more cross-country misadventure. Just Baltimore. Just poverty. Just lentils and tuna and waiting for the huge paycheck that was going to make everything better.

But it was only Wednesday. Or maybe Thursday. I was still dead-ass broke until payday. So I opened the door and started walking. The same walk that I had taken almost every night during June. But nothing helped. My mind was racing. To spend or not to spend? To eat or not to eat? To write or not to write? What am I going to do? Not just next week. Not just at the grocery store. Not just with the $4,800. What am I going to *do?* And how am I going to *pay for it?*

And when the hell am I going to get some pants that actually fit?

The decisions I faced required a special kind of wrestling. The sort of intellectually serious, emotionally charged decision-making that a man can only undertake deep in the wilderness. In front of a refrigerated truck crammed with kegs. With a bunch of old ladies drinking Manhattans and complaining in the background.

It's a damn good thing my family reunion was that weekend.

My extended family rents a camp on the outskirts of Ridgway for one weekend every July. The local Elks Club owns it. It's nothing fancy, but my father has eleven brothers and sisters. So it's a big deal as far as family reunions go.

We gather there for a few days of baby cooing, card playing, and rumormongering. Highlights include a huge table covered with home-made pies and cookies. And the beer truck. It's a trailer, really, with three taps sticking out the side. We usually go through eight or ten kegs. It's fantastic.

But I knew it was going to be different that summer.

I parked my car in the gravel lot and strolled toward the camp, then onto the patio and through the crowd. I got some looks but nothing serious. Mostly because nobody recognized me. I was making my way over to the beer truck when the cry went up.

"OH MY GOD!"

My cousin Mary had spotted me. She organizes the reunion and collects the money. She was holding a plastic cup full of beer in one hand, a fistful of cash in the other. With both still firmly in her grasp, she spread her arms wide and started bullying her way toward me— never spilling a drop of beer.

"IT'S SAM!"

Everyone turned from their cards and their babies and their goodies and their beer to see for themselves. At the last second, right before I got sucked under, I saw the telltale wisp of smoke, the Carlton 120 bouncing in between the faces. "I told you!" Aunt Virginia shouted. "I told you! A hundred pounds!"

She had done the advance work for me. As had Gracie and Skippy. So it's not like I took anybody completely by surprise. Still, I suppose it's strange to see someone show up a hundred pounds lighter than he used to be. There was no stopping it.

"Lentils?"

"Tuna?"

"Eight hundred calories?"

"Are you nuts?"

"I can't believe you did it."

"Show me the belt!"

But it was okay. I set up shop by the beer truck with Skippy, my dad, and a few of my uncles. Aaron was there. He had shown up the night before with the pictures. Which was perfect. The pictures were good. And they gave people something else to talk about.

So we sat and talked and drank. Like real people. I forgot about calories and money and deadlines. I just let it go. I told people about Punch and Bosnia and I showed them my belt. Again and again I showed them my belt and told them about the awl. People took turns estimating my total weight loss. And we had fun.

My mom expressed serious reservations. She hadn't seen me for months. She admitted that I looked fine, though. Strong, even. But she wondered.

"This lentil thing," she said. "Are you done?"

"That's what I am trying to figure out," I told her.

"But you'll be fine once you get the money from the merger, right?"

"I don't know," I said.

Because I didn't know. The $4,800 would just about cover my credit cards. That's all. I still had to deal with the student loans. And back rent. And eventually I would have to deal with the taxes, which I had deferred. I had to find money to pay all those bills.

And then all that other stuff . . . That stuff I hadn't even really even thought about yet . . . The stuff that was *really* going to change everything . . .

Again.

So I sat by the beer truck, listening to the ladies gossip and the babies coo and the men compare stories about cars and tools and work. I watched Skippy flip through the pictures of our trip out west. And I came up with another plan.

I decided not to kill the Urban Hermit. At least not yet. There was still a lot of work to do. And he was the only one dumb enough to get it done. I didn't tell anyone about it, though. I knew they would all think I was nuts.

I wasn't all that sure about it myself.

The reunion ended like it always does.

I woke up on Sunday at the camp. I had an excellent homemade breakfast. I played with the kids in the creek, making dams and catching crayfish until the priest showed up. He said Mass in a clearing in front of the beer truck. Like he always does.

Then I left. But I didn't head straight to Baltimore. I had some shopping to do. At my parents' house.

It was strange, like diving into history. My old room had changed very little. There was a crib, because my mom and dad watched my nieces and nephews a lot. But apart from that it was the same. The old iron bed, still painted green. Decals from my high-school football helmet, still attached to the headboard. The dartboard, still surrounded by hundreds of little pockmarks documenting my bad aim. A poster of a Lamborghini Countach. Several of Jim Morrison. The plastic crucifix. The metal one. The green dresser. And the clothes.

The clothes I hadn't seen since college. Toward the end of freshman year. All folded neatly, arranged in perfect little rows. T-shirts, extra-large. Pants, size 36. Slightly out of fashion, maybe, but they were never all that cutting-edge in the first place. Levi's. Some Dockers. Hard to go wrong.

I yanked out a pair of khakis. They were in remarkably good shape for pants that had been crammed in a dresser for nine years. I slid off the huge size-40 shorts I was wearing and slid the pants on, one leg at a time. I buttoned them. They seemed a little big, but they would do. Same as the rest of the pants. Same as the polo shirts in the closet. Same as the dress shirts.

My old wardrobe was my new wardrobe. And I didn't pay a penny for it.

I packed it all into a huge garbage bag and headed down the stairs. My mom was watching the news.

"Did you find everything?" she asked.

"Right where I left it."

"Does it fit?"

"Fits perfect."

"That's amazing."

"I guess so," I said.

"You're lucky," she said. "I almost threw it all away."

· **16** ·

The Tipping Point
A New Plan Takes Shape

*Gladwell introduced the idea of the "tipping point"—that, as
with epidemics, only a slight push might send a trend soaring or
plummeting—in a 1996 article about the decrease in Brooklyn's
crime rate. The premise for the tipping-point theory is the counterin-
tuitive, nonlinear relationship between effort and results. To illustrate
nonlinearity, he recalls his childhood frustration with an unrespon-
sive ketchup bottle, and he quotes the ditty his father recited: "Tomato
ketchup in a bottle. None will come, and then a lot'll."*

—Review of Malcolm Gladwell's *The Tipping Point*
in *The American Prospect*, July 17, 2000

July 17, 2000. Monday. I strolled into work, sat down in my old-
ass new pants, and waited.

Then someone showed up and handed me something. Maybe it
was an actual check. And maybe I hightailed it to the bank and
deposited that sucker. But I can't say for sure. Maybe the company
deposited the merger funds directly into my account. So maybe all
they handed me was a stub.

I might remember the whole experience in more detail—more
fondly—if the money had been mine. If I could have touched it. Let
it stew in the bank for a few days. Or a few hours, even. But it wasn't

mine. I had already spent it. Months and months and months ago. Some of it at Safeway. A little at gas stations here and there. But most of it at Kisling's. I took some solace in that. At least I enjoyed it. I enjoyed the hell out of it, as a matter of fact. So no crying. No complaining. No bellyaching. You get what you deserve.

After getting the check or the stub or whatever it was, once I was sure the money was real, I walked to the post office in Laurel to mail the envelopes. The ones that contained the huge checks I had written to the credit card companies the night before.

Maybe I ended up a few hundred dollars short. Or maybe I had a few hundred of the $4,800 left over. Either way, it was close. And for all intents and purposes, I was out of credit card debt. Broke as hell. Still behind on all the other bills. Still living paycheck-to-paycheck. But at least some of the bastards who harassed me on the phone every day would finally have to stop.

The painfully thin envelopes slid through the slot and—*phlit*—landed in a plastic bin, safely out of reach.

Pricks. Take that. I paid your ass.

Later that day I scratched a few dollars together and made my way to the grocery store to purchase more Urban Hermit supplies. They were cheaper, though. Because things had changed.

I still had money coming. The paper had to reimburse me for my hotel expenses. And *Reason* was supposed to be sending a check for the Rainbow article. When? I had no idea.

I hated having no idea. It drove me nuts. Worse than the hunger and the boredom. Because I had become addicted. *To the cushion.*

It paid to have a little leeway. Some resources in case of emergency. Need to get to Europe? Need gas money for a cross-country trip? Need to cobble together a drug deal with strange bikers? You need some liquidity. That's an elementary observation to most people, but it was a revelation to me.

And I was going to need some resources. Soon. I had been at the *Leader* for almost a year, just about as long as a twenty-seven-year-old guy can stay in an entry-level journalism job. I had generated some good clips. It was time to start shopping my résumé around. Which was weird. I switched jobs a lot, but this was the first time I was staying in the same profession. It seemed impossible, but it was true: I had finally staggered into what I was going to do when I grew up. Journalism. I never would have guessed it.

I figured the best-case scenario would be a full-time gig at the *Baltimore Sun*. I liked Baltimore. My roots had sucked up a little too much whiskey over the years, but they were roots nonetheless. But shifting from a small weekly newspaper to a major metropolitan daily was no sure thing. Especially a major metropolitan daily that had just been taken over and was probably looking to cut costs.

That damn merger. I knew it was going to screw me somehow.

I talked to Joe. He figured I would be looking around eventually. He even offered to help. He knew a guy at the *Sun*. He sent an e-mail introducing me. Made a call, too. But the odds were stacked against me. If I had to take a job somewhere else, I would have to move. And if I had to move, I was going to need money. Money that would come from . . . where? I sure as hell didn't have any.

The plan was . . . to eat some lentils until all the checks came in.

I had made a lot of headway. All that money and weight and all those inches and the awl. But I wasn't *finished*. I wasn't done paying. The bills. Or the pipers.

I was close, though. So . . . close . . .

It had been a rough couple months.

I could handle the physical stuff. I was young. Twenty-seven years old. The fatigue? I had never been much of a sleeper. The hunger? It was bad. Still that constant, empty pain, the churning, grinding sensation of a body feeding on itself and withering away. The stomach growling, protesting, demanding *more*.

But screw the hunger. Screw the noise. When I saw something I wasn't supposed to eat, I didn't pick it up. When I saw something at the store that looked good, I didn't buy it. Easy? No. Simple? Yes. And simple was exactly what I needed.

Still, a man can only take so much. And I had my limits. So it was time to be reasonable.

It was time to start drinking again.

I had the slip-up in England. That one almost cost me. But come on. One disaster in all that time? Besides, I survived. I got the story written. And since then? I'd been a model of moderation. There was some debauchery in Montana, but that was work-related. And on the way home . . . Pizza Hut. McDonald's, even. Then a whole week of work and deprivation. Then the reunion. The beer truck. Greasy breakfast. Then more work. More lentils.

Hell, I had my filthy mitts on $4,800. And instead of building a ridiculous cache of narcotics and firearms, I paid *bills* with it. *All of it*. That's what I call discipline.

So why not use it? Why not keep the Urban Hermit around just long enough to build up a little stash? Just enough money to keep my options open. Enough to pay for a plane ticket if the job search leads to an interview somewhere. Enough for a coat and tie that fits. Enough to chip away at the bills—new and old—until the big money arrives.

And enough, dammit, to pay for some beers on Friday and Saturday night.

Enough to *live*.

It was a revelation: Live on lentils and tuna from Monday through Friday. That would cost about six dollars a week. And on weekends? Back to Kisling's. Eat like a real person. Until Monday.

I would end up saving less. Maybe three hundred dollars a month instead of six hundred dollars. But that was enough. I would send some of it to the creditors and start an emergency fund with the rest. It wouldn't be easy. Things would really suck during the week. But who cares? It was only until all the checks came in.

It was a dicey proposal. The only thing that had made the Urban Hermit plan possible was the totality of it all. There were no decisions to make. No back and forth. Just do it. The new plan meant temptation. Tantalizing whiffs and glimpses of the good life. Slippery slopes. Roads to hell paved with good intentions and meat loaf. But to hell with all that. I couldn't stand being holed up like a stupid, sober animal anymore.

There would have to be a few adjustments, of course. Especially at the bar. I would have to get the shots under control. Same as the drugs. So . . . lentils all week. Let loose on weekends. Easy on the shots. No drugs.

Airtight.

But what about my health? How much longer could I hold out? I only knew one way to judge: I fell on my face and did push-ups.

I did a hundred of those suckers. I struggled with the last few.

But dammit, I did a hundred freaking push-ups. Probably for the first time in my life. I was good to go.

My return to Kisling's.

I thought about it all week. In bed. At work. In the shower. I was going *home*. Where everybody knew my name. Where they were always glad I came. I couldn't wait.

Literally, I couldn't wait. I didn't go home after work on Friday. I was planning to. Because that's what reasonable people do. I didn't want to go overboard. But . . .

I left the office early. I fought traffic. I parked my car. It was only four-thirty. Maybe five. It was warm out. So I strolled down past Kisling's. Just to take a look. To prepare myself.

Somebody had propped the door open to air out the place. I peeked inside. It was mostly empty. But I heard a few familiar voices. Saw a few familiar faces. Took a whiff. Yep. Saloon.

My saloon.

I put one foot on the concrete step. I inched forward and put the other foot on the threshold. Then I swung that first foot up and over and dropped it silently on the dirty green mat beside the video poker machine.

I was inside the bar.

I continued moving my feet—left, right, left—until I was standing next to the stool. My stool. In the bottom crook of the L-shaped bar. I put my fingertips on the deep brown wood in front of me to steady myself, then maneuvered my nine-year-old khakis into the sweet spot on the bar stool. I heard the clunky hum of the kitchen. The white noise of the radio. The empty banter of people getting ready to tie one on. And I waited.

Which was new. I never waited at Kisling's. For anything. There was always a Rolling Rock waiting for me by the time I sat down. Always a fresh one by the time I was halfway done with the first. And if I hadn't ordered shots in a while, somebody would do it for me.

But not that day. I just sat there, drinking it all in. God. I loved that place.

Then the bartender saw me. She was about my age. Long dark hair. Short. Cute. Familiar. She gave me a blank stare, a generic smile, and made her way over.

"What can I get you?" she asked.

"What do you mean?" I said.

"Can I get you a drink? A menu?"

"Michelle . . ." I said.

I saw a glimmer of recognition, then nothing. Then the glimmer returned. Then she lit up. Smiled. And hollered.

"SHUT UP!"

"Michelle . . ." I said again.

"SHUT THE HELL UP!"

She took off running toward the top of the L-shaped bar, rounded the corner, and came running back down its full length to where I was sitting. She leaped through the air and flung her arms around my neck.

"Sam!" she said, quickly tearing herself away and shouting back to the kitchen. "Sam's back!"

And then . . . It was hectic, like I expected. But there were only a few people in the bar. Things settled down once I got through the initial reaction, those first frantic questions about where I'd been and how much weight I'd lost. Michelle got me up to speed on all the gossip. Who was sleeping around. Who got punched in the face. Basic bar talk. Every once in a while she'd stop, look at me, and smile. "I just can't *believe* it. You look *so great*." But it was subdued, in a nice kind of way. I didn't even get drunk. I just had a few beers and went home.

I probably returned later that night. And I probably got shit-housed. But to be honest, my triumphant return wasn't all that re-markable. Nothing sensational happened. No cops showed up. Nothing burned down. No mariachi bands or knife fights. All I re-member is the sensation of *being there*.

Which was enough.

· **17** ·

George Bush, Black Beans, and the Summer of Survival

There are those who fear that when Dennis Miller takes over the microphone for his first football broadcast this Monday night he will say something outrageous, will fail to show proper respect for the game, and will do anything for a laugh. We can only hope.

Let's face it, the best thing about the debut of this year's version of Monday Night Football *is that it is taking place on the night of the opening of the Republican Convention. Talk about your no-brainer. Let's see, would you rather hear Miller talking and mocking football, or George W. Bush explaining the school voucher system? The only more snooze-inducing choice would be Al Gore on the environment.*

—C. W. Nevius,
San Francisco Chronicle, July 29, 2000

We should get great viewership. Who wants to see the coronation of George W. Bush? The guy thinks Croatia is the show on after Moesha.

—Dennis Miller

I t was a weird summer.

The 2000 presidential election heated up in August. Both major conventions. Intriguing questions about Ralph Nader. Nagging choices to make about foreign policy, the economy, and the Culture War.

Survivor had become a phenomenon. Breathless television reporters descended on Silicon Valley to profile the latest pimply-faced teenager to make his first $500 million. Or the latest to lose it. Smiling analysts predicted that the NASDAQ crash—30 percent since March!—was finally over. Dour analysts warned that it had only just begun. Either way, it was only a matter of time. The Napster case proceeded in court. Heinz announced plans to sell green ketchup. High drama, all around.

Even for the Urban Hermit.

Safeway. I had already scored the bread and the cheese and the cabbage. I had just made the hard right into the dry-goods aisle. I was scanning the nasty sacks of legumes when I started to wonder.

"Is there any reason it has to be lentils?"

If the plan could be five days a week instead of seven, if I could be a part-time hermit instead of a full-time one, then . . . *No, it doesn't have to be lentils.* As long as there's enough protein, and as long as it's cheap, who cares?

Look around. Pinto beans. White beans. Black-eyed peas. They had to be better than lentils. So I kept looking, considering this whole new world of possibilities, until I saw them: exotic, alluring, delicious . . . black beans.

Screw elections. To hell with the NASDAQ. *Black beans.* And *rice.*

I snatched two bags of beans off the shelf and tossed them into my cart. Ha! They cost the same as the lentils. I scurried two feet down the aisle and pounced on a big sack of white rice. Then I retraced my steps and put the cheese back in the cooler, the bread back on the rack. No more sandwiches. I would eat the tuna plain, right out of the can.

Tee hee!

I soaked the beans overnight. Just like the instructions said. I didn't add any salt. Someone on the Food Channel said soaking beans in saltwater would make the skins tough. I sure as hell didn't want tough skins. These beans were going to be perfect.

If only.

I came home from work and got the beans simmering. I tasted one. They were still hard. I turned the heat up to a rolling boil, but all that action ripped the skins apart. I ended up with a pile of mushy gray stuff and chewy black skins. Enough for a week.

I made some rice, mixed it all together and parceled out enough for my Monday meal. What the hell? It was something different, and it wasn't nearly as bad as the lentils. Besides, I could see the potential. Next week, I'd just let them simmer longer.

For a long time, people attributed my tolerance of liquor to the fact that I was so enormous. That's crap. I knew 130-pound guys who could drink a case of beer in one sitting. And I knew 350-pound guys who started puking like schoolgirls after two wine coolers and a shot of Rumple Minze. Heavy drinking is, at least in part, a mental exercise.

And I proved it. I was still pretty good at drinking, even after losing all that weight. People were impressed. I could belly up to the bar and hang in there like a champ. No more drugs, though. And I cut way back on the shots. But I was a barfly again. The life I loved. Exactly like before. Only a little less. And a little less often.

But then, out of nowhere, something strange. Something foreign. I mean, it was downright shocking.

What I mean is, when I looked down the bar, I would see something a little . . . off. Yeah, there was Skippy throwing ice cubes into the ceiling fan. There was JJ and the crew from the fish warehouse telling me I was a huge pussy, betting who could kick my ass now that I wasn't such a Fat Bastard. But I was used to all that. What got me was, as I looked down the bar, all of a sudden there was this . . . girl.

A straight-up, honest-to-goodness human being of the female persuasion. A bona fide woman, soup to nuts. Sitting there and smiling and saying things like it was the most natural thing in the whole world to be doing. Despite the fact that everyone knew it was bizarre.

Not that there had never been girls. In high school and college and beyond, they would show up on occasion, usually unannounced, and endure the idiotic shenanigans until they wised up. Like drinking buddies, only shaped different, with more interesting parts. But Skippy and I were not the kind of guys who maintained "girlfriends." Sure, not a lot of girls went out looking for ridiculous drunk guys. But it went beyond that.

The warehouse guys were just as ridiculous as we were, but they always had girlfriends. They were constantly handing out their phone numbers to chicks at the bar. Going out on "dates," engaging in melodramatic blowouts about every other week until they'd show up at the bar all weepy, complaining that they never should have talked to that bitch in the first place. We'd buy them a beer and listen until they scurried off to hand their grubby business card to

some other pain in the ass. But not me and Skippy. We were drinkers.
If some chick wanted to sign up for a while, so be it. But that was
about it.

So imagine everyone's surprise when I started talking to that girl
at the bar. And she talked back. Like we might be together or something.

She was a waitress at Kisling's. I liked her. She was nice. She
drank beer and smoked cigarettes. Gave nasty looks to the cus-
tomers who made rude remarks or tried to cop a feel. Worked a few
days a week to pay her way through college. I think she was a year
older than I was. Or maybe a year younger. Her name was Kim.

I am not sure how it happened. I think we just started talking
one night and I told her my Rainbow stories. She listened. And she
didn't make me show her the belt. Maybe she thought I looked
dashing after losing all that weight. Maybe we were drunk.

Before I knew what was happening we were renting a movie.
Renting a movie? I hadn't had a membership at Blockbuster my
whole life. Who rents movies? Well, we did. And then we were drinking in Fell's Point and none of my friends was there. Neither were any
of hers. Then, one day, we decide to *do something*. I think we went for
a walk in a park or something outrageous like that.

One night she called and Skippy answered.

"Who the hell was that?" he asked later when I got off the
phone.

"Kim," I said.

"Kim?"

"From the bar."

"Holy shit."

"I know."

"What's going on?" he said.

"I have no idea."

And I didn't. She told me I was weird. She told me I needed to stop losing weight. I told her I was still broke. She had a crazy dog. We made a bet about whether rats can climb trees. She showed me pictures of her family's Thanksgiving dinner. Half the people wore pilgrim costumes, half dressed as Indians. Her grandmother had made the outfits. They had been wearing them for years. I made fun of her, but I thought it was pretty cool.

It wasn't anything serious. We were just . . . hanging out.

Then one day I went to the bar and someone told me that Jeff was going to kick my ass. Jeff. One of the local contractors who refurbed old row houses for a living. I had known him for years. He was a good guy. But he was big. Brutal. The kind of guy who really could bring the hammer down on a candy-ass like me if he put his mind to it.

"Why the hell would Jeff want to kick my ass?" I asked.

"Because you're fucking around with his girlfriend."

"His girlfriend?"

"Kim."

"Kim's his girlfriend?" I asked.

"He thinks so."

"But I'm not fucking around with her."

"That's not the word around here."

"What's the word?"

"That you're fucking around with her."

Jesus. That threw me for a loop. The last thing I needed was an ass-kicking, and I could feel one coming on. Fast. But there was no place to run. No place to hide. The only place I ever went was

Kisling's. Same with Jeff. So I ordered a beer and waited for him to show up. I knew it wouldn't be long.

It wasn't.

"Dude," I said.

"What's up?" Jeff asked as he slid onto a bar stool next to mine. He didn't sound like he was going to kick my ass.

"You all right?" I asked.

"What are you talking about?"

"I heard you're pissed."

"Oh, Jesus Christ."

He did not stomp me into oblivion. In fact, he bought me a beer. And he told me some long and terrible story about he-said and she-said and the rumor mill and if anyone was going to get his ass kicked it was going to be so-and-so who started this whole thing and nobody is anybody's girlfriend and go ahead and do whatever you want and let's get another beer.

So we got another beer. And while I drank it, it occurred to me that Skippy and I had been right all along. Bars are for drinking. Who needs all that other bullshit?

The romance fizzled, of course. Not because of any ruinous fisticuffs. Just because. All of us hung out at the same place. One of us worked there. One was an up-and-coming carpenter/tycoon. One was a strange journalist who ate a lot of beans to save money for beer. Throw in all the rumors and innuendo and it got way too complicated. So we all went back to Rolling Rock. It was nice. And not nearly as awkward as I feared it might be.

So August just sort of limped along. I got better at cooking black beans, and that helped a lot. Then Safeway had this unbelievable sale on yogurt. They were almost giving it away. So I traded in some of my rice and the tuna and made the switch for a week. It was an outstanding change of pace.

The *Baltimore Sun* idea didn't pan out. Joe's guy at the paper sent me some e-mails. I sent him some clips. He said they were good, but the paper wasn't hiring. They were cutting staff, not adding it. So I looked online for jobs. Chicago? Pittsburgh? New York City? I didn't really care. I just sent out a few résumés and hoped for the best while I slowly wasted away.

I say slowly because the weight loss was no longer precipitous. It was merely . . . alarming. The size-36 pants I got at my parents' house didn't start to get loose for a few weeks. Maybe even close to a month. So I poked another hole in the belt. Everything seemed fine.

Maybe even better than fine. At least physically. One day I flopped onto my belly and did push-ups. Just to make sure I wasn't dying. I stopped when I got to 150. Seven and a half push-ups for every one I could do three months earlier.

People were starting to worry, though. And they were starting to ask questions. I kept telling them about the push-ups. I kept telling them to watch me toss huge boxes of flounder at the warehouse. I kept telling them to watch me belly up and kick the hell out of a Rolling Rock keg for a few hours. Fit as a fiddle. Strong as an ox. Drunk as a skunk, you silly sumbitches! It's not like I was starving. Hungry, sure. But I had a lot of energy stored in that big old belly of mine. And I was using it up. I wasn't frail. I wasn't sunken or pale or weak or defeated. They had to admit it. I looked pretty good.

But how much longer could I keep it up? That was the question. Could I really make it until I was in the clear financially? Was there enough of the Fat Bastard left to really make it? I was beginning to wonder.

So was Skippy.

He was sitting in the recliner watching the news, getting ready to go to work. I was heading down the stairs, getting ready for my nightly walk. He looked at me like he hadn't seen me in years.

"Holy shit, dude," he said.

"What?"

"You've lost a lot of weight, man."

"I know," I said.

Losing and Winning

The Numbers Game

You're going to like the way you look. I guarantee it.
—George Zimmer, founder and CEO,
The Men's WAREHOUSE

Early September. Steamy, sticky air rolling across the asphalt. The crowded parking lot of the Laurel Shopping Center, where those five bullets crashed into George Wallace in 1972. But Wallace was long gone. Now there was a grocery store. A liquor store. A barbershop. A bookstore. A Chuck E. Cheese's. That shopping center had just about everything, as a matter of fact. Including my destination: Marshalls.

Acres of shirts, shoes, and housewares. Incredible specials on Christmas decorations. The peculiar plastic scent of damaged goods. And the selection. Perry Ellis. Bill Blass. Calvin Klein. They sounded prestigious. But were they? Or was it a pile of crap they couldn't sell at regular stores last year? I didn't care. I just needed some pants. Size 36 was the end of the road at my mom's house. As much as it pained me, it was time to spend some money.

Here's the thing, though. *I had some money.* Not Brooks Brothers money. Not Nordstrom money. Not even Sears money. But enough for some pants from the bargain basement. So I meandered through the aisles looking for size 34. I found them. Tried them on.

Too big.

I ventured back into the store and grabbed a pair of Tommy Hilfiger khakis. Size 32. The Holy Grail of American male fitness. I grabbed a pair of darker khakis, some brand I'd never heard of. I walked back to the dressing room. I slid into the Hilfiger one leg at a time. Zipped up.

Perfect fit.

I carried the pants to the counter. A young girl rang me up: thirty-six dollars for both pairs. Thirty-six dollars? I could have bought a whole month of black beans and rice with thirty-six dollars. Even a night at the bar if I was careful. Stupid fucking pants.

It had to be done, so I handed over the cash. But as I grabbed the bag and walked to my car I felt a strange sensation creeping up on me: It was time to think about the Urban Hermit's future. Sure, the plan had simplified my life. It had paid for Bosnia. It had paid for Montana. And it had paid for the pants. But I had just lost twelve inches off my waist in four months. There weren't a lot of inches left to lose. I needed to make some hard decisions.

And I was preparing myself to do just that. But that's when everything blew up in my face. The baby, the job interview, the hot chick from upstairs, the drugs, the cat, the duck, that bizarre encounter with the Dukes of Hazzard, and . . .

And that was only the beginning. Of the end.

But I'm getting ahead of myself again.

My sister's baby arrived on September 16. A girl. They named her Rena. Just like my cousin, the dietician who told me I would die if I did the Urban Hermit plan for too long.

Gracie was a wreck. Her husband worked full-time. They had a little boy who was eighteen months old. They lived in a little two-bedroom apartment. It was madness, especially that first week. My mom set up shop on their couch and took care of whatever she could. Cooking. Cleaning. Getting up with the baby.

I tried to help. I brought lunch. I took little Joseph out to play in the grass. But mostly I kept my mom company while Gracie tried to get some rest. I distinctly remember sitting on the couch, watching the 2000 Summer Olympics, waiting for the baby to cry. I distinctly remember my mother lambasting me about my weight.

And then I was standing on the bathroom scale with my mother looking over my shoulder, watching the numbers scream past, then come to rest.

I weighed 202 pounds, 23 pounds less than I weighed when I got back from the Rainbow Gathering.

"I knew it," my mom said. "You're too skinny. Way too skinny."

"But—"

"Too skinny!"

I offered to do some push-ups, lots of them, to prove I was healthy. She wasn't interested. She wanted to see me put some flesh on my bones.

My mom would have been relentless under normal circumstances, but she was so busy with the baby that I managed to keep her at bay. I told her the check from *Reason* was sure to arrive soon. That I had even started spending a little money. I showed her my new pants. Every day and in every way, I was getting better and better.

It was enough to hold her off, but only for a while. I was running out of time and I knew it. But there was nothing I could do . . . except go to work.

. . .

Route 1 was humming with activity.

Howard County officials inspected the porn store and fined the owner for operating the video booths. The porn store retaliated with a lawsuit, but things looked grim for the whack-shack crowd.

John Stafford, the would-be senator who heated his trailer with televisions, still wasn't satisfied. He wanted the porn store shut down. It occupied his every waking moment until he discovered that he wouldn't be living next to the porn store after all. Not because the law was on Stafford's side, but because his landlord decided to close the trailer park and kick everybody out.

It was big news in Laurel, but it didn't surprise me. The place was rough. There were about fifty trailers. Some of them were well-kept, but others were disasters. One had recently burned down, in some sort of crystal-meth mishap.

The owner said that 50 percent of tenants owed him thousands in back rent. One guy who hadn't paid in twenty-seven months owed more than ten thousand dollars. The owner said he had to give residents only thirty days to leave, but he was letting them stay until the end of the year—as long as they didn't owe any money.

I wasn't very sympathetic to the residents' plight at first. The dilapidated trailers. The cars up on blocks. One of the trailers flew a Confederate flag. The place was like a caricature of itself.

Then my mind turned to John Stafford's family. He had bought his trailer two years earlier from a woman who had lived there for years. It was so old that it would almost certainly fall apart if he tried to move it. As for the place being a dump, Stafford argued that it was the owner's job to deal with abandoned trailers. Just like it was the owner's job to remove rusting refrigerators and other debris. But the owner hadn't done any of that. Why *should* people pay rent if they lived next to a burned-out death trap?

Touché.

Half the people living there paid their bills. A lot of them took care of their trailers. Three months seemed like a raw deal for them. For guys like John Stafford. Sure, he heated his trailer with televisions. Which was weird. But he had three kids.

"There ought to be a law," Stafford complained.

So I dug around and discovered that there was a law.

In Maryland, owners who want to sell a trailer park or change the use of the property have to give tenants a full year to vacate. I called the owner. He said that didn't apply because he didn't plan to change the use of the property or sell it. He just wanted to close the trailer park.

I called county officials. They said the owner told them he was selling the property. I called the owner back. He said that was 100 percent false. He also said that anyone who abandoned a trailer and left it behind would receive a bill for disposal. He planned to sue anyone who didn't pay.

It was Community Journalism 101. I did a lot of interviews, made calls, spent hours tracking down all the regulations involved. Which was exactly what I needed. It kept me occupied. Besides, editors love that kind of shoe-leather reporting. Journalism with a purpose. It was sizing up to be just the kind of story that would sound great in a job interview.

And I was going on one.

. . .

The call came from the *Annapolis Capital*. An editor had received my résumé. He wanted to talk.

Joe called someone he knew there and put in a good word for me. I thought I had a chance, only . . . I didn't have anything to wear to the interview.

I had a sports jacket that I had bought in 1999, when I was at my fattest. I tried it on. I could have used it as a parachute. My dress shirt was even worse. It was at least five inches too big. *In the neck.* My gosh. I never even thought about how much smaller my neck had gotten.

I got in my car and drove to my sister's apartment. I needed to talk to some women.

My mom and my sister were enthused. An interview sounded a lot like a career move. Which implied I had a career. Which smacked of—growing up. They said the occasion called for a suit. You can never be overdressed for an interview, they said.

Yeah, well . . . no way. What little money I had in my account was there because I starved myself, and I didn't intend to shoot it on a wardrobe. Especially something I'd wear only once. Journalists don't wear *suits*.

I already had those pants from Marshalls, so I countered with the idea of going back for a sports coat. I sold them on the general idea, but not Marshalls. The women couldn't help me go shopping. They were stuck traveling between the apartment and the doctor's office for the foreseeable future. But there was no way I could go by myself. Matching a jacket with a shirt? I had a better chance of spontaneously combusting.

My sister suggested Men's WAREHOUSE. It would be cheaper than a department store, but I could get some help from the staff. That sounded like a plan to me.

"Do you need some money?" my mom asked as I got up to leave.

"No," I said. "I got it."

The numbers. The old man in the impeccable gray suit kept sending them my way, wave after wave, never seeming to notice that I was drowning. Or maybe he just didn't care. Salesmen seldom do.

Chest measurement: 44. *My jacket at home was a 56.*
Neck measurement: 16. *My dress shirt at home was a 22.*
Navy blue jacket: $149. *Eighteen weeks of Urban Hermit supplies*
White oxford shirt: $29. *Twenty-nine beers at Kisling's.*

I was in a daze by the time I got to the counter. But the salesman wasn't done. "Do you have a tie for this jacket, young man?" he asked.

"No," I said.

"You have to have a tie."

"Right," I said. "Of course."

"Can I recommend one?"

"Just grab one that matches," I said. "I don't know anything about ties."

He grabbed me a real humdinger. Silk. Forty-eight dollars.

"Wow," I said. "Is that how much ties cost?"

"Yes," he said.

"What the hell," I said. "You might as well throw in some socks."

Total damage: $240

I fantasized about strapping twelve twenty-dollar bills to my fist and punching that bastard right in the face. Just to show him. A left uppercut, maybe. Or a straight right. "I got your $240 right here, jerkass!"

Kapow!

But I didn't. I paid with my debit card.

And to be honest, I felt good about that. He was a good sales-man. And I was a good customer. Because I actually had money.

For once in my life.

Ha! It was a damn good thing I didn't ditch the Urban Hermit plan when everybody told me to.

· **19** ·

Good Times

The Moon, Antarctica, and a Duck

In the time since the band's last proper album (1997's The Lone-some Crowded West, *on Up Records), Brock has found himself quite a bit to write about. During the hiatus, he has lived as much like a wandering hobo as possible.... At one point during his time off from the band, Brock worked at a truck stop, cleaning blood off meat-delivery trucks. "I liked cleaning out meat trucks a lot," he says. "I got to work drunk. I'd do it again."*

—"Moon Shot: Major-Label Status Becomes Modest Mouse," *Baltimore City Paper*, September 20, 2000

I t was time to do something. Finally.

Modest Mouse was coming to Baltimore. They had played in D.C. earlier that year, but I missed both shows. That was right after I started the Urban Hermit experiment. When I had *nothing*. But I was weaning myself off of nothing. I was trying to start living again.

So I bought the new album. It was called *The Moon & Antarctica*. I also bought three tickets for the concert. One for me, one for Skippy, and one for Pat, a drinking buddy who tossed fish with us. It was an all-ages show at a bingo hall called Sher-Wes Gardens in the industrial strangelands of East Baltimore.

We didn't care about the opening acts, so Skippy, Pat, and I trudged across the street to a local watering hole called Bill's Café.

We were the youngest people there by about two decades. Everyone was Slovakian or Polish—at least it seemed that way—and they knew we didn't belong. I thought things might turn grim, but I was thirsty. Besides, we were experienced drinkers. All we needed was a diversion.

Luckily, kids from the concert were filing in with their fake IDs and tattoos and piercings. So we acted crusty and rolled our eyes at the youngsters to fit in better with the regulars. We kept getting drunker until someone came in two hours later and said that the band had arrived. We chugged our beers and stumbled across the street.

Sher-Wes Gardens was a weird place to see a concert. Low ceilings. No real stage. No pyrotechnics or laser light show. The band just stood there and played their instruments. We were the oldest people there. The cool kids rolled their eyes at us when we stood in the wrong place or shouted the wrong nonsense. But we didn't care. We had fun. I even bought a T-shirt. It was brown, with MODEST MOUSE stenciled across the front. It had a picture of a buffalo on it.

I got the Annapolis job.

The editor wanted me to work a neighborhood beat out in the suburbs. He said he might promote me to a general assignment slot at the main office in a year or so. It was a good offer, I guess. But I was almost twenty-eight. Neighborhood beats are for kids right out of college and pay accordingly. The journalistic equivalent of junior varsity, I figured. If I took the job, in two years I'd be a thirty-year-old reporter looking for my first real beat. About ten years behind schedule.

I wasn't sure I could find anything better. But I had a good feeling. So I said, "No thanks."

I thought I was taking control of my life. I was wrong.

I got my first hint from Harold, my coworker. He was a stylish guy, a few years younger than I was. The sort of fellow who chatted with the hot girls upstairs—the sales reps who sold space in the local phone directories. Harold knew their gossip. He knew which ones were cheerleaders for which professional football team. He also knew a few things about me, apparently.

Harold was chuckling when he walked by my cubicle one evening. We were the only two people left in the newsroom.

"Oh, man," he said, looking at me, shaking his head.

"What's going on?" I asked.

"You have no idea, do you?"

"Huh?"

"I knew it," he said. "You have no clue."

"What the hell?"

"She's after you," he said.

"Who's after me?"

"One of the girls upstairs."

"What are you talking about?"

"I'm not supposed to say anything," he said. "I'm just supposed to ask if you have a girlfriend."

Oh, man. No way. I just went through that with the girl at Kisling's. And this was way worse. The girls upstairs were dangerous and strange. Upscale in a way that made me confused and dizzy. Perfectly coordinated outfits from Banana Republic, all khaki and perfectly pressed. Hair perfectly coiffed. Makeup perfectly applied.

Skin plumped with lotion and perfectly tanned, even in October. Brand-new compact cars, perfectly washed and waxed.

Self-consciously stylish girls. Aggressive. Ambitious. *Intense*. I had never said a word to any of them, but I knew the score. Dramatic girls. Highfalutin girls who lived with their parents so they could afford better compact cars and wintertime tans. Or girls who lived on their own in perfect town houses within striking distance of the mall. Girls who tried out to be NFL cheerleaders. And succeeded. Not the kind of girls who dated fat guys. Not the kind of girls who appreciated hermits, urban or otherwise.

Besides, someone sent Harold to do recon. To ask if I was dating anyone. What was this? Sophomore year?

All I wanted to do was take my skinny ass to the bar. Why wouldn't anybody just let me take my skinny ass to the bar? Is there anything wrong with a guy starving himself so he can pay for a trip to Bosnia, a trip to Montana, a bag of weed, a stupid fifty-dollar tie and a few drinks for his skinny ass at the bar? All I wanted was a little peace and . . .

"So?" Harold asked.

"So what?"

"Do you have a girlfriend?"

"No."

"I didn't think so," he said. "Okay, then."

"Okay what?" I asked. "I don't understand what's going on."

"You don't need to."

"It's not one of those cheerleaders, is it?" I said.

"No."

"Thank God," I said. "They're terrifying."

"She's hot, though," he said.

"This is bad."

. . .

I was working on a story when a woman named Nita poked her head into my cubicle. She was maybe forty-five years old. Her job was collecting money from people who bought advertisements.

"What are you doing?" she asked.

"Writing," I said.

"I need some help," she said. "Come with me."

So I did. I followed her through the newsroom. I figured she needed me to lift a box of paper, or maybe put a jug of water in the cooler. But we walked past the copier. And the watercooler. Then we walked out the door.

"Where are we going?" I asked her.

"Right here," she said as we rounded the corner of the building.

"Right where?"

"Sam," she said. "This is Michele."

"What?" I said.

"See you later," she said.

Then Nita was gone and I was alone with the girl from upstairs. It was awkward. Embarrassing. I was pissed off at Harold. At Nita. The world. But I had to say something.

"Hello," I said.

"Hello," she said.

Harold was right. She was a very attractive young lady. Or hot, as they say in the vernacular. Perfectly blond. Perfectly coiffed. Perfectly fashionable leather coat with a belt. The glasses. The kind of girl who could kill an Urban Hermit just by looking at him. Ye gods.

"What's your name again?" I asked.

"Michele."

"Michele what?"

"Duck," she said.

"Duck?" I said.

"Yeah," she said. "Duck."

"You work upstairs?"

"Yeah," she said. "You're a reporter?"

"Uh-huh."

"Are you new?" she said.

"No," I said. "I've been here over a year."

"Really?" she said. "I don't think I've seen you around."

"I guess I keep to myself."

"Well," she said. "I have a meeting."

"Okay," I said.

And she left.

I limped back to my locker to grab my geometry book and get ready for football practice. I mean . . . I went back to work.

There was a message on my office phone the following morning. From Michele. She said I should give her a call. I guess all my smooth talk paid off. Or maybe she wanted a closer look at my suave Marshalls wardrobe. Or maybe she was nuts. I was pretty sure she was nuts. Because let's be honest here, I had no business talking to any chicks.

And say I did call her. What would we talk about? Stocks? Bonds? Cars? Yeah. I could tell her about the beat-up Ford Taurus my parents bought for me. She could tell me about her cheerleader friends. Maybe I could conjure up a charming anecdote about starving myself half to death, or invite her over for a single serving of boiled lentils and a can of tuna. I was at a loss. So I did what all idiots do. I waited until I got home and asked my drinking buddy for advice.

"So," Skippy said when I got done detailing the situation, "she's hot?"

"Yeah," I said.

"Where do these chicks keep coming from?" he asked.

"I have no idea."

"What are you going to do?"

"I don't know," I said. "What do people do?"

"I don't know," he said. "Tell her to meet you at Kisling's."

"That's what I was thinking."

"Then it's probably a bad idea."

"That's what I figured," I said. "Should I call her?"

"How the hell should I know?"

So I called. Her brother answered the phone. They were having a cookout. I heard him teasing her as he handed her the phone. It all seemed perfectly scripted. So upper-middle-class suburbia that I almost cried. But it was too late.

We talked. She said she lived with her mom somewhere in Laurel (Of course!). She just paid a great big pile of money (Yes!) for a puppy (Told you so!). An English springer spaniel (Why not!) named Lucy (What else?).

I could hear Lucy playing in the background. Even the dog sounded uppity, like it was barking in French. And I could tell it wasn't drinking whiskey. These were sober-pet people. Pretty people. People with ambition and expensive animals.

I have no idea what we talked about, but eventually I said goodbye and hung up the phone. I told Skippy that the whole thing was spinning out of control. He laughed at me. Then we turned on the news.

The USS *Cole* was refueling in the Yemeni port of Aden when two men pulled alongside in a boat and detonated an enormous bomb. The blast blew a thirty-five-by-thirty-six-foot hole in the destroyer's hull. It also killed seventeen sailors, injured thirty-nine more. Various terrorist organizations were suspected in the attack, including a group called al-Qaeda.

October 12, 2000.

The absurd cat-and-mouse game with Michele went on for days, and one thing became painfully clear: I was not the cat.

I'd walk through the parking lot and there she'd be. Or I'd run into her in the conference room. It's not like avoiding her was an option. We worked in the same building.

Besides, she actually seemed kind of nice, despite the whole highfalutin problem. Plus she smoked cigarettes. Which made her even hotter.

I had no idea what to do, so I tried to force the issue. I suggested that we meet at Oliver's after work. It was a bar right next to the office. If I started making an ass of myself I could just claim I didn't want to drink anymore because of the drive. And I could bolt. It was a brilliant maneuver. Except she said no.

We talked again a few days later. I suggested Oliver's again.

"No."

She clearly had no interest in going to a bar. And I had no interest in going anywhere else. So screw it. Until . . .

We were standing near the parking lot, by the back door of a Chinese restaurant. I was getting ready to go cover some kind of meeting when she dropped the bomb. "Hey," she said. "How about that rough little trailer park over on Route One? The one you keep writing about?"

Finally. Here we go. Little Miss Upscale is going to start talking smack on the trailer trash. The last straw. I knew where this was headed and I didn't like it one bit, so I unleashed a rambling defense of John Stafford and his neighbors. "Okay, maybe it's a little rough," I said. "But some of those people are really getting screwed."

And I kept going. I told her about people like Rose. Sixty-three years old and tough as nails. She got married when she was fifteen and had seven kids before her husband up and left her. She raised them on her own in an old rented farmhouse until the government seized the land to expand an airport and kicked her out. She survived, though, and moved to the trailer park in the early eighties. Kenny, the live-in companion she referred to as "my old man," was in the hospital recovering from heart surgery when she heard the trailer park was closing and she was getting tossed again.

Rose was proud of the home she had made for herself. Her trailer was clean and orderly, decorated with pictures of her grandkids. She said the trailer park was never a paradise, but there were some good people there. Like Miss Kaiser, Rose's good friend. Miss Kaiser, retired from the army, hadn't missed a rent payment in twenty years. She had the canceled checks to prove it. And then there was Rose's son Larry, who lived a few rows down. He stopped by for dinner almost every night.

But not for much longer. All of them were going to be out on their asses. It didn't seem right. The losers who refused to pay their bills were getting evicted at the end of October. Rose paid her bills faithfully and she got to stay until the end of December. Two extra months. That's what she got for doing the right thing.

Bullshit. Rose was mad as hell. She almost cried when she talked about it. But she didn't. Because she was stronger than that.

So, yeah. Okay. The trailer park was a little rough. But there were worse places. And there's a law that says the owner can't—

"Hey," Michele said, derailing my tirade.

"What?" I said.

"I have to tell you something."

"Okay."

"I know Rose," she said.

That didn't make any sense at all.

"Really?" I asked. "How?"

"She was my neighbor."

"When?" I asked. "She's been in that trailer park for eighteen years."

"She was my neighbor in the trailer park," Michele said.

"You lived in the trailer park?"

"Yeah," she said. "Until I was twenty-three, about two years ago. I lived there almost my whole life."

"Holy shit," I said.

Holy shit was right. What do you say to that? *You don't look like you grew up in a trailer park.* What the hell would that mean? Or something like, *Hey, I assumed you were a real jerk before, with all your stylish stylings. But now that I know you're from the trailer park, I think you're kind of nice.* Good God. Just keep staring ahead. Don't say anything. Keep your mouth shut. Silence!

But I *did* like her more once I found out she was from the trailer park. There was no way to say that without looking like a real asshole, though. Thank goodness she was still talking.

". . . and I kept seeing these articles about the trailer park in the *Leader*," she said. "So I started asking around about the reporter. Who turned out to be you."

"Really?" I said, trying to buy some time.

"Yeah," she said. "It started when you wrote that article about John Stafford. You interviewed him at the Bottom of the Bay."

John Stafford. My favorite political candidate. Ever.

"Do you know John Stafford?" I asked.

"Yeah," she said. "He lives in my old trailer."

"What?"

"My mom sold it to him a few years ago," she said. "When we moved out."

"John Stafford's trailer used to be your trailer?"

"Yeah."

"You know," I said, grasping at straws, "he heats it with televisions."

"What?"

"John Stafford," I said. "He heats the trailer with televisions. He has like twenty of them. Keeps them running all day."

"Really?"

"That's what I hear."

Silence.

"Why'd you move?" I asked.

"You've been there," she said. "That place is a dump."

"Well . . ."

"It wasn't always that bad," she said. "But the last couple of years—we had to get out of there."

"Okay."

"I just thought I ought to tell you," she said.

"All right," I said, paralyzed. But then an idea . . .

"Hey," I said. "Maybe we should go to Oliver's after work. I can tell you about what's going on at the trailer park and you can—"

"No."

"No?"

"I'm not going to Oliver's with you," she said.

"Oh," I said. "Okay."

"You're going to have to ask me out on a real date."

"A real date?"

So I set up a date with Michele Duck. Friday night. I figured I would take her to Baltimore and . . . huh. What was I going to do with her?

"Take her to Kisling's," Skippy said.

"I'm in trouble," I said.

And I was. But apart from that, things were looking up. I was still hungry, still wasting away little by little. But I had a date with a very attractive piece of work who turned out not to be the annoying, high-society type after all. The check from *Reason* was due any day, and that was going to change everything. It wasn't a fortune. Just two thousand dollars. But that was enough to give me a little breathing room. Enough to pick up and move on if I felt like it. Or enough to make a stand in Baltimore. Enough to take a girl on a real date, whatever that meant.

I'd be scraping by, just barely. But I'd be able to pay my own way. To do things on my own terms. And I earned it, dammit! The months of starvation and saving. Busting my ass to get from Bosnia to Montana. The Tribune buy-out. It was a perfect storm of virtue and discipline and good fortune. I got my shit together when it counted, and now I was cashing in. I was finally getting what I deserved. I could feel it.

No, really. I could feel it.

Again.

No. Please. *Not again.*

· **20** ·

The Comeuppance

The universe is shaped exactly like the earth, if you go
straight long enough you'll end up where you were.
—Modest Mouse, "3rd Planet"

Wednesday, October 18, 2000. Savage, Maryland. Route 1, two miles north of the trailer park. Half a mile east of my sister's apartment.

Confidence? High.

Cares in the world? Few.

I was stopped at a red light in front of a new CarMax and a grocery store. It was early afternoon. The road was busy but not packed. The Taurus was pointed north. Why? I can't recall. Maybe for a story. Maybe to visit the new niece. It doesn't matter either way. Because I never got where I was going.

Green light. Foot on gas.

Stillness.

More foot. More gas.

Still nothing. What the . . .

Turn down that racket on the stereo and . . . "WWWHH-AAAAHHHHHHHHH . . ."

Engine racing. Wheels of stone. A horrific loose feeling in the right leg, like it's falling through the floor and through the asphalt and into the dirt and straight to hell.

The transmission. Great Holy Mother of God. *The transmission.* Gone.

I couldn't even muster a profanity. Not a *shit.* Not a *fuck.* Not a *damn.* No expression. No tears. Like I had known it was going to happen. Like I had planned it all along. I just sat in the left-turn lane, shifting the car from drive to park. Park to drive. Hit the gas. Nothing.

Park. Drive. Gas. Nothing. *Park. Drive. Gas.* Nothing.

Parkdrivegasnothingparkdrivegasnothingparkdrivegasnothing.

I thought about putting it in reverse. That's when I looked into the rearview mirror and saw the traffic piling up behind me. I sat through the green light. Then a red light. Then another green light. People were honking their horns. Government workers. Angry rednecks. Soccer moms. Accountants in SUVs. They were driving around me. They were flipping me the bird, shouting:

"You're holding up traffic!"

"Move your ass, jerk!"

"Fuck you, buddy!"

Yes. Exactly. Fuck *me.*

21

Payday

In the Zone

Laugh hard, it's a long ways to the bank.
—Modest Mouse, "Paper Thin Walls"

Car parts are expensive. I learned that the hard way. This was the third time the transmission on the Taurus hit the shits.

My parents knew, too. Better than I did, even, because they paid to have it fixed the first two times. About $1,400 a pop. Would it make sense to dump that much into an old junker again? How long would it last? Where would the money come from?

Excellent questions. But they would have to wait. Until Saturday. Because I had to take care of a few things.

First, I had to borrow a car so I could get to work. My sister was still laid up with the baby, so she didn't need to drive. Her husband took their Chrysler to work and left me his old pickup. A green Dodge Dakota.

Next, I had to get a grip on myself. I was frantic. The check from *Reason* was on its way, and that was supposed to be the Urban Hermit's fatal blow. I was planning to kill him off for good. But now what? Do I spend all that money on a fucking transmission? Do I keep eating lentils until I weigh as much as I did in third grade? Until I go completely insane? Six months of scraping and starving and now a stupid hunk of metal that I don't even understand is going to . . .

Well, it's going to do what it's going to do, I told myself. For now, pay attention. Straighten up. Or at least try. Because someone is watching. From the passenger seat of the borrowed pickup. And she's asking a lot of questions.

Dates are for normal people. Not Fat Bastards. Not Urban Hermits. And certainly not a Fat Bastard trapped in an Urban Hermit's starving body.

I gave it a go. But I was terrible.

"So I'm not sure what to do for a car," I was telling Michele as we screeched to a halt in the Friday traffic. "I can't afford a new one. But I can't afford to fix the transmission, either."

"Oh," she said.

Wait. Did I screw up? Maybe the first thirty seconds of a date isn't a good time to start yammering about abject poverty. Maybe I should keep my mouth shut. But she kept making conversation.

"So," she said. "What do you do?"

"I'm a reporter," I said.

Wow. It was sizing up to be a long night.

"I know you're a reporter," she said. "I mean, what do you do for fun?"

"I go out drinking a lot."

"What?" she said.

Dammit.

"Oh," I said. "It's not like it sounds. I mean . . . I go out a lot less than I used to. I used to go out drinking every night just about. But I don't anymore."

"What's that mean?"

"I ran out of money," I said. "I can't afford to drink all the time anymore."

Dammit.

"So what do you do?" she asked again.

"Sit around and eat lentils, mostly," I said.

"Lentils?"

Dammit.

"Well, not just lentils," I said. "I've been eating a lot of black beans lately."

"Beans?"

Oof! What the hell am I doing here? I never should have mentioned the lentils. Or the beans. But . . . what the hell is this chick's angle? And why is she looking at me? Good grief. *She dressed up.* A sweater. Khaki pants. That leather coat and the blond hair. Zow! She looks like danger and smells like math. Or maybe that's some kind of strawberry-avocado shower scrub. How would I know the difference? Is there one? Either way, it seems calculated. *Intentional.*

And this traffic! Rush hour. I never counted on rush hour. I should have planned this better. I don't even know where we're going. Which way do I turn the wheel when I get off the exit ramp? And . . . and then I realized that my mouth was still moving.

". . . so I just decided that I would live on eight dollars a week, because it would save me a lot of money. And besides, I was pretty fat, so I figured I would just live off reserves while I got my finances straightened out and—"

"You were fat?" she asked.

"Yeah," I said. "Enormous. At least a hundred pounds heavier than I am now."

"When was this?"

"About six months ago."

"You lost a hundred pounds in six months?"

"At least," I said. "I haven't really had anything to eat since April. Except I eat on the weekends now. Like I said."

"That's weird," she said.

Dammit.

Why is she still here? Why hasn't she jumped out the window? Man. There's about a 96 percent chance I'm going to get Maced in the next half hour or so. Because . . . wait . . . "Look," I said. "There's our exit."

"Where are we going?" she asked.

"You'll see," I said.

Yeah. You and me both.

I had lived in Baltimore for four years and I had been to the Inner Harbor maybe twice. It sucked. The place was crammed with tourists buying fudge and wacky hats. Beers cost five dollars apiece. It wasn't my scene at all.

But good grief. I needed to think of something. I zipped past Camden Yards, took a right on Conway Street. The Inner Harbor. Lots of lights. Lots of pedestrians. I figured there was safety in numbers, so I eased into a parking lot and turned off the engine. "We're here," I said.

"Where?" she asked.

"We're going to the ESPN Zone."

"What's it like?"

"I don't know," I said. "I've never been there."

"Can we eat there?"

"I don't know," I said. "Probably."

We made polite chitchat as we crossed President Street, walked over a footbridge, and headed to the ESPN Zone. And then . . . *Wham!* I never guessed the place would be so noisy. Good gracious. Twenty-nine thousand gargantuan televisions blasting football and baseball news at top volume. Wild hordes of sweaty softball players jockeying for position at the bar.

And the video games. It was like a casino hopped up on crank. Digital race cars, twice as loud as the real thing. People—competitive people—jumping up and down and slamming buttons and screaming. Tinkles and gongs and crashes and the lights and the flashing and the dizzy, deafening NOISE of it all!

Dammit.

I stood there for a second, jostled this way and that by the waitresses and regulars. I wondered what would happen if I said goodbye, tossed Michele the keys to the truck, went outside, and jumped into the harbor. How long would it take me to swim to Fell's Point? Could I make it? But then I spotted a kiosk with a sign that said TO-KENS. Or something like that.

"Let's go get some tokens," I screamed.

So we went and got tokens. Which weren't really tokens. I got a plastic card with credits on it. Ten dollars for the video games. I also paid ten dollars for two beers.

I grabbed everything and led Michele through the chaos, up a flight of wide stairs, into the heart of the action. We hollered more polite chitchat as we raced imaginary jet skis and played other games we didn't understand. The only one that made any sense was a big-screen TV with two fake fishing rods in front of it. For catching fake fish. I swiped my card and we played. She was good at it. Good enough to beat me, at least. It was kind of fun until we ran out of credits three minutes later. My beer was gone. She hadn't touched hers. So we found a corner and stood there.

"So," she said after an awkward silence. "You're a reporter."

"Yep."

"Did you go to college?" she said.

"Yeah."

"University of Maryland?"

"No," I said. "Yale."

She looked confused. Like I just told her I was in the mafia or the French Foreign Legion. "You never said you went to Yale," she said.

"You never asked."

"You just . . . You don't seem like a Yale guy."

"What do you mean?" I asked. "What's a Yale guy like?"

"I don't know," she said. "But you should have told me about the Yale thing."

"Why? Would it have made a difference?"

"I don't know."

And then more silence. Maybe fifteen seconds of it. Excruciating. "You want to play the fishing game some more?" I asked.

"I don't know," she said.

"Maybe we could get some dinner."

"Okay," she said. "But it's kind of crowded in here."

"All right," I said. "I'll think of something."

I blazed a trail through the bodies. She followed. I looked back and noticed that she still hadn't touched her beer. "Something wrong with that?" I asked.

"No," she said as she handed it to me. "It's kind of warm, though."

I drank the whole thing before we got to the door. It was a five-dollar beer. I didn't care how warm it was.

"Where are we going?" she asked.

"There's this place I go a lot," I said. "It's called Kisling's."

"Do they have good food?"

"Sure," I said. "Probably."

We climbed into the truck. We drove for ten minutes. We parked and started walking. "It's a bit of a dive," I said, doing my best to soften the blow. "But it should be quiet. We should at least be able to talk and . . . What the hell?"

There was a huge crowd on the sidewalk in front of the bar. There was a line. At Kisling's?

Dammit.

October 20, 2000. Mike Tyson versus Andrew Golota. The bar had the fight on pay-per-view. I completely forgot about it.

It was a ten-minute wait just to get inside. Plus it was already getting rowdy. Five deep at the bar and sinking fast. Way worse than the ESPN Zone. Plus there was a cover. Two bucks a head.

"Are we going in there?" Michele asked.

"I guess," I said. "But we're not waiting in line."

I led her around the corner, nodded to one of the regulars who was watching the side door, and pushed my way in.

"You don't have to pay the cover?" Michele hollered.

"No," I shouted back.

It was a madhouse. The worst of the bunch had been drinking for hours. I could tell. These were people I knew, shouting, slurring, dropping shot glasses on the floor. I would have been one of them under normal circumstances. They knew it, too.

"Hey, asshole! Where you been?"

"Someone get this shithead a drink!"

"Who the hell's that chick?"

Whoops. Time to go upstairs.

Which wasn't easy. The place was packed. Hot. Nasty. We pushed our way to the staircase in the back and we climbed to the second story—only to discover that the upper bar was just as bad. I saw my buddy JJ, the guy who ran the fish warehouse.

"Duuuuuuuude!" he shouted. "Where's your beer?"

I was wondering that myself. But Michele—my perfectly coiffed, perfectly terrified date—was getting kicked, jostled, and otherwise abused by the bloodthirsty drunks who were screaming at the television as the undercard got underway. Muhammad Ali's daughter was fighting.

I wanted to watch and drink and scream, too. But I knew when to cut my losses. "We just stopped by to see what's going on," I hollered at JJ. "We have to go."

"Duuuuuuuuude!" he shouted.

Indeed.

I rescued Michele—who was pinned between a drunk rugby player and an even drunker electrician—and forced a path down the stairs, out the door, onto the crowded sidewalk and . . .

"Sorry," I said.

"Yeah," she said.

I had no choice. There was no more getting into the truck. No more video games and saloons. I had to take her down by the water. Down to the converted American Can Company, with its fancy shops and new restaurants. Down by the new Safeway where I bought my lentils. Down where the sober-pet people roamed.

"Ever been to the Austin Grill?" I asked.

"No," she said.

"Me neither. I think it's Mexican. That all right?"

"Sure," she said.

"Good. We can walk."

Michele ordered some kind of salad. I got a chicken dish with black beans. I told her about being a redneck at Yale. She told me about the trailer park. I told her about the Rainbows. She told me about John Stafford. And then we were done.

We strolled down to the fancy promenade by the marina. We looked at the yachts, the fancy condos, and the expensive people with their expensive dogs. I told her that's where I walked when I had nothing better to do. Which was most of the time. And then the date was over.

It was a little rough, but we made it. And she didn't even blast me with pepper spray. I drove her back to Laurel. She told me to give her a call. I said I would.

The crowd was gone by the time I got back to Kisling's. The fight was over. Golota went down in the first round after a series of head butts and forearms. He got pummeled in the second. He refused to leave his corner for the third. He forfeited. Mike Tyson won by TKO.

Boxing officials later changed the decision to "no contest" when Tyson submitted a urine sample that tested positive for marijuana.

Either way, he won $10 million.

My dad was skeptical about getting the Taurus fixed. It was ten years old, it had more than a hundred thousand miles on it, and it kept killing transmissions. I wouldn't get any more than a few hundred on a trade anyway, so I gave it away to a tow-truck driver. I told him he could keep the stereo—an Alpine CD player—if he just hauled the whole damn thing into oblivion.

He agreed.

Bye-bye, Ford Taurus. Hello, humiliation.

On Saturday, October 21—the morning after the date—my mom and dad drove down to my sister's apartment from Pennsylvania. I met them there. I got in my dad's van and he drove us to a Mazda dealer in Baltimore.

I test-drove the cheapest vehicle on the lot: a green pickup left over from the previous model year. It didn't have four-wheel drive, but it had air, automatic, and a decent factory CD-player. They were selling it for something like $13,000. I talked them down to something like $12,500. My dad thought it was a pretty good deal.

While I signed the papers, he sat down and wrote a check for $2,000. The down payment. Which I couldn't afford.

But what the hell? I couldn't afford anything.

Again.

The check from *Reason* came early the next week. I think it was Monday. It was in the mail when I got home. Two thousand dollars.

I drove to my sister's apartment. I signed the back of the check and handed it to my mother.

"Why don't you keep it?" she said. "Just in case. You can pay us back later."

"No way," I said. "Take it."

"You might need it if you get a job and have to move," she said.

"Maybe. But you should take it."

And that was the end of the Rainbow money.

Just like the merger money. I had been thinking about it for months, but it was already spent by the time it showed up. I missed financial solvency by two days. Forty-eight hours. I thought about it while I drove my shiny new truck back to Baltimore. It was a hell of a thing.

In a way, I was happy about the timing. If I had gotten that check a week earlier, I would have shot a ton of money on something stupid. Like maybe a whiskey-soaked funeral for the Urban Hermit. Maybe I wouldn't have spent all of it, but Skippy and I would have had a big night out on the town. Maybe two. So I was lucky the Taurus broke down when it did.

And I was happy about being able to swing a new car. Six months earlier? No way in hell. But I was in better shape now. I was out of credit card debt because of the Urban Hermit scheme and all the ridiculous things that went along with it. If I hadn't starved myself, I wouldn't have saved up that money. And I wouldn't have been bored enough to pitch the Rainbow story to *Reason*.

But I was still screwed. Turns out when you buy a car, the down payment is . . . just a down payment. The bank expected me to keep paying. Every stinking month: $269. And then the insurance. The Taurus wasn't worth anything, so I hadn't been carrying collision. Now I had to. Another hundred dollars a month out the window. Plus the truck was hard on gas, and I drove a lot.

I had to come up with an extra four hundred a month *just to pay for the truck*. But how?

I drove to Safeway. I made my way to the dry-goods aisle. I tossed two bags into my cart. None of the fancy stuff, either. No black beans and rice. Just lentils. Back to basics. Until I could come up with a better idea.

22

Put Up Your Dukes (of Hazzard)
Doing Business with the World's
Smallest Drug Dealer

Against a backdrop of post–Summer of Love angst, Thompson con-
jures skewed visions of flower children, off-duty hookers, weightless
typewriters, crashing planes, and memories of terror at the Cana-
dian border while transporting a shoe full of grass. Even more dis-
turbing and affecting is "Death of a Poet," which recounts the
story of a Thompson crony, Leach, a "bad drinker and wife beater"
who introduces Dr. Gonzo to his two rubber blow-up dolls before
running amok, upon the arrival of police, in a bloody orgy of vio-
lence. The title entry emerges as the collection's sole disappoint-
ment, with its quasi-coherent narrative of Thompson's affection for
his black tomcat.

—Review of Hunter S. Thompson's *Screwjack*
in *Publishers Weekly*, October 23, 2000

I had just lost a hundred pounds or so. My job situation was up in
the air. I was going out on strange dates with some girl who came
out of nowhere. And all of a sudden my plan to be off the Urban
Hermit snide fell victim to the transmission.

Skippy and I talked about skipping town. Anything to get away.
Maybe a camping trip. But the weekend was still a few days off, so I
went to work in the morning, came home in the evening, and tried to
keep busy.

"These are tumultuous times," I thought to myself as I settled into a recliner and watched our cat swat a piece of fuzz it had pulled out from underneath the television stand. And I got to thinking about the situation. Is this fair? Did I bring it on myself? Should I be grateful I started fixing things when I did? Or have I finally earned the right to start bitching and moaning?

The cat didn't give a shit either way.

She was jet black. Her name was Sophie, but we never called her that. We called her . . . well, it was kind of a drawn-out, high-pitched warble. A highly stylized version of the word *kitty*. It sounded like "MMRRRIIITTTTTEEEEEE."

She was one of many bizarre felines we had taken in over the years. The first was an enormously fat tabby that walked through our door one day and stuck around for a few weeks. Then left for a few weeks. Then returned for a few weeks. We named him Goble, after one of our favorite bartenders at Kisling's. The orange hair. The round face. The resemblance was striking.

Skippy bought Sophie at a pet store when we lived on Bank Street. I can't remember why. I just came home one day and discovered that Goble had a little buddy. (Turns out they didn't get along at all.) Then there was Steeler Kitty, a tiny black-and-yellow stray that showed up a few months after Goble disappeared for good. We didn't keep track of them. They were happy. We were happy. It worked.

So there I was, contemplating the mess I was in as I watched little Sophie bat that fuzzball around on the floor. She rose up on her hind legs and juggled the fuzzball in her front paws, rolled onto her back, and mauled it with her back paws. Such a simple, carefree life. Imagine, passion for a fuzzball. What was it about that thing?

Yeah. What is it? Doesn't seem very fuzzy for a fuzzball. Come to think of it, it seems kind of . . . yeah. It looks kind of like . . .

Holy shit!

"MMMRRIIITTTEEE!"

I leaped out of the recliner and grabbed Sophie in mid-pounce. She was perplexed but powerless. I snatched her little bauble off the floor. I examined it. And I declared it my own. Then I called the fish warehouse.

"Skippy," I said. "You still up for camping this weekend?"

"Sure," he said. "Why?"

"Because the cat just found a hit of Ecstasy."

"Cool," he said. "I'll get some scotch."

The Ecstasy was a little ragged around the edges but not bad considering the beating it had taken. It must have been there for months. Maybe a year. The television was huge. We never moved it. And we never vacuumed. It was there all along. Waiting for the cat to find it.

I guess I could have swallowed it immediately. That's what I would have done six or seven months earlier. But things had changed. Maybe sobriety had become a habit. Or maybe I knew if I got all ripped up on Ecstasy I'd walk down the street and spend $250 at the bar. Or maybe I just didn't feel like it.

I could have thrown it away. Or given it away. Or sold it. But there was a good chance I had already paid for it. And I was there when the cat found it, so it was mine. Fair and square. And . . . *and I was trying to save some money and if I didn't get out of town I'd probably end up at the bar and I already had a date scheduled with Michele on Friday and there was no way I could afford to go out two nights in a row and . . . and . . .*

And I convinced myself that I deserved the pill.

So I kept eating lentils. I kept filing stories at work. And on Friday

THE URBAN HERMIT • 248

I took Michele to a touristy little historic district in Ellicott City. We walked around. Got some coffee. Browsed through some cozy shops. We got a beer at a brew pub. (One beer!) It was nice. A real date. It dawned on me that I might actually like her. She asked me to call her when I got back from camping. I told her I would.

Then I went home and packed all my gear for one night in the woods, taking special care to cushion the Ecstasy from any unnecessary abuse.

Skippy and I were looking for deep woods. We didn't want predug fire pits and flush toilets. We wanted to hike. To find our own place in the Big Wilderness.

We thought about going to Shenandoah National Park. The fall foliage was in full bloom, but that was the problem. Shenandoah would be packed with sightseers. We'd never get a moment's peace. So we decided to bypass Shenadoah and find a secluded spot in George Washington National Forest.

Saturday morning. We packed our stuff into Skippy's Saturn and hit the road. We slid past the Inner Harbor and Camden Yards, hopped onto 95 South and blazed past Laurel. Then the D.C. Beltway, and onto 66 West. We were making great time. Unbelievable time. Until Skippy suggested that it might make more sense to take it slow and soak in a little culture. See some sights. I agreed. We were supposed to be having fun. Contemplating. Besides, it was early. There was plenty of time. For everything. The bullshit would be waiting for us when we got back.

Skippy took a hard right off the highway when we got to Manassas. We dug through a pile of CDs for some mood music—Neil Young,

Willie Nelson, Johnny Cash—and headed for the country. It was perfect.

Route 211 was a crooked little two-lane through the Virginia countryside. Small towns, horse farms, and cabins. The place was lousy with character and charm. Locals had set up folksy roadside stands about every half mile, selling pumpkins, apple butter, and homemade jelly. We sang along with the stereo—"Powderfinger," "Coward of the County," "Whiskey River"—and joked around about anything that came to mind. We were pleased with our decision to take it slow. Until we saw it. In front of us.

A traffic jam in the middle of nowhere.

"What the hell?" Skippy said.

"Is there a wreck or something?" I asked.

And then we sat there. Stop-and-go for ten minutes. Then twenty minutes. Then thirty. We couldn't see more than a few hundred yards in front of us because of the twists and turns in the road. We were okay with it at first, but we still had a long drive ahead of us. We had to clear this traffic jam, or the trip would be a bust. I was starting to get nervous when I noticed a break in the action.

"Wait," I said. "What's that?"

I saw the corner of an enormous orange sign poking above the trees. We inched closer and saw cars pulling in and out of a field along the road. Then we noticed cars parked along the shoulder, people getting out and walking.

"What's going on?" Skippy asked. "Is there a fair or something?"

"I don't know," I said. "That sign . . . It kind of looks like a bar."

"A bar? Out here?"

"I'm not sure. But I think the sign says 'Cooter's.'"

"Cooter's?"

"Yeah," I said. "Cooter's."

But it wasn't a bar. No, no, no. We were in Sperryville, Virginia. The hometown of Ben Jones—the actor who played Cooter the mechanic on *The Dukes of Hazzard*.

Jones had more recently served two terms in the House of Representatives, but nobody in Sperryville seemed to care much about his political career. The enormous crowd had gathered at a museum devoted to memorializing *The Dukes of Hazzard* and all it stood for—especially any and all things Cooter-related.

Skippy and I hit the jackpot. We came through Sperryville on a special day. Cooter's was hosting a Bluegrass Festival. It was such a huge event that organizers had called in the cultural reinforcements. Cooter was on the scene, of course, but so was Enos the cop and a host of other characters from the show. They were sitting in booths beside the museum, signing autographs and kissing babies.

My gosh! Ten replicas of the General Lee—television's finest bridge-jumping Dodge Charger—graced the parking lot. They were lined up about fifty yards away from us, separated by hordes of the show's biggest fans. I bet there were five thousand people there. At least. And not a single one of them was an ironic hipster nostalgia freak. The place was packed with mullets and bleached-blond teenage girls smoking menthols. Scores of heavy women wearing Blue Oyster Cult T-shirts, men decked out in Tasmanian Devil and Lynyrd Skynyrd gear. We weren't in Northern Virginia. We were in 1982.

It was awesome. I walked around that place like I was ten years old. Cooter walked right past me. I waved at him like an idiot. He waved back, then hopped into a General Lee, fired that sucker up, and did a huge doughnut in the parking lot. The crowd went wild.

"Jesus," Skippy said. "It's a good thing we didn't take that Ecstasy yet."

"Damn straight," I said. "Talk about overload."

We watched Cooter do some more doughnuts.

"Hey," I said. "You have that camera?"

Skippy nodded and pulled out a little disposable we bought at a gas station that morning.

"Cool," I said. "Get a shot of me with Cooter in the background. No one's going to believe this shit."

I stood in front of the General Lee, my arms raised high in triumph. Skippy took the picture. We switched spots and I took a picture of him. Then we went through the museum, which was more like a gift shop. Tons of memorabilia, some of it incredibly expensive. But they had some offerings for the common man. Skippy got a baby-blue T-shirt that said COOTER'S: SPERRYVILE, VA. It had a picture of a tow truck on it. I was going to get one, too, but I didn't have any money.

And for once, it didn't matter. We just kept walking and gawking and soaking it all in.

We decided to leave after about an hour. It was a tough call. There was a beer truck, and the bluegrass was just getting started. We had tents to sleep in, even a car. But we knew ourselves well enough to know what would happen if we stayed, and we figured backwoods Virginia would be a terrible place to get arrested. Especially with Maryland plates, a hit of Ecstasy, and a fifty-dollar bottle of scotch. So we took a last, long look and hit the road.

We drove for another hour, up into Shenandoah National Park, down the other side, and finally into George Washington National Forest.

By two-thirty we were parked along a dirt road, right next to a big pile of stones. A scraggly path disappeared up a steep hill to our right. "How about we walk for a few hours, then make camp when it starts getting dark," I said.

"Sounds good," Skippy said.

And then we walked.

It was brutal. Straight uphill, almost. Then down. Then back up. Over rocks. Jumping tiny streams. All with an overstuffed pack that must have weighed fifty pounds. Then up some more, stopping occasionally to snap a picture of the flaming foliage on the opposite side of the valley. I got tired. Tired like I couldn't take another step. But I put a hand on my knee and *pushed*. Then we took another picture and *up*.

We started out in some oak and maple trees that had just started losing their green. Then up into some trees that were in their full fall color. And then I'm not sure what happened, but Skippy and I noticed it at the same time: All the trees around us were bare. It was creepy, like something out of a science fiction movie.

"What the hell?" Skippy said. "Was there a fire up here or something?"

The trees looked dead. Rickety. They crackled and wailed when the wind blew. We heard branches crashing to the forest floor. We weren't real woodsmen by any stretch, but it didn't take Grizzly Adams to figure out that this was not an ideal place to pitch a tent.

Or . . . Grizzly Adams wasn't a real woodsman either, was he? He was the greenhorn, right? Wasn't Uncle Jesse from *The Dukes of Hazzard* the same guy who played Mad Jack on *Grizzly Adams*? Was he on both shows at once? Or did *Dukes* come later?

We kept walking as we discussed those questions and others, but we never made it out of the dead trees. "I don't think it's getting any better," I said. "And it's not going to be light out much longer."

"Nope," Skippy said.

"You feel like walking back down into something safer?"

"Think we'd make it before it gets too dark out?"

"Probably not," I said. "Besides, I'm tired."

"Me too," he said. "Let's just camp here."

"What about the trees?"

"It'll be all right."

We found a decent clearing on a rocky overlook. I unpacked my gear and started putting my tent together. Skippy didn't. He decided he would just crawl into his sleeping bag and sleep under the stars. So he collected a bunch of wood—which didn't take long since all the trees were dead—and started a fire. He broke out the scotch just as I finished with my tent.

"Give me a pull off that," I said as I sat down beside him on a thin foam camping pad, about three feet from the flames. I took a swig from the bottle. It was good scotch. Then I leaned back and pulled a plastic bag out of my backpack. I took out the Ecstasy and put it on the bottom of a small aluminum camping pan. I reached down to my waist, pulled my Swiss Army knife out of its leather holster, and extended the blade. I measured up the little pill and cut it in half.

"Today was a good day," I said as I finished the delicate operation.

"Yes, it was," Skippy said.

Then we talked. Ate trail mix. Drank scotch. Fed the fire. Laughed. Sang "Powderfinger" without the benefit of a stereo. And generally had a good time until all hours of the morning. Nothing outrageous. Just two guys in a bad camping spot, enjoying some time away from it all.

Then we went to sleep. And not a single tree limb came crashing down on us.

23

Worlds Collide
The Long Unconscious Fall

The only question left now is: Who gets the Sock Puppet?

Pets.com, the online retailer whose cheeky TV mascot gained it widespread fame, said yesterday that it had fired most of the staff and was shutting down.

The failure was the first for a publicly traded dot-com.

Amid disappointing sales and a lagging stock price, Pets.com executives said yesterday they planned to sell the site's remaining assets. . . . The fire sale also includes the Sock Puppet character. Although the company auctioned off the actual puppet on eBay earlier this year for about $20,000—which it donated to charity—it remains among its most valuable properties. . . .

The company's lavish ad spending also helped make Pets.com synonymous with the dot-com money mania that characterized 1999, and the ubiquitous Sock Puppet became one of the more well-liked symbols of the Internet economy. . . .

—New York *Daily News*, November 8, 2000

Skippy and I enjoyed the camping trip, but it didn't really change anything. So it was back to the grind.

Except we had the election to think about. Our guy was Libertarian candidate Harry Browne. We knew he wasn't going to win, but we thought it would be cool if he managed to lead in our precinct. At least for a minute or two.

I'm not sure why we thought that was important or funny. But we did. So on November 2 we dragged ourselves out of bed at some ungodly hour and headed to the polling station, just to be sure we'd be first in line.

It's a good thing, too. A seventy-five- or eighty-year-old bag of bones wrapped in a pale green shawl shuffled into line behind us about thirty seconds after we got there. Normally I would have let her ahead of me, but she didn't look like a Libertarian. She would cost Harry Browne his two-vote lead if she got the jump on us. So she had to wait.

Or would she? When the door swung open about ten minutes later, I was horrified to see two volunteers set up to process voters, each on opposite ends of a long folding table. I skipped up to the closest one and took my rightful spot in the lead, but Skippy never had a chance. That old biddy zipped right past him like a flash of lightning. The race was on.

I figured I could outpace her, but she was hustling. What the hell? Was she there to give Lyndon Larouche an early bump or something? I whipped out my registration card and tossed it to the old man sitting at the table. He smiled at me, looked at my card, and opened a huge book with the names of all the registered voters. He put his finger at the top of the *M* column and started sliding through all the entries. Sloooowly.

I looked over at the old lady. She knew the volunteer, so checking her name was a formality. She was good to go. Drat! I looked back down at my guy. Wait . . . What? He was scanning through the names . . . McConnell, McDevitt, McDonnell . . .

"Sorry," he said. "Your name's not listed. You sure you're registered?"

"You're looking in the wrong place," I said. "I'm not a *Mc*Donald. I'm a *Mac*Donald. With an *A*."

Come on, dude! The old lady was already heading into the booth. I looked at Skippy. He looked at me. Defeated.

But we were still okay. She had one vote. We were two. It didn't matter which jerk she was backing. Harry Browne would take the lead once Skippy followed me and pulled the lever. We were sure of it.

Except by the time the old man found my name and waved me through, another old lady had arrived and teetered up to the other processing station. The first old lady had already voted, so her guy was in front.

I pulled the curtain aside in a rush, but I fumbled with the ancient machine. All those levers. It looked like the dashboard of a Model-T Ford. I got confused. I faltered. And I failed. By the time I exited I had already heard the other machine register two more votes with resounding *ca-chunks*. Another old lady had already entered the booth. I looked up and saw Skippy still standing at the table, explaining to the volunteer that he, too, was a MacDonald. Not a McDonald.

What a disaster that election turned out to be.

Florida. Recounts. Hanging chads. An honest-to-goodness Constitutional crisis. But Harry Browne wasn't in the running anymore so I tuned it out and went to Safeway. Sure, for the lentils. But I was also there for something new.

Pictures. Electronic pictures.

When I dropped off our little disposable camera the guy who took it asked if I wanted a CD. I hadn't had pictures developed in years, so that option was entirely new to me. "It's pretty cool," he said. "They put everything on a CD. You can look at your pictures on a computer. You can even e-mail them."

E-mail? Excellent. "I'll take the CD," I said.

And then, two days later, I had it. The CD with the pictures from *The Dukes of Hazzard* experience. Pictures of me, standing with my arms raised high. Cooter in the background, turning doughnuts in the General Lee. It was fantastic. Bizarre. Perfect.

I hurried home and ripped off an e-mail to my college friends. I had dodged them earlier in the summer when they demanded my presence at our fifth reunion. When I was mired in the opening weeks of the Urban Hermit plan. They were pissed.

But I was back, see? The old me. The real me. The cat and the Ecstasy! Who else but your old college drinking buddy could pull off something like that? Who else would stumble across a full-blown Cooter rally in backwoods Virginia? I threw in some details about Bosnia and the Rainbow Gathering and the bikers and the big sack of marijuana. It's *me*, I told them. And I'm *alive*. As reckless and stupid as ever.

I attached the photos. I sent that sucker. And I started getting responses almost immediately. But none of them said a word about the cat or the Ecstasy or Bosnia or the bikers. Nope. They all had one question:

"Holy shit. How much weight have you lost, dude?"

And then I had to explain it all over again. For the millionth time. The lentils. The tuna. The belt and the awl and the numbers.

Turns out Sam MacDonald—that old Fat Bastard—wasn't nearly as alive as I thought he was.

Michele tolerated my stories about Sperryville. She even laughed at the pictures. It looked like she planned on sticking around.

She said she wanted me to meet her brother. And her friends. I didn't know what to make of that. It sounded like a disaster. Until she said the most amazing thing I've ever heard: "Maybe we could meet you at Kisling's."

Well, then. Kisling's it is! Seriously. What could go wrong?

It was Saturday. The first weekend after the elections. I got to my regular spot at the bar around seven P.M. I felt spent. Maybe it was the lack of food. I'd been eating even less than normal. I just couldn't stomach the lentils anymore. Or maybe I was still reeling from the hike up the mountain with Skippy.

The beer helped. It buoyed my spirits, like it always does. So I ordered another, which I was just leaning into when Michele and her brother, Doug, walked through the door with Allison, his girlfriend. Followed by Michele's friend Dawn, and Dawn's boyfriend, Chris.

The girls were a little out of place, a shade blonder than people at Kisling's were used to seeing. A bit more done up. But that was fine. And the guys were a perfect fit. Doug painted cars for a living. Chris was in the elevator union. Both of them drinkers, both eager to tie one on. So we ordered drinks and got ready to watch my worlds collide.

We were making real progress. Having a grand old time. After another round I suggested to Michele that we ditch her posse for a few minutes so we could head over to the Sip 'n Bite and grab something to eat. I was feeling better. My appetite was back. I might have even talked her into it. Only that's when we heard those two enormous, terrifying thuds.

The first was the sound of my head bouncing off the bar. The second was my head bouncing off the floor.

And then all the screaming. Which I didn't hear at all.

It's not like I was hammered. I had a few beers. That's all. I wasn't slurring my words. I wasn't feeling dizzy. But I knew something was wrong when everything went black and I kept hearing my name.

"SAM!"

"SAMMY!"

"SAM MACDONALD!"

slap slap slap slap slap

"SAM MACDONALD!"

The voice belonged to Justin, one of the guys who owned the bar. When he saw my eyes flutter open, he turned his attention to the phone in his hand.

"Should I call?" he said to nobody in particular.

Michele was the one slapping me. "Sam," she said. "Are you all right? Are you all right?"

Doug was looking over her shoulder. "Is he dead?"

"I think I should call," Justin said.

I was laying flat on my back in a booth. I was confused. My head hurt. Bad.

"What's going on?" I asked.

"You passed out," Michele said. "You hit your head on the bar. Are you all right?"

"Yeah," I said. "Yeah. Just . . . let me get up."

Justin put his free hand on my chest and pushed me back into the seat. "No," he said. "Stay down. I'm calling an ambulance."

"Ambulance?" I said.

"You hit your head really hard," Michele said.

"How long have I been out?" I asked.

"A few minutes," she said. "We thought you were dead. But just wait. We're calling nine-one-one."

"No," I said, snapping to attention. "Hell, no."

I sat up.

"Wait!" Michele said. "You hit your head really hard."

I thought she was going to cry. But that didn't matter. Neither did my headache. I stood up. I was wobbly, but I managed to keep my balance. I collected my wits. And then I lunged at Justin. "Give me that phone," I said.

"Lay down!" he yelled, dodging my advance.

"Give me the phone," I said.

"You hit your head," he said. "Why don't you just let the paramedics—"

"No paramedics," I said. "I'm fine. I'm standing. I'm talking. I'm fine."

I put on my best face and tried to explain that I pass out all the time. Which was true. Especially when I get nervous about stuff. Years earlier, when I was an altar boy, I hit the deck two or three times, in front of the entire congregation. Once I was carrying the big glass pitcher of water for the washing of hands and . . . *bloop* . . . down I went. But I was fine. And I was fine all the other times.

So, yeah. I was fine.

"Listen to me," I said. "I don't need an ambulance."

"Just let them take a look at you," Michele said.

Right. I knew they'd cart me off to the hospital. I had seen it happen to people at college. They had a few too many drinks or smoked some pot and got all wigged out, then some nancy-pants got worried and called the paramedics. Then all of a sudden it's the next day and they have a $1,500 ambulance bill to explain to their parents. All for nothing.

"I'm telling you right now," I said. "I'm fine. If you call an ambulance, I won't be here when it shows up."

So they didn't call. They just loaded me into Michele's car and took me home.

Maybe it was just a normal fainting spell. Or maybe the Urban Hermit plan was finally getting to me. I didn't know what to do about it either way. Cracking my head off the bar had me a little worried, though, so I went to my sister's house after work on Monday and got on the scale.

I weighed 198 pounds. Under 200 for the first time in something close to fifteen years. Twenty pounds less than my playing weight senior year of high school. More than fifty pounds less than when I got back from Bosnia.

But I felt great, apart from the two huge goose eggs on my head.

When I got home from my sister's I rattled off 175 push-ups in about two minutes. I did a clap on every tenth one. I was strong.

And even if I wanted to dump the Urban Hermit plan, I didn't know if I could. The bills were still piling up. The truck payment and the insurance were killing me. Plus I was trying to save some money in case I had to move. I was still looking for a new job. I was still . . . waiting.

So I came up with a plan to get everybody—my mom, my sister, Michele, the people at work—off my back. I promised that I would stop losing weight when I got to 180 pounds. I don't know where that number came from. I just invented it. I'm five feet eleven inches tall, and 180 sounded reasonable. Plus, I figured the final eighteen pounds would buy me some time.

It did. But not much.

At some point in November an editor at the newspaper in Atlantic City called and invited me to New Jersey for an interview. I envisioned mobsters, casino owners, and high-stakes poker players. Maybe even some down-and-out hookers. So I gathered up my new sports coat, took a day off work, and made the long drive.

They offered me the job. Only they wanted me to work a neighborhood beat, about an hour north of Atlantic City in some kind of summer resort community. They wanted me to work there for at least a year before considering me for the main office.

I turned it down.

Then my sister moved. Living in a tiny apartment with a toddler and a newborn was too much for her. So she packed up her husband and her kids and they headed to Ridgway and moved in with my parents while they looked for work.

Then the holidays. I went home for Thanksgiving. Old friends who hadn't seen me in years kept babbling about my weight and how great I looked. People in my family kept hassling me about how skinny I was and how I needed to gain some of it back.

But I showed them. I proved how reasonable I was, how things were getting back to normal. I ate turkey, and loads of it. Stuffing. Cranberry sauce. Homemade rolls with butter. Beer. Wine. Pumpkin pie. I was ravenous. And I wasn't paying for any of it. So screw the Urban Hermit. I really packed it in.

Then I contracted a vicious stomach virus from one of my sister's kids and spent three days throwing it all back up.

Then Christmas. How am I supposed to pay for Christmas? Michele, stubborn Michele, was still hanging around, despite the poverty and the passing out and the lentils. I had to get her something. Plus her birthday was a few days before Christmas. Of course! Why not?

So I just kept plugging away. Writing stories. Slinging fish. Applying for jobs. And disappearing little by little, pound by pound.

But I knew I was almost out of weight to lose.

24

The Gun That Was Not Fired, the Accidental Pundit, and the Outrageous Sensation of Moving On

And finally two young ladies appeared, blissful at having been se-lected for the honor, to help the hunger artist down the few steps leading to a small table on which was spread a carefully chosen in-valid repast. And at this very moment the artist always turned stub-born. True, he would entrust his bony arms to the outstretched helping hands of the ladies bending over him, but stand up he would not. Why stop fasting at this particular moment, after forty days of it? He had held out for a long time, an illimitably long time; why stop now, when he was in his best fasting form, or rather, not yet quite in his best fasting form?

—Franz Kafka, "A Hunger Artist," 1922

I left the woods for as good a reason as I went there. Perhaps it seemed to me that I had several more lives to live, and could not spare any more time for that one.

—Henry David Thoreau, *Walden*, 1854

January 28, 2001. Super Bowl Sunday. Time to go to work.

The Baltimore Ravens had made it to the big show. People all over the city had been drinking for a week straight. Television reporters swarmed the streets to document the debauchery.

Grim-faced city officials warned of riots, win or lose. Everyone remembered the year before, when the Super Bowl was in Atlanta. Ray Lewis, the Ravens star linebacker, was leaving a party with friends. Shots rang out. A man died. Authorities charged Lewis with murder.

He later pleaded guilty to obstruction of justice, a misdemeanor.

There was tension in our neighborhood on January 28, 2001. Amateur fireworks. Bottles smashing. Screeching tires and indiscriminate hollering. Cars of all sorts thundering the ridiculous, ubiquitous song that had become the Ravens' anthem:

"Who let the dogs out? Woof, woof, woof . . ."

It would have been a great day for a drink. To join in the revelry. But Sundays were warehouse days. No exceptions. So when early evening arrived, Skippy and I laced up our boots and got ready to sling some fish.

Michele was dubious. She had been hanging out at our house all day. She had seen the news. "I don't want to drive through this mess," she said. "You care if I watch the game here?"

"Go ahead," I said.

"What if there's a riot?" she asked.

"The .357 is on the floor next to my mattress."

"Are you serious?"

"It's loaded," I said. "Don't mess around with it unless someone kicks down the door or tries to light the house on fire."

"Shut up," she said. "You know I'm not touching that thing. I hate it."

"And don't just start shooting through the door," I said. "You have to wait for them to get inside the house. If you shoot through the door, you're going to jail."

"I can't believe you're just leaving me here," she said. "The whole city's going to go nuts."

"You can come stack fish with us if you want," I said.

"See you later," she said.

While Skippy and I were knee-deep in frozen fish guts, the Ravens stomped the New York Giants 34 to 7. Ray Lewis earned MVP honors. But nobody let the dogs out in Baltimore. There were no serious riots. Michele never fired a shot.

And then . . . more work.

Maryland authorities had hammered out a deal with the owner of Michele's old trailer park. The residents who paid their bills would get an entire year to vacate. So John Stafford and his kids got a reprieve. Rose, too. Which I was glad to see.

But that was all background noise, the result of work already done. I was more worried about what was going to happen next. Life—especially the job search—had slowed to a crawl during the holidays. Maybe it was exhaustion. Maybe there weren't any jobs. Or maybe I just needed to get off my ass.

I got a boost right around the time of the Super Bowl. *Reason* finally ran the Rainbow story in its February issue. So instead of shopping around a crappy-looking Word file to prospective employers and promising that the article would appear sometime soon, I had a real clip. I started sending out more résumés and cover letters.

In the meantime, I stuck to the revised Urban Hermit scheme. Starving during the week, living on Friday and Saturday. Building up a pathetic little nest egg because . . . well, you never know. I kept promising Michele and my mom that I would stop when I got to 180 pounds.

I still didn't have a scale, though, so there was no way to check.

I can't recall the sequence, exactly. But here's how it all shook out.

Some guy from *The Wall Street Journal* read the Rainbow article and posted his reaction on OpinionJournal.com, the venerable newspaper's daily online roundup, on February 12, 2001. It was headlined, "Why We're Not Libertarians," and it wasn't exactly kind:

> *Reason* magazine publishes 4,000-plus unironic words on something called the "Rainbow Gathering," an annual assemblage of hippies. Sam MacDonald's groundbreaking article reveals that hippies do lots of drugs (a good thing, by libertarian lights) and are naive about economics (not so good, but kind of endearing).
>
> MacDonald's central argument, though, seems to be that the Rainbow hippies are heroes because they refuse to apply to the U.S. Forest Service for a permit to use federal land. This makes no sense at all. We understand that libertarians oppose public ownership of land, but how does it follow from this position that if land is publicly owned, it is commendable to defy the rules governing its use? It's as if MacDonald were saying he's against welfare and therefore in favor of welfare fraud. Frankly, we don't understand how such flawed logic could have found its way into a magazine called *Reason*.

Ouch.

I didn't understand what the hell the guy was talking about.

Welfare? Who said anything about welfare? But I was pretty sure he didn't like it. He singled me out as the one writer whose work explained why "we"—journalists at one of the world's most influential newspapers—rejected the notion of libertarianism. *Libertarianism.* Which happened to be the guiding force of the magazine that hired me to write the story. I figured my career in political magazines was over. Unless . . .

Nick Gillepsie, who had recently taken over as *Reason*'s editor-in-chief, called me that afternoon. He was laughing. He seemed happy about getting slammed by the *Journal*. He asked if I had any more story ideas.

I said sure. I made some up on the spot and e-mailed them to him. And then I waited.

Gillespie called me a few weeks later. He said the magazine's Washington editor was moving to New Haven. (His wife had landed a teaching job at Yale.) He asked if I was interested in interviewing for the job. A full-time gig with the magazine.

Sure, I said. I'd be interested in that.

Then everything started going a hundred million miles an hour again.

I got the job.

I had to move to Washington, D.C. Skippy thought about coming with me. We even looked at a few places. But then he decided against it. He couldn't afford it.

Neither could I. The position paid a lot more than I was making at the *Leader*, but my rent would likely triple. I'd need first and last months' rent up front. A security deposit. My car insurance would go through the roof. And dollar Rolling Rocks? In Washington? Forget it.

I figured I could make it once I got settled. But first I had to get settled. So I gathered what little money I already had stashed away. I saved as much as I could by ratcheting down on the Urban Hermit plan. And a few weeks later—in May 2001—I moved to a studio apartment in Washington, D.C., and started a new life.

Work was cool. My office was a block away from the White House. I shared it with a bunch of free-market types who ran a civil liberties law firm called the Institute for Justice. I wrote about politics and culture. I talked about guns and drugs on radio shows in cities I'd never been to. I went to events and dinners. I listened to important people talk about important things.

President George W. Bush was cutting taxes. The whole city was going nuts trying to track down a missing intern named Chandra Levy. Congressman Gary Condit, who was allegedly having an affair with her, lived a few blocks away from my apartment. I had absolutely no idea what any of it meant. But I was there. In the middle of it.

At the same time, my new life felt an awful lot like the old one. Especially my aching belly. The Urban Hermit followed me from Baltimore. I had to keep him around because I was still dead broke. So I ate lentils.

And I walked. I lived close to a subway station, but I would have had to switch lines to get to my office. I thought about taking the bus, but . . . screw it. The bus cost. Not that much, but enough to add up. So I hoofed it to work every day. Two miles each way through the hot, sticky Washington summer.

Anything to save a few bucks.

And then I got my tax return. I got it late because I had deferred filing. (I had been interviewing for the job in April, and the deadline had snuck up on me.) The total was less than I had hoped because I hadn't paid any taxes on the Rainbow money. But I got a check.

I can't remember how much, exactly. Probably because I didn't have any fun with it. I used it to pay off the taxes I owed from the *previous* year. And my student loans. And my parents.

That really sucked, but I was done.

Out of debt. Completely.

Finally. The car repairs and the taxes and the student loans and the credit cards and all the rest. Finished. It took me more than a year of starvation, hard work, and blind luck. But it was over.

Mostly.

Michele stepped up her harassment campaign over the course of the summer.

She saw me on weekends, when she rode the Metro in to visit. She claimed that I was wasting away. That I was getting smaller and smaller every time she saw me.

I still felt great, though. I tried to prove it. I fell on my face and hammered out push-ups. A lot of them. And fast. I did them one-handed. See? Stronger than a *bastard!* Wanna see me do a pull-up? Oh, I'll do pull-ups. You just watch. Because . . .

"Sam," she said.

"Yeah?"

"You're too skinny," she said. "You don't look weak and you don't look sunken or pale. But you look like you don't weigh enough. You're a big guy. Or . . . you're supposed to be bigger than you are. I can tell."

I tried to explain that things were different. And they were. I never really killed the Urban Hermit, but living that way was pretty impractical in D.C. I was always heading out to dinners and conferences and other bullshit like that. For work. People fed me for free, but nobody ever asked if I wanted a cup of boiled lentils. So I ate whatever they had.

And the booze. It's not like I was back at Kisling's with Skippy and all the blue-collar tycoons, sucking down Rolling Rock every night. But working in D.C. required a good deal of social drinking. Five beers here, four glasses of wine there. So I drank.

I had moved beyond the Urban Hermit. There was never any fanfare. No grand funeral with whiskey and fireworks. But I was eating more. And I hadn't had lentils in weeks.

Michele thought otherwise and really laid into me about it. She complained about my rib cage. She said she could feel it. She said it was weird. She pointed out that even if I was eating more, I was also walking about ten miles a day. She reminded me that I promised to stop at 180 pounds.

"There's no way I'm down to one-eighty," I said. "My skeleton weighs one-eighty."

"How much do you weigh, then?" she asked.

"I don't know," I said. "But my waist is still thirty-two. It was thirty-two when I weighed two hundred pounds. I can't be at one-eighty yet."

She had me curious, though. I still felt fine. But my pants . . . They were actually sagging a little. So the next day at work I asked one of the lawyers how to get to the gym in our building.

I went there. I located the scale. I stepped on it. I shifted the counterweights left and right.

I weighed 169 pounds.

"Gadzooks," I thought. "I better put on some weight."

. . .

So I started eating more. My pants got a little less loose. Michele said I looked a lot better. And that was good enough for me.

I never abandoned the Urban Hermit plan completely, though. Lentils? Yeah. I sent them packing. Because lentils suck. But black beans? Hard-boiled eggs? They weren't great, but they were cheap. And money never stopped being an issue. I'd go to the grocery store and I'd eye up the tuna steaks. I'd want them. But I never wanted them bad enough to pay sixteen dollars a pound.

Even simpler things. I started buying coffee again, but I couldn't bring myself to put sugar and creamer into the shopping cart. I drank it black. Because it was cheaper.

Besides, the Urban Hermit plan was *simple*. I cooked once a week. Maybe twice. It was nice not to think about making dinner day in and day out. Same with lunch. I never, ever bought lunch for myself. There was always someone offering food if I'd go listen to a speech or attend a conference. Or someone willing to take me out and expense it as "networking." So I ate lunch, but only when it was free. Some days that didn't work and I'd go home hungry. But that didn't bother me anymore.

From time to time I'd get really busy and forget about food altogether. I'd go two days and realize I hadn't eaten anything at all. At which point my pants would get a little loose and Michele would start hollering and I would eat some more until she stopped.

It was a good system. And it worked.

I was settled in and I was making progress. I was getting a feel for what it meant to be a libertarian writer in a hyper-political town. It required a deft touch. What to take seriously? What to poke fun at? When to be a journalist? When to be a jackass?

I thought I was doing all right.

My boss must have thought so, too, because he called one day and told me take the subway to National Airport and fly to New York City. To the CNN studio. It was time for me to become a television pundit.

My flight got canceled because of thunderstorms, but that didn't matter. A producer told me to head to the studio in Washington, right next to Union Station. They would connect me via satellite.

They plunked me down in a makeup chair. Then they plunked me down in front of a camera. And before I knew what was happening, I was on the air. It was a show called *Greenfield at Large*, hosted by veteran news correspondent Jeff Greenfield. Jake Tapper from Salon.com and Tish Durkin from *National Journal* were on with me.

We talked politics. Which wasn't easy. Congress was in recess. There wasn't a lot going on. So we made baseless predictions about what might happen next. We talked about how the tax cuts might play out, and whether the rumors about Chandra Levy and Gary Condit would have any wider political impact.

And then we yucked it up. I think I started it.

GREENFIELD: Is there something out there that we haven't been talking about that's not filling the papers that you think may turn out to be a very significant issue as we get into this autumn?

MACDONALD: Well, it's kind of lighthearted, but I think it could be important. Representative Phil English from Pennsylvania has proposed a bill to slash the beer tax, which means billions of dollars. But it makes sense. The beer tax is incredibly high. And if you can't sell the American people on a tax cut on beer, the tax cuts are done. So we'll see how it plays out. I hope it works.

GREENFIELD: All right, well, we'll adjourn to our favorite watering hole and keep an eye on that. Jake Tapper, is there an issue that you're seeing and saying yes, that one's going to play?

TAPPER: I don't know how significant it is—but it's certainly fun to cover. There's a bill by Senator Allard, a Republican of Colorado . . . which would ban the transport of roosters for use in cock-fighting. As I'm sure you know, Jeff, having gone to many cock fights. . . .

GREENFIELD: All right. Well, I think we're already demonstrating that at least the male members of this panel may have a little too much time on their hands: beer tax and cock[fights]—I guess there might be a bill to legalize beer sales at cock fights.

MACDONALD: I would be all for it.

And then it was over. When the cameras stopped rolling, before we all parted ways, I asked Greenfield to say hello to his daughter Casey for me. She had been in my class at Yale.

My mother's phone started ringing almost as soon as the segment aired. People couldn't believe it.

"Dolly, I was just watching CNN and—"

"Yes," my mom would say. "That was him."

"Oh, my goodness," they would say. "He's lost so much *weight.*"

I got the same reaction from people I hadn't seen in years. I got e-mails from high school and college buddies. People I used to work with. None of them asked what I was doing in Washington or what I was doing on CNN. None of them congratulated me for turning the show into a forum on beer and cockfighting. It all boiled down to the lentils. The weight loss.

But I had come to terms with that. And I was happy.

I was debt free. I was a political journalist. I was camera-ready. A fellow with a job and a girl and a future. I had struggled. But I had emerged from the Beast of the American Belly. And I had emerged victorious.

I had moved on.

August 27, 2001.

I was in the Senate Hart Office Building. President Bush had nominated John Walters to head the Office of National Drug Control Policy and I was there to cover his confirmation hearings.

I thought Walters was a bad choice, and I thought that the ONDCP was a silly office in general, so I planned to poke fun at the proceedings. I was walking to the hearing room when I spotted a like-minded soul from the National Organization for the Normalization of Marijuana Laws. We were chatting about the Drug War and all its absurdities when he noticed that something wasn't quite right.

Everybody was running toward the door.

"What the hell's going on?" he said.

September 11, 2001.

I did some decent work in the chaotic months that followed. Some reporting. Some commentary. But everything had changed. There wasn't a lot of call for snarky libertarians anymore. The world had turned serious. *Reason* closed its Washington office and gave me my walking papers a few days after Christmas.

They let me stay on for a few weeks, just to cushion the blow. But by the end of January I was unemployed and dead-ass broke.

Again.

Epilogue
Don't Try This at Home

Three bullwhips, twenty rolls of bubble wrap, four croquet mallets, two flesh-colored thongs, two pairs of size-sixty pants, one jockstrap and cup, two plastic babies, one briefcase with several thousand volts of built-in shock power, one first-aid kit and one straitjacket are pushed to the side of a Holiday Inn hotel room in West Chester, Pennsylvania, where P. J. Clapp is about to start his working day. These things are the raw materials of his trade. Soon he will transform them into "magic," as he sometimes calls what he does, and soon thereafter this magic will find its way to the public, by way of MTV, on the show Jackass, *which is currently among the most popular cable programs in the country, with about 3 million viewers tuning in each Sunday night to watch Clapp, who goes by the name of Johnny Knoxville on TV, and a few other* Jackass *regulars do what they do best. They swallow goldfish and barf them up; they dive into stinking hills of elephant poo; they strap on electric dog collars and zap themselves silly; they get pummeled by professional boxers named Nigel; they drink sludge-thick bong water; they try to jump the L.A. River on roller skates and mangle their ankles; they listen as a doctor intones, "You've got a lot of healing to do."*
—Rolling Stone, *March 29, 2001*

These scenes of voracity recall Balzac or Belushi, frenzies in which "eating" is shoving, gorging, devouring, cramming. In The Fat Girl's Guide to Life, *Wendy Shanker consumes cookies by the boxful and bread by the loaf. In* It Was Food Versus Me . . . and I Won, *Nancy Goodman gobbles a dusty, gnawed bagel from the floor of her car.*

Betsy Lerner in Food and Loathing: A Life Measured Out in Calories *stuffs herself until she's "bloated, drugged, transported." In* Passing for Thin: Losing Half My Weight and Finding Myself, *Frances Kuffel, for whom eating is a stinging, gum-tearing orgy, sits on a toilet, sucking on Wheat Thins until they "soften into goo," eating a whole box and stuffing more food in her underwear for safekeeping. She envisions herself, always, a "colostomy bag overflowing."*

—Review of ten new diet and health books

in the *New York Times*, July 4, 2004

I decided to stop drinking with creeps. I decided to drink only with friends. I've lost thirty pounds.

—Ernest Hemingway

Let me be perfectly clear: This is not a diet book.

Why not? Diet books sell like crazy. And by "crazy" I mean sheer, unadulterated cuckoo. Americans spend more than $50 billion a year on diet products, and they spend a huge chunk of that total on books. Go to a bookstore and see for yourself. Everybody has a theory that promises to help you shed pounds without going hungry. Without giving up your favorite foods. Without a moment's discomfort of any kind.

Almost all of them are based on the same, comforting notion: *It's not your fault.* You just need some help from an expert. From a scientist. From a psychoanalyst. From Dr. Phil. From French women. (They don't get fat, see? And whose fault is it that you're not a French woman? Not yours!) The Barnes & Noble next door to where I am writing at this moment offers eleven shelves of "secrets," "strategies," and "solutions" to your weight-loss conundrum. Don't buy the notion that French women never pack on the pounds? Another book promises to explain why Japanese women never get fat—*or old*.

So if you envision yourself as "a colostomy bag overflowing," or if you are seeking diet guidelines for any other reason, try one of those books. I really must insist. Anyone stupid enough to view *The Urban Hermit* as a diet book and use it as such will probably die of kidney failure. And deservedly so.

Seriously, don't try it. You'll get hurt.

Besides, it really sucks. Especially when you end up living like a hermit for years. Which happened to me.

Sort of.

I managed to line up a few freelancing gigs after *Reason* pulled the plug. Enough to pay the bills for a while. But eventually I had to get a real job, and I did. I became a reporter for a newsweekly linked to the *Washington Times*. I'm not sure I was a great fit with the editors' political leanings, but the people were all very nice to me. And I appreciated the work.

I only lasted there a few months, though. I quit to accept a journalism fellowship that I applied for and, inexplicably, received. It paid $50,000 for one year. (More than I had ever made.) To write a book.

Which I did. Only it took two and a half years to finish it.

But that was fine. I stretched the fellowship money and made it last the whole time by taking a job as a bartender and . . . yes, by basically not eating anything.

Things were a little different, though. I relaxed my standards. I accepted lots of free meals from kindhearted people. I drank beer with regulars at the bar where I worked. But during the week I ate a few black beans, rice, and whatever was on sale. Usually to the tune of about eight hundred calories a day.

So I lived a regular life, more or less. I just spent less money and got used to being hungry. And I got used to the routine. When left to my own devices, I would often forget about food entirely. Sometimes for two or three days in a row. Until the stomach-growling got louder or someone told me I was too skinny.

It was almost always my mother. Or Michele.

Yeah. Michele stuck around. I bought her an engagement ring with the last of the fellowship money. We got married on June 5, 2004.

When we got back from our honeymoon—which consisted of driving around for a few days, because that's all we could afford—we settled into an apartment on the eleventh floor of an enormous residential complex in Silver Spring, Maryland.

Our first night there, we were standing on our balcony, sober as all get-out, when . . . *boom!* Down I went.

Passed out. Cold.

I smashed my head off the railing on the way down. Michele called 911. I woke up just in time to grab the phone from her and cancel the ambulance.

I guess some people never learn.

We struggled financially. I was doing some corporate work. Michele was in nursing school. Then she got pregnant and we started worrying even more about money. Then we found out she was pregnant with twins.

Then someone started talking to me about a speechwriting job. It paid more money then I ever dreamed of making. I said I was interested. The interview process took months. I had to go on three interviews. One of them was in Wichita.

They offered me the job.

The place I was working countered with a competitive offer. Then the people offering the new job offered me even more money and gave me until the end of the week to decide.

On Thursday night our apartment building caught fire. The alarms didn't work. We crawled through a dense cloud of smoke to the fire escape. My wife was five months' pregnant with twins, so getting out wasn't easy. The elderly couple in the apartment next to ours died.

Someone from the University of Pittsburgh called my cell phone the next morning to offer me a free ride in the school's creative nonfiction MFA program. He offered me a teaching spot to boot, and it came with a small stipend.

I was confused. So I called all the job people and told them that my house just burned, we were homeless, we were broke, and my wife was five months pregnant with twins. I asked if I could have until Monday to figure things out. They said that would be fine.

Michele and I talked about it over the weekend and made our choice: We decided I would bail on both jobs, go to grad school, and write a great book.

I wrote this one instead.

But Michele is still nice enough to remind me to eat from time to time.